Critical Muslim 4
Pakistan?

Critical Muslim is published quarterly by C. Hurst & Co (Publishers) Ltd on behalf of and in conjunction with Critical Muslim Ltd and the Muslim Institute, London.

All correspondence to Muslim Institute, CAN Mezzanine, 49–51 East Road, London N1 6AH, United Kingdom
e-mail for editorial: editorial@criticalmuslim.com

The editors do not necessarily agree with the opinions expressed by the contributors. We reserve the right to make such editorial changes as may be necessary to make submissions to *Critical Muslim* suitable for publication.

C. Hurst & Co (Publishers) Ltd.,
41 Great Russell Street, London WC1B 3PL

ISBN: 978-1-84904-223-9
ISSN: 2048-8475

To subscribe or place an order by credit/debit card or cheque (pounds sterling only) please contact Kathleen May at the Hurst address above or email kathleen@hurstpub.co.uk
Tel: 020 7255 2201
A one year subscription, inclusive of postage (four issues), costs £50 (UK), £65 (Europe) and £75 (rest of the world).

The British Museum

Discover the Islamic World

From early scientific
instruments to
contemporary art,
explore how Islam
has shaped our
world through objects
for centuries

Great Russell Street,
London WC1B 3DG
⊖ Tottenham Court Road,
Holborn, Russell Square
britishmuseum.org

Mosque lamp. Enamelled glass.
Syria, c. AD 1330–1345.

OUR MISSION

Critical Muslim is a quarterly magazine of ideas and issues showcasing ground-breaking thinking on Islam and what it means to be a Muslim in a rapidly changing, increasingly interconnected world.

We will be devoted to examining issues within Islam, and Muslim societies, providing a Muslim perspective on the great debates of contemporary times, and promoting dialogue, cooperation and collaboration between 'Islam' and other cultures, including 'the West'. We aim to be innovative, thought-provoking and forward-looking, a space for debate between Muslims and between Muslims and others, on religious, social, cultural and political issues concerning the Muslim world and Muslims in the world.

What does 'Critical Muslim' mean? We are proud of our strong Muslim identity, but we do not see 'Islam' as a set of pieties and taboos. We aim to challenge traditionalist, modernist, fundamentalist and apologetic versions of Islam, and will attempt to set out new readings of religion and culture with the potential for social, cultural and political transformation of the Muslim world. Our writers may define their Muslim belonging religiously, culturally or civilisationally, and some will not 'belong' to Islam at all. *Critical Muslim* will sometimes invite writers of opposing viewpoints to debate controversial issues.

We aim to appeal to both academic and non-academic readerships; to emphasise intellectual rigour, the challenge of ideas, and original thinking.

In these times of change and peaceful revolutions, we choose not to be a lake or a meandering river. But to be an ocean. We embrace the world with all its diversity and pluralism, complexity and chaos. We aim to explore everything on our interconnected, shrinking planet — from religion and politics, to science, technology and culture, art and literature, philosophy and ethics, and histories and futures — and seek to move forward despite deep uncertainty and contradictions. We stand for open and critical engagement in the best tradition of Muslim intellectual inquiry.

Wider Concerns of Halal

You think you know what is *halal*?

It's not just about '*halal* meat' and '*halal* food'.

In fact, *halal* is one of the most sophisticated concepts of Islam. It is best translated as 'praiseworthy' and has a direct relationship to public interest, environment, business ethics and moral behaviour. During the 'Golden Age of Islam', the concept of *halal* was used to generate policy and legislation for city planning, protection of flora and fauna, trade and commerce and was a driving force behind social and cultural productions of Muslim civilisation.

We aim to advance a more holistic understanding of what is *halal* and what it means to lead an ethical, socially responsible life in the twenty-first century.

Look out for our workshops, seminars and school visits.

Halal Food Foundation is a charitable arm of Halal Food Authority.

Halal Food Foundation

109 Fulham Palace Road, London W6 8JA, UK
Registered Charity Number: 1139457
Website: www.halalfoodauthority.com
E-mail: info@halalfoodauthority.com

CM4

October–December 2012

CONTENTS

ET CETERA

PAKISTAN?

THAT QUESTION MARK

Ziauddin Sardar

Like the sword of Damocles, a perennial question mark hangs over Pakistan. Can Pakistan survive? Can it continue to endure the 'war on terror'? Will it see out drone attacks, the Taliban, violent fundamentalists, the insurgency in Balochistan, inter-provincial rivalries, rampant corruption, economic meltdown and twenty-hour daily electricity blackouts? Given that it ranks high on the Failed States Index and is characterised by 'perversity', US-based journalist Robert Kaplan goes as far as to phrase the question as: *should* Pakistan survive?

No, is the proper answer, according to US military analyst and novelist, Ralph Peters. 'Pakistan's borders make no sense and don't work', Peters testified before the US House of Representatives Committee on Foreign Affairs. Instead of 'defending the doomed relics of the colonial era', the US should actively promote the balkanisation of Pakistan. In his testimony Peters suggests that Pakistan should be divided into a Free Balochistan and a Pakhtunkhwa for all Pashtuns – 'despite their abhorrent customs'. One presumes that by this logic there should also be a Sindhistan for all Sindhis, leaving what's left of Pakistan to the Punjabis. According to yet another expert, Michael Hughes writing in *The Huffington Post*, a fragmented Pakistan will be 'easier to police and economically develop' and thus its 'rapid descent towards certain collapse' could be avoided. In this best of all possible worlds, breaking Pakistan into small pieces is necessary to 'fix it'.

Questions arise, and are asked, in a context. There are good reasons why certain questions should be asked about Pakistan. However, questions, by their very nature, can also lead to a restricted set of answers. When a question is framed in such a way that an answer, or a set of specific answers, becomes inevitable it serves not as inquiry but as ideology. 'Can Pakistan survive?' has only two possible answers: yes it can, no it can't. Either answer frames Pakistan as a problem now and for the future. US policymakers asking the question perceive the problem to be that Pakistan cannot be 'policed', managed and controlled, which is what makes it 'perverse'. By equating Pakistan with survival, the question automatically consigns Pakistan to history. The country becomes an entity whose survival is permanently at issue, an insoluble problem. Implicitly, it is a problem that needs to be feared. So we move naturally to the next question: 'should Pakistan survive?' This is essentially an ethical question based on the assumption that as a problem to be feared perhaps Pakistan ought not to survive. The stark fact that Pakistan is still there, despite numerous predictions of its imminent demise by countless pundits, does not affect the logic of these questions.

Certain questions are thus not questions at all. To answer them is to reinforce the assumptions they are based on and accept these suppositions as self-evident truths. Questions about the survival of Pakistan are in fact an act of violence towards an already beleaguered nation. The best response to such inquiries is provided by the Victorian poet Robert Browning:

> Well, British Public, ye who like me not,
> (God love you) and will have your proper laugh
> At the dark question, laugh it! I laugh first.

So, what then are the appropriate questions to ask?

Let's begin with: why are things the way they are? The crisis in Pakistan is certainly a product of what Ayesha Siddiqa, the Islamabad-based security analyst and author of *Military Inc.: Inside Pakistan's Military Economy*, calls a 'chain of deep state'. It consists of an alliance of the military, the feudal landlords and the politicians. Pakistan's military is not just a conventional army but also a corporation, which produces all varieties of goods and services from soap and banking to cornflakes and housing development. Its main concern seems not so much to defend the country, on which its record is rather poor, but to maintain and enhance its business interests. The military siphons off a sizable chunk of the country's revenues and virtually all of its foreign aid. Its spy arm, the Inter-Services Intelligence Directorate (ISI), is above the law and human decency; it has become a murderous institution that has targeted not just dissidents but also human rights lawyers. Both the military and the ISI have nursed and nourished the Taliban, promoted extremists and violent organisations, and supported al-Qaida. Pakistan is an

agricultural state; around half of its GNP and most of its exports are based
on agriculture. The feudal landlords, consisting of a few thousand extended
families, control the bulk of Pakistani agriculture. The land is worked by
peasants or tenants who are virtually in bondage to the landowners. To
preserve their wealth and privilege, the feudals fight hard to keep the landless peasants on their fiefdoms uneducated and dependent. Both the military
leadership and the politicians come from this feudal class of *Zamindars*,
Jagirdars, *Nawabs* and *Vaderas*. Political parties are structured on feudal patterns and led by feudal leaders who run them as their private property,
passing on what they regard as inheritance to their children. Pakistan Muslim League, the party that established Pakistan, was dominated by feudal
lords from its inception. The Pakistan People's Party is the fiefdom of the
Bhutto family. President Asif Ali Zardari has already declared that his eldest
son, Bilawal Zardari Bhutto, will succeed him as Chairman of the Party. The
bulk of the lower house of parliament, the National Assembly, consists of
feudal landlords; there are certain individuals from this background who
always win elections – no matter what. Key posts in the executive also go
to the feudals. The army itself has evolved a feudalist structure. Much of the
judiciary too comes from the same feudal class. So the same group of families are in power whether the country is ruled by a military dictator or
sustained by an illusory democracy.

The 'deep state' uses Islam as an instrument to maintain the status quo.
Allegedly, Pakistan was created in the name of Islam. But Islam in Pakistan
is not a faith or a worldview but an ideology. Like all ideologies, it is an
inversion of truth: whereas Islam, in theory at least, is about justice and
equality, in Pakistan it functions as a mechanism for oppression. In other
words, it has gone toxic. While Islam values mercy, forgiveness, compassion, pluralism and diversity, in 'the Land of the Pure', ideological Islam has
jettisoned all that is humane. Almost everything that carries the adjective
'Islamic' in Pakistan is associated with puritanism, intolerance, chauvinism
and phobia of the Other. Women, the Shia, the Ahmadis, Christians and
Hindus are all harassed and killed in the name of Islam. Suicide bombers kill
countless innocent people to promote their Islamic cause. All the elements
identifying themselves as 'Islamic', from religious seminaries to political
parties such as Jamaat-e-Islami and various brands of Jamiat Ulema-e-Islam,
to the outright psychotic groups like Lashkar-e-Taiba, Sipah-e-Sahaba,

Khatm-e-Nabuwat and Lashkar-e-Jhangvi, have authoritarian or semi-fascist tendencies. For those with little hope, Islam serves to provides a sense of moral superiority, a brand of soap that washes whiter than white.

The irony is that the brand of Islam which has become dominant in Pakistan is no friend to the poor and the marginalised. It is an aggressively capitalist and ugly enterprise, a natural ally for the conservative middle class by which it is eagerly embraced. This toxic Islam is one of the biggest hurdles to land reform in the country. One would expect the feudal landlords to be against reforms of any kind. On numerous occasions when efforts have been made to tackle land reform, the feudalists have argued that the problems of the peasants are their own creation, hence land reform could actually increase their plight. Despite resistance from the feudal quarters, land reform has been undertaken in Pakistan under various governments in 1959, 1972, and 1977. Limits have been introduced on how much land can be owned by individuals. Millions of acres of cultivated land were redistributed. It was a small, incremental advance. But in 1986, the Federal Shariat Court, created by the military dictator Zia-ul-Haq with 'specific authority to carry out judicial review of all laws' and ensure they were not 'repugnant to the injunctions of Islam' declared that a ceiling on land holdings was un-Islamic. In a famous August 1989 judgement (Qazalbash Waqf v. Chief Land Commissioner, Punjab and others), the Federal Shariat Court ruled further that the Shariah places no limit on the land that can be owned by a feudalist. Moreover, the state is not obliged to spend any surplus on the poor. So Islam is specifically constructed in Pakistan as an instrument that promotes feudalism and oppresses the poor and the marginalised. Shariah rules OK. The poor and landless peasants are only there to shout slogans at demonstrations against blasphemy or some other perceived insult to Islam, and serve as cannon fodder for the Jihadi groups.

Despite the suffocating stranglehold of the 'deep state' and the poison of toxic Islam, Pakistan is still there. An appropriate question would be: why has Pakistan not disappeared into a black hole? How does it manage to survive? Or as the German philosopher Martin Heidegger would say, why is there something rather than nothing?

Equipped with a few tomes and a few sentences of Urdu, Robin Yassin-Kassab sets out to answer this question. He travels by bus, rickshaw and plane from Karachi to Bahawalpur, Lahore and Islamabad. He attends literary festivals, joins protest rallies, participates in Sufi dance sessions, and talks with intellectuals, academics, writers, politicians, journalists, ordinary citizens and the occasional 'naked madman'. He is quite overwhelmed by the diversity and complexity of Pakistan; it is certainly not a place that can be seen through a single lens, say that of religion or the Taliban. Good and bad things are happening simultaneously:

Pull up at the lights and there's a disabled child (possibly kidnapped and then tortured) begging, or a boy washing the windscreen, or a man making a monkey clap for a few rupees, or a man banging a drum. Alternatively park at some shop fronts, wind down the window, order some samosas or juice, and watch the people buying and selling, joking and fighting, singing and praying, smoking and snoring. And playing cricket, for Pakistanis are playing cricket wherever you cast your gaze.

The real strength of Pakistan, concludes Yassin-Kassab, is the resilience of its people, who always find the inner resources to rise above the turmoil. The state may be weak, but societies are strong. The country may be ruled by one of the most corrupt governments in its history, yet it does function as a democracy. It is being torn apart by violence, yet somehow held together by men and women who value peace and integrity. Instead of looking for scapegoats to blame, Yassin-Kassab suggests we should find time to praise its people. 'The country is overflowing with the bright and the beautiful.'

Of course, not all the people of Pakistan are praiseworthy. Karachi, major port and economic hub, is plagued with a culture of political violence and the antics of vicious gangsters. The city, as Taimur Khan notes in his brilliant excursion into its underbelly, is enveloped with fear and foreboding. Khan takes us to the parts of the city that are largely invisible not just to outsiders but also to most of Karachi's inhabitants. In Lyari we meet the gangsters who run protection rackets but who also hope for better education and amenities for their neighbourhood. In De Silva Town, Khan spends some time with a taxi driver caught in ethnic violence and plays pool with members of the Christian community. We meet the body builders of Federal B Area and the bookies and the violent land developers and property magnates of Guru Mandir. In Karachi, 'there is room for everyone.'

There is also hope. Khan asks Imran, a young high school student from Qasba Colony, if he would like to live somewhere else? 'I never want to live anywhere else but here', Imran responds without hesitation. Why would a young man wish to live in city noted for its lawlessness, political and ethnic violence, targeted killings and culture of fear? Perhaps because there are other things in Karachi the young man values. Karachi is noted for its entrepreneurial spirit. Wherever you look, says the journalist and activist I A Rahman, 'everybody, from a coolie to an industrial baron, is engaged in utilising all his time to do something.' The inhabitants of the city place a high premium on time.

The public dismay at any enforced suspension of work — caused by a call for *hartal* (strike) or disruption of power supply — is to be seen to be believed. Whenever a strike is called, workplaces have to be closed and vehicles kept off the roads to avoid heavy losses. But everyone remains keen to break the ban. As the evening approaches and the vigilantes retire to report success to their superiors, the vendors rush to their posts, shops reopen and streets come alive with fast-moving, noisy traffic.

Karachi is also a city that takes social service, charity and philanthropy seriously. Indeed, I have been out with the volunteers who manage the ambulances of the Edhi Foundation, which provides the only viable emergency service in the city. I have seen the dedication and passion of the citizens who organised the Orangi Pilot Project, and worked tirelessly to build schools, improve drainage and water supply, set up micro credit schemes, and establish health facilities in a million-strong shanty town. I have visited the schools built by a charity called The Citizens Foundation; and the offices of the Urban Resource Centre, which highlights the problems of the city through research and documentation. All of these institutions are run by the kindness of donors and the generosity of volunteers.

In Peshawar civic culture is not as strong as in Karachi. As elsewhere in Pakistan, the ruling party in Peshawar, the capital of the northern province of Khyber-Pakhtunhwa and the administrative centre of the Federally Administrated Tribal Areas (FATA), is using its 'power as an extended opportunity to seize patronage from the state and distribute it to its supporters'. More and more wealth, notes Muhammad Idrees Ahmad, is being 'squirreled away into gated communities of extraordinary opulence'. Even railway tracks are not spared by thieves. Idrees revisits the city of his birth after several years of absence to discover that the employment situation has become so bad that labour is forced to migrate to Afghanistan. There is a great deal of sexual frustration amongst the youth, 'instances of child abuse are frightfully high', and oppressive tribal traditions continue to make life difficult for most people. Yet, there is hope in Peshawar too. The 'dignity, hospitality, generosity, irreverence, humour, compassion and grace under pressure' of the people of Peshawar 'remain matchless'. There is a dynamic women's movement, a broader awareness of political issues, and the city's culture of self-sacrifice is alive and thriving.

Life in Quetta, the provincial capital of Balochistan that borders Afghanistan, is even more precarious. Quetta provides a good illustration of the mindboggling ethnic diversity of Pakistan. Mahvish Ahmad visits the city at considerable risk to herself and discovers an ethnically divided city 'under attack from all sides'. The ethnic communities of the city, the Pakhtuns, Baluch, Hazaras, Punjabi and Urdu-speakers, 'live in their own exclusive enclaves'. The city is 'a thoroughfare for food and weapons to NATO forces across the border and the headquarters of the notorious Taliban Leadership Council'. There is a constant shadow of imminent violence from the 'war on terror', ferocious extremist groups, the Baloch groups fighting for secession, and Pakistan's paramilitary Frontier Corps constantly on the lookout for 'suspicious' individuals. Ahmad visits a graveyard where the bodies of Hazara victims of the extremist group Lashkar-e-Jhangvi lie: 'bodies were buried in straight lines, with the same headstones inscribed with the same dates.' Ahmad tracks down Baloch separatists who claim to be secular and progressive and feel frustrated at being ignored and marginalised. They complain about the domination of 'treacherous Sardars', the tribal leaders, and blame the government for pitting the ethnic minorities of the city against each other. She talks to Pakhtun leaders who want Balochistan to split into two provinces, so they can have their own province and their own governance. Both sides use history to justify their claim to dominate and control the provincial capital city of Quetta.

The relevant question for Quetta is not who is a Baloch, a Pakhtun, or Hazara but who is a Pakistani. While questions of ethnic identity are obviously important, they seldom lead to a viable, inclusive politics. What confines peoples' thought, and limits their scope for action, are the questions they consistently ask themselves. Questions based on fragmented and isolationist ideas can only produce yet more fragmentation and isolation. To change one's outlook on life, to move from despair to hope, one needs to ask bigger questions. That's why Ahmad's suggestion that all sides in Quetta come together in a new secular alliance, based on the model of the old National Awami (People's) Party (NAP), makes sense. NAP, a united alliance of all ethnic groups in Balochistan, advocated provincial autonomy, recognition of different ethnic groups as 'nations' and demanded certain rights on the basis of ethnicity. Such an alliance, based on a progressive politics, could provide true hope for the troubled people of Quetta and Balochistan.

Merryl Wyn Davies is concerned with perhaps the biggest question of all: what is Pakistan? To the first-time visitor it is a place known through received ideas: myths, legends and innumerable stories, many represented in the work of artists or portrayed in cinema and on television. None of these, apparently, include mention of peaches. Davies travels to the small North West Frontier village of Pir Sabaq, devastated by the great flood of 2010. What she discovers is totally unexpected: despite great odds, the people of Pir Sabaq have rebuilt their village and their lives. Davies is moved by the courage, resolve and the will to succeed demonstrated by the women of the village. From the disjunction of her expectations of the North West Frontier and the encounter with peach orchards, Davies begins a reflection on the power of imagined landscapes. In her travels she encounters a variety of 'imaginariums', coherent world pictures each laying claim to being the reality of time and place that once was and now comprises Pakistan. She is aware not only of a plurality of imagined worlds but the tenacious hold even the most discredited ideas have on her expectations. She notes the subtle way in which Pakistan as a newly created country dislocates the past. To India belongs antiquity and heritage, to Pakistan the predicaments of modern politics. This newness, she argues, even affects the investigation of the most ancient past, the remains of the Indus Valley civilisations found within Pakistan. Imagined landscapes, Davies suggests, do not evaporate in the face of contradictory reality. The real potency of imaginariums is their power to influence and direct response in spite of reality, their ability to cause people to act and react as if what was imagined and expected is, nevertheless, actual. The question is not which imagined world is right, nor what is the correct answer. Imagined landscapes, the idea of a place, is always multiple, seen with different expectations of past, present and future by everyone. What is important is acknowledging and accepting the coexistence of these multiple realities. The Pakistan Davies finds is a compound reality in which whole galaxies of imagined landscapes are in play and all exert their influence. It is in tracing the outlines of imagination for the variety of people and place she encounters that Davies finds that complex location called 'Pakistan'.

This complex Pakistan has an abundance of intellectual and cultural resources that provide us with hope and inspiration. Take Pakistan's media: a phenomenon to behold. Numerous television channels, such as Geo TV, ARY, Dunya and Samaa, writes Ehsan Masood, are 'relentless in their coverage of corruption, and in their dogged questioning of officials, including the army'. Not surprisingly, many journalists have paid a heavy price for their bravery: from being roughed up by police to murdered by the intelligence services. But despite the threats and intimidations, 'no politician of any party can expect an easy ride from journalists'. They are grilled not just in a plethora of daily talk and analysis programmes but also mercilessly lampooned in razor-sharp satirical shows. Then, of course, there are what Pakistani viewers call the 'dramas', the soaps, mostly focused on cultural, social and political issues, and largely designed to be a mirror to society. Quite simply, these dramas, which can run as serials for months if not years, are among the finest and most hopeful things Pakistan has to offer. They can, and often do, bring entire cities to halt, generating intense debate and discussion. Freedom, in the domain of the media or elsewhere, often has its consequences. Masood highlights some of the recent amusing and not-so-amusing scandals of the media, and the travails of Pakistan Electronic Media Regulatory Authority (PEMRA), one of the few institutions in Pakistan seemingly not short of cash. Regulating hundreds of channels would be a nightmare for any regulator even in a highly developed country. For PEMRA, with all its resources, 'trying to regulate Pakistan's new electronic media is like trying to be the sheriff in a cowboy movie.'

One reason why Pakistani television dramas are so apt and brilliant is that they are, as Aamer Hussein shows, either based on classical Urdu novels or written by mostly female successful writers. Hussein relates how, as a young adult living in London, he discovered the 'house of treasures' that is Urdu literature. He began by laughing at the prose of Razia Butt's novel *Saiqa* – 'lushly descriptive of landscape and emotions alike, the situations lachrymose' – but soon realised that 'the world-behind-a-curtain Butt portrayed was far closer to the lives of most of her young readers than our "modern" way of living or our anglicised tastes.' He moves on to A R Khatoon's *Nuru-lain* and remembers that his mother used to read this story to him when he was seven. Through Hussein's personal story, we discover the great works of modern classic Urdu fiction, most of which chronicle 'the struggle for justice and human compassion throughout history'. A charming story from Khatoon's *Kahaniyan*, 'Princess Mahrukh and the Magic Horse', is included in this issue of *Critical Muslim*. Mahrukh is a headstrong princess who receives a horse as a gift from her father, but the horse is only a horse by day and becomes a seductive prince by night. When the horse prince elopes with her slave girl, Mahrukh follows his tracks through inhospitable terrain before she reaches the land of Kanggan, where she avenges herself.

Hussein briefly mentions one particular writer who is as indigenous to Pakistan, and as ubiquitous as *paan* (a betel leaf concoction). The nation's answer to Ian Fleming is one Ibn-e-Safi who at the peak of his productivity produced two detective novels a month. His most famous series are *Jasoosi Duniya* (The World of Spies), which began in 1952, and *Imran Series,* which first appeared in 1958. Ibn-e-Safi, who suffered both at the hands of the British and Indian authorities because of his progressive views, wrote 232 novels in all. He kept a whole generation of Pakistanis, including myself, enthralled right up to his death in July 1980. He appealed equally to the young and the old, and the story of his life and works is told through another story: the discovery of a fake Ibn-e-Safi (yes, in Pakistan they can fabricate anything, including novels) by my grandfather, Hakim Abdul Raziq Khan, in the small town of Bahawalnagar, where I grew up.

Ibn-e-Safi and the writers discussed by Hussein are the literary heroes of my generation, but Pakistan is also blessed with a new generation of equally inspiring writers. Bina Shah asks the question: is there a boom in Pakistani literature? If so, is it something genuine and deep-rooted or something that will eventually fizzle out? Certainly, talk of a boom makes little sense if the focus is on the so-called 'Corona of Talent', invented by Britain's literary magazine *Granta*. The 'Big Five' are said to be Kamila Shamsie, author of *Burnt Shadows*; Mohsin Hamid, whose *The Reluctant Fundamentalist* (2009) is being made into a film; Mohammad Hanif, who wrote *A Case of Exploding Mangoes* (2009); Nadeem Aslam, the writer of *Maps for Lost Lovers* (2005);

and Daniyal Mueenuddin, whose collection of short stories In *Other Rooms, OtherWonders* (2010) has been much praised.

Shamsie has been writing for two decades, which hardly qualifies her to be 'new talent'. I encountered her in 1998, when her first novel *In the City by the Sea* came out, around the same time as I was regaling myself with Aamer Hussein's stories in *This Other Salt* (1999). Aslam, in contrast, is likely more British than he is Pakistani. And Daniyal Mueenuddin has yet to make himself heard outside a small circle of English-speaking writers and editors. Some of these writers display a tendency towards stereotyping women and falling back on lazy 'terrorism' narratives, which Shah dissects. If this 'corona' is compared to the writers considered by Hussein, the boom turns out to be not much louder than a fire cracker.

Literature is indeed thriving in Pakistan but rather like the 'New World' of Columbus, it has always been there, and did not need 'discovering'. In literature, as in other fields, constructed imaginariums and the limiting logic of the questions they promote serve as traps that prevent us from seeing the whole picture. Pakistani literature, as Shah rightly says, is 'a long-standing movement with history and depth'. Indeed, one may find genera-tions of writers in one family as Muneeza Shamsie, Kamila's mother, shows in her essay 'Discovering the Matrix'. It's a tradition that nurses, nourishes and provides hope. And represents 'the long and continuous struggle of Subcontinental women to assert their voice and claim their right to speak'.

However, it is not just literature that is flowering in Pakistan. The coun-try's truly phenomenal tradition of music continues to flourish. No one in Pakistan, writes Bilal Tanweer, 'needs to be told What Coke Studio Is and What It Does': its status as 'a cultural behemoth' is confirmed. Since it was first broadcast on TV in June 2008, Coke Studio has been a sensation. What it does is profoundly simple: it synthesises tradition and modernity in 'a clear attempt to bridge the cultural fragmentation of Pakistan'. And it succeeds.

Literature and music, the foundations of culture, can be a great source for healing a nation. But Pakistan needs to change its politics too. Here, some hope is offered by Imran Khan, the celebrity cricketer turned charity fun-draiser, who has discovered latent charisma now as a politician. Khan, in Ali Miraj's assessment, 'has captured the zeitgeist'. He has managed to mobilise tens of thousands of young volunteers (with some assistance from music), and speaks their language. Miraj is impressed by Khan's clean record, probity and determination; but he is also troubled by his religious zeal, naked nationalism and naïve analysis of the problems of the nation. On the whole, he offers a 'real alternative' to the 'dynastic merry-go-round of the Bhuttos on the one hand and the Sharif brothers, the leaders of the Pakistani Muslim League (N), on the other, with smatterings of military rule in between'. He has articulated an 'attractive vision of a country based on meritocracy rather than nepotism'. However, we would be unwise to put all our proverbial eggs in one basket. Khan, as Miraj notes, faces tremendous obstacles: from the 'Obama syndrome' of promising too much and delivering little, to dirty politics; entrenched operators; the feudal structure of Pakistani politics to the threat of assassination. If Khan fails, there will be others to fill his shoes.

However, no action can be undertaken if individuals or nations are suffering from a mental paralysis. As Taymiya R Zaman discovered, certain questions allow no room for sensible answers. Constantly bombarded by her American students with questions, which were actually aggressive statements about the failure of Pakistan, Zaman retreated into herself and refused to talk about her country. She was so paralysed that she was not even sure of her own feelings about Pakistan: 'the sheer fatigue of deflecting questions left me with little room to know what it was I would say if allowed to speak on my own terms, or even what these terms would be.'

Like Zaman, Pakistan too seems to be paralysed by questions constantly thrown in its direction by America and the way it is framed in the West. Most Pakistanis blame the US for all the country's problems. There is, indeed, a great deal to blame, not least the fact that the US has dragged Pakistan into its 'war on terror' and continues to order drone strikes on Pakistani territory, very likely in contravention of national and international laws. If the two countries weren't supposed 'allies', then the actions of US military commanders would in effect be tantamount to a declaration of war on a sovereign nation. But America is an imperial power, and imperial powers do not have friends, they have only 'interests'. The main religion in America is an aggressive notion of 'national security', a cult of death of which robotic killing is the latest fetish. So it is delusional to believe that America can be a friend of Pakistan. Equally, being paranoid about America, or perpetually looking for conspiracies (a favourite pastime for Pakistanis), can be fatal for Pakistan. Nothing consumes one more thoroughly or easily than hatred of something over which one has little power.

Zaman's paralysis is only cured when she visits Pakistan on a sabbatical. The 'images of suffering, helpless brown people waiting for Angelina Jolie's benevolence' evaporate. It was 'like running into the arms of a lover you've been forbidden to see for years'. There was nothing menacing about the immigration officer; students in Lahore are more amiable and trusting than their American counterparts; and she felt safer in the streets of Karachi than San Francisco. In Lahore, she comes face to face with the real Pakistan and has an epiphany:

A woman is walking in our direction, obviously agitated, pounding on car windows. She comes to Haniya's window and raps on it. Haniya rolls her window down. The woman says her sister has been burned in an accident and she needs to get her to the hospital. Will we help her get the road open? 'Yes,' we say. Car doors open, women and men rush out into the night. The woman argues with the police. The crowd backs her up. The policemen say they are doing their job. 'Is this politician's life worth more to you than my sister's?' she yells. They seem shamefaced. The crowd gathers momentum. A man says he is recording this because he is a journalist from GEO. The policemen open the road. This is the Pakistan I know and love, I'm thinking. These ordinary victories, nothing short of heroic. When the long-awaited winter fog descends on Lahore, I am convinced that the city is magic, and the magic is compounded because it will never make it to newspapers abroad. This magic is ours, you think, disappearing into the night with your secret lover, and no one needs to know.

Self-discovery. That's what liberates Zaman and restores her true self. Pakistan too needs to discover itself and reflect on the testimony of the magic of its societies and the heroic deeds of its ordinary citizens. Pakistan needs to consider what determines the fate of nations. Can a nation exist as a surrogate of an imperial power or can it determine its own destiny? Ultimately, Pakistan's problems are its own creation; and only Pakistan can solve them. The country is in dire need of questions that focus the mind towards self-reliance and self-assertion. Those who live in history look backwards; they can only repair their self-image by imagining that they are morally superior to others. A better way for a nation to improve its self-esteem is to correct its deficiencies, to reorient itself by ditching obscurantist dogma and reinventing tradition; rebuilding with the resources of heritage and culture is a much bigger challenge.

The question all Pakistanis should be asking is: what can be put right? Or, more appropriately, what can we put right? The answer is: almost everything; and every segment of Pakistani society has a share of responsibility. Take the military. How can an army protect its own people when it becomes a cancer on society, consuming its host? Where would that leave the military itself? Or take the issue of Balochistan. Would it not be better to grant Balochistan, and other ethnically-based provinces, full autonomy? Would this not only give them the freedom they crave and remove the torment of Punjabi majority domination, but also redirect the energies wasted in ethnic struggle and violence towards building civil society? Central authority imposed by force never works; rather, central authority is effective only if it is clearly demarcated.

Numerous other options become possible provided the civilian elite begins to pay in tax what it owes and realises that stealing from the nation is against its own self-interest and will eventually lead to its own demise. A country cannot develop or maintain its infrastructure or function as a viable state unless its citizens pay their taxes. The need for infrastructural improvements in Pakistan is verging on the cataclysmic. Roads are crumbling, the railway is over a century old, large segments of the rural population are not connected to electricity grids and water supplies, the sewage systems are overwhelmed, and the national airline is too expensive for domestic and too unreliable for international travel. Pakistan needs to rebuild its public transportation system and invest in railways. Power is not only unreliable, it is also very expensive. There is an over-reliance on a handful of very old dams, and a couple of ageing nuclear power plants. Yet, there is plenty of potential for solar and other renewable sources of energy. Why isn't Pakistan investing more in alternative sources? Of course, it would help if the army, which has siphoned off much of the country's wealth, and the feudal landowning elite, who have looted the nation for decades, paid their outstanding energy bills. The country also needs serious measures to stop deforestation which is among the reasons for the floods we have witnessed in recent years.

But citizens have responsibilities too and there is much evidence that, regardless of the failures at the top, these are being taken seriously. In many cities, citizens are delivering services where the state is failing, for example establishing schools as in the case of The Citizens Foundation charity; encouraging alternative sources of energy supplies as the many environmental groups are doing; or organising sanitation and waste collection, pioneered by the world-changing work of the late Akhtar Hameed Khan, who founded the Orangi Pilot Project.

This is closer to the reality of Pakistan than what you might read in an essay in *The New Yorker* or in *Granta* and this is the reality we have tried to convey in this issue of *Critical Muslim*. Our stories are by no means complete because we, too, are mostly outsiders rather than participants in the nation's daily life. And, like all observers, we too flew into the nation's airports with pre-conceived ideas. But, as Yassin-Kassab, Davies, Zaman, and the London-based comedian Shazia Mirza have all shown, we were willing to have our own baggage challenged, opened up, replaced, or thrown out.

Mirza in particular had no hesitation in shattering her perceptions of a country, 'famous for Imran Khan and terrorism but not comedy'. 'There was no shouting or fighting or war of any kind,' Mirza writes, tongue firmly in cheek. Perhaps most surprising of all, she discovered that Pakistanis laugh at bawdy sexual jokes. 'I should never have listened to people who kept telling me, "don't tell jokes about sex, politics, religion, terrorism, or news"', Mirza declares.

Pakistan too should stop listening to people who triumphantly announce its collapse, or to those who childishly describe it as a 'cartographic puzzle'. Instead, it must continue to ask questions of its own, and continue to demand answers from its rulers and from its paymasters. If you internalise what imperial power says about you and play dead, you should not be surprised to see vultures circling above you.

Pakistan needs only to listen to itself. And ask questions that matter.

WHY ISN'T IT EXPLODING?

Robin Yassin-Kassab

Brown hawks crowding the sky. Mangroves. Trapped black Arabian Sea water in the Creek. Dusty virtual streets in the planning and early settlement stage; behind them boulevards and hospitals and flyovers; behind those mile on mile of tower blocks and shanty towns, a city of almost eighteen million souls.

But closer than that: supersize puppets nodding to pumping dance music, and conference halls crammed with chattering people, and tent-loads of poets. What's this? It's the Karachi Literature Festival.

Failed states, Pakistan-specialist Anatole Lieven declared afterwards, don't hold literature festivals. Perhaps Lieven assumed too much: there are festivals in Iraq and Palestine. And novelist Mohammad Hanif provided a grimmer perspective during his very well-attended and gently provocative session when he said 'even places that don't have running water want to have a literature festival now.'

But this one was big. One hundred and forty five producers of reportage, academia, analysis and fiction had been invited, most of them Pakistani or South Asian. The media was there. Bigwigs, students, business people, families and bright young things were also present in great numbers. Hanif Kureishi and Vikram Seth were the biggest draws.

Sessions were held and works were read in Urdu, Punjabi, Sindhi, Pushto, Seraiki and Balochi, but the dominant language was English. The attendees were highly literate English speakers and readers. Did this make the festival elitist? Of course it did, said Mohammad Hanif. 'We live in a country where half the people can't read – in any language.'

Pakistan's toiling masses were discussed but not represented. Still, the festival was representative of something, and something very large indeed. In the halls and corridors, in the gardens and in people's homes, I met novelists, actors, painters, singers, film makers, dancers, poets, and combi-

19

nations of the above. Not everybody was part of an elite, or at least hadn't been born into one. The coteries that had formed were meritocracies and included people of various social origins. The general public was articulate and bright: the students and teachers who came to my writing workshop, and the import-export people who questioned me after the Arab Spring panel, and the endless supply of bloggers.

Furthermore, the water was running in the taps of the prosperous, spacious inner suburbs near the sea, Clifton and the DHA and around the Creek. The traffic was flowing in an organised fashion down tree-lined avenues into well-numbered side streets.

Karachi

The last time I arrived in this city was the summer of 1993. Nineteen years ago, long enough ago to have been someone else. Karachi was my first exposure to 'third world' chaos. I remember the crush of bodies waiting at the airport's exit, and the unsurfaced roads snarled with buffalo and burning rubbish. This time was quite different. This time I was driven in from the airport on a red and turqoise dawn, through clumps of sea mist and a mild stink of sewers; depending on the breeze that stink still remained, and there were familiar sights too – rickshaws and painted buses, crowds dressed in shalwar qamiz picking their morning route across railway tracks. But the infrastructure had most definitely improved, the roads and buildings, the refuse collection. This time it felt like an organised, working city, like the commercial capital it is. The central zone was also smoothly functional. One post-festival afternoon I drank orange juice in Bohri Bazaar, inspected the carcasses and caged birds in Empress Market, then strolled south past the Atrium Mall with its multiplex cinema and boutiques with names like 'Fiction'. I crossed a broad park free of plastic bags where boys and men were playing cricket. A pleasant urban wander.

The tower block zone, part of which I was driven through later, while crowded and befumed, does not compare unfavourably with that of Cairo, a similarly sized megacity. The air pollution in the centre was less bad than in Tehran, which has a much smaller population.

The relevant chapter of Anatole Lieven's book *Pakistan – A Hard Country* suggests the Muttahida Qaumi Movement (or United National Movement) city administration is to thank for the progress. Despite its involvement in criminal and ethnic violence (before 1997 'MQM' meant Muhajir Qaumi Movement, identifying it with the communities which migrated from India at Partition), the movement's mobilising and organisational skills are tangibly proved by the cityscape. But perhaps it's better to thank that which has been mobilised: Karachi's hardworking technical middle class, and its resilient and long-suffering working class. Perhaps it's best to acknowledge the spirit of the city itself. Something has gone right here.

Last time the place was ablaze with ethnic conflict. This time the violence occurs on a much more modest scale. Dead gangsters are found in 'gunny bags'. Tit-for-tat killings are perpetrated by the activists of 'banned religious organisations.' Shia professionals are assassinated, as they are throughout the country, in a low-level war that's persisted since the reign of General Zia. A Punjabi told me he'd never felt safe living in Karachi – thrice his phone had been snatched at knife-point. Even in the city centre there are triggers aplenty to set off a worrying type: convoys of Rangers manning truck-mounted guns, and soldiers in tin helmets peering from street-corner shelters. As in other parts of Pakistan, the nervous wealthy are accompanied by armed bodyguards. It isn't comfortable like Europe. But neither is it anywhere as dangerous as Caracas or Mexico City. Given its rapid growth and its population of often competing ethnicities, this is quite an achievement. And Karachi's a lot more comfortable than it used to be.

It contains signs of the discomforts suffered in the vast country beyond. Outside the Press Club a protest tent was displaying pictures of Balochistan's abducted. That morning the mutilated body of Sangat Sana had turned up at the side of a Balochistan track. Sana was a Baloch Republican Party leader and he'd gone missing in 2008. He'd been shot thirty times in the head and chest.

There are more Baloch in Karachi than there are in Quetta, Balochistan's regional capital. There are more Pathans here than in any city except Peshawar. The Pathan population is swelling as refugees arrive from the wars in the North West. In Karachi as elsewhere, Pathans dominate the transport business. Their tough but showily dressed-up trucks (wearing portraits of soldiers, eagles or beautiful women, and surrounded by mosaic, then layered and bedecked in whirling windmills, bells and streamers) offer one immediate image of Pakistan.

Contrast this image to that of Riyadh airport's soulless transit zone, where I spent five hours before flying for Karachi, and which reminded me unpleasantly of Saudi Arabia beyond the transit zone. It consists of two identical wings arranged identically to house identical coffee outlets. Not one bookshop or paper stall. And the internet was disconnected. There was one television screen, showing sport. But in Karachi, having left the barren for the fertile, I met not only Pakistani truck art but also Pakistani slogans, authored by the Pathan nationalist ANP, the three versions of the Muslim League, the dead martyrs and living looters of the People's Party, and Imran Khan's party. Plus the black and white striped flag of the Jamiat Ulema-e-Islam.

There were slogans saluting the MQM's London-based leader Altaf Hussain. The Sindhis, who remember riots and the threat of ethnic cleansing, don't respond well to this. The Shia don't respond well to the sectarian Sunni Tehreek flag. Indeed there's a flag or a slogan to insult just about everyone. I recognised the Arabic word *intiqam* – revenge – among the Urdu, Sindhi and Pushto graffiti.

And now, fresh from holding the literature festival, Karachi was hosting a Difa-e-Pakistan (or Defence of Pakistan) rally. The newspapers spent ink counterposing the two events, casting them as products of two separate worlds. The purpose of the rally seemed to be to articulate a list of grievances – some understandable, some incomprehensible – against America, India and Israel. The organisers were a motley crew of religio-nationalist rightists, including pro-Taliban parties, proponents of Pakistani jihad in Kashmir, and sectarian hate organisations (like the 'banned' ones which do the tit-for-tat killings). Plus Hamid Gul, retired chief of the ISI, Pakistan's influential intelligence agency. The Tehreek-e-Insaf (Justice Movement) led by Imran Khan – to the chagrin of Imran's liberal supporters – also sent a delegate. According to a later newspaper report, one excited speaker at the rally threatened to 'make this ground a graveyard of the media.'

However much fun this sounded, I didn't have time to stay. The first of my three weeks in Pakistan was being eaten up. I'd been bravely considering an epic bus trip, but my Islamabad host's work schedule was pressing. So I flew north, over Sindh and the Punjab, to Pakistan's political capital.

Islamabad

I flew with Air Blue rather than the state-owned PIA, which, like the railways, nobody seems to trust anymore.

Emerging from Martyr Benazir Bhutto International Airport, I regretted wearing sandals. Here the weather isn't the Arabian Sea anymore. It's the edge of the Margalla Hills, which are the edge of Indus Kohistan, which is the edge of the highest agglomeration of mountain ranges in the world – the Karakoram, Hindu Kush and Himalaya. North from here the mountains rise until Kashgar and Tibet, and just thirty-six miles north in Murree three feet of snow had fallen the day before.

I was met by the Kashmiri driver employed by my old friend Ejaz. I hadn't seen Ejaz for eighteen years. We'd studied at the same Oxford college, and it was Ejaz who'd first invited me to come to Pakistan. I came, in 1993, and worked for the *News*, an English-language daily which had just started up. Maleeha Lodhi, the founding editor and later Pakistan's ambassador to the UK and the US, gave me my first sensible job, as subeditor and writer. The office was on the Murree Road in Rawalpindi, right across from the park named after Liaquat Ali Khan, Pakistan's first prime minister, who was assassinated there in 1951, and where Benazir was also assassinated in December 2007. I stayed at the *News* for a year and a few months, writing stories, enjoying myself, travelling in the tribal areas and in the high mountains.

Ejaz and I lost touch. Years later we were put back in contact through an uncanny chain of coincidences which involved a Pakistani novelist, an academic, the South Bank Centre and a pub in Earl's Court. Since then we'd talked several times on the phone. I knew he'd married, had daughters and a son, and was working as a lawyer.

Islamabad and Rawalpindi, formerly separated by the Islamabad expressway, have now joined up. Islamabad was built from scratch, starting in 1960, on a grid system, so its neighbourhoods boast names like F7 and G3. When I lived on its edge the city was still very obviously a work in progress, a virtual city of pauses and spaces. Now the gaps have filled in, the gardens are a little wilder, the streets more lived in. They used to say Islamabad was fifteen minutes from Pakistan. It used to be a city of civil servants who went to bed at nine. Now it has something of a social life, even at the weekends when the political class has gone home.

Some things have improved, others have not. In parts of Rawalpindi people live in shanty constructions of straw and plastic, or in tents, some of canvas, some of poorly-patched rags. Some of the campers are full-time nomads, but most are urbanites whom the city has failed. Or who have failed the city, depending on your perspective. A decades-old mulch of decaying plastic bag lies underfoot and all around in these areas. It blocks the water channels. It forms the mounded earth on which people build and play.

But Ejaz lives in a gated community next to the expressway. In the dark I had the impression of arriving at a cold Scottish mansion. At the top of the steps the door swung slowly open and Ejaz appeared in coat and scarf, well wrapped up against the chill. They'd been encouraged to convert to gas heating, he explained. Then the gas ran out. (It does come, but intermittently.) 'Except it hasn't run out. It's mismanagement.' The lack of gas coincided with a power cut, the daily 'loadshedding'. A back-up system kept the lights on for another hour.

'Now we're waiting for water loadshedding,' Ejaz complained. 'That'll complete it.'

We ate and we talked. I learnt what had become of our old friends.

Faisal is doing well in the foreign ministry. Dr Atif works in Birmingham. Dr Asim has his own hospital in Islamabad and a beard long enough to cover his chest. Hassan runs a medical college in the Emirates.

Iftikhar is very happy to have left the army. His batchmates still serving are being asked to 'murder Pathan tribesmen', and their consciences are wracked. These days Ifti does IT for an NGO. Mudassir, who was a journalist back then, works for an NGO called FAFEN – the Free and Fair Election Network.

Babur died young of a heart attack.

Ejaz lives in luxurious surrounds. He runs a successful legal practice specialising in telecoms – a boom business in the last decade, so competitive that a Pakistani phone call is now the cheapest in Asia. He'd 'worked his hair off,' he said (and he had, like most of us, grown much thinner on top and somewhat thicker round the middle), 'making the rich richer.' He is much more religiously orthodox than he was. He's an intensely moral and self-disciplined man. He always was, but now there's a structure to his discipline. He's a disciple of an American sufi, Shaikh Nuh Ha Mim Keller.

One day Ejaz took me into the countryside to see the land his father recently bought and the farm he's building on it. We drove through the very distinctive landscape of the Potohar Plateau, once the heart of the Buddhist Gandara civilisation (ruined stupas still stud Taxila and other sites), and favoured recruiting ground for the British and Pakistan armies. The current Chief Of Army Staff, General Ashfaq Kiyani, comes from a village nearby.

At its wildest the plateau is a labyrinth of canyons and gulleys running with hare and wild boar. At its tamest its fields of wheat and mustard erupt brick kilns and intensely eroded rock and clay towers. In the villages strung out along the vaguely surfaced, single-track road, everyone was wrapped in blankets against the bitter morning cold. The ground was dust which turns to mud slurry when it rains. The dust was occupied by goats and camels, water buffalo, and absurdly overloaded trucks.

We visited a state agricultural institute near Chakwal to hear professional advice on planting groundnuts. There was an electric fire in the office but the air was colder than Scotland. And the Punjabi farming talk baffled me twice. So after an obligatory cup of *doodh putti* (tea and milk boiled together) I went out and walked through the institute's working garden, hugging the sun and perusing a line of olive trees which were there to be grafted to suit the local climates.

Then we drove to a village where dung cakes were drying on top of neat brick walls. We weighed out and bought groundnuts to plant. Once business was concluded the farmers drew our attention to their impressive bulls, which on festival days they dress up and show at the local shrine. They brought out photograph albums as we drank our *doodh putti*, and they pressed us to stay for lunch. But we pressed on and had oily stuff on a roadside *charpoi* (rope bed) instead.

On the track to the farm we passed an older farm with a traditional donkey-operated well. Ejaz wants the same, plus beehives, plus a thatched roof on the wattle house he's building. His workers think he's strange. He can afford brick and concrete, so why does he want to live like an old-school peasant? But there are more like Ejaz. In Lahore I heard about Kamil Khan Mumtaz, an architect and an adherent of the perennialist philosophy, who works in traditional styles and materials.

The tethered cows and calves were doing well. The citrus trees, on the other hand, had been blighted by frost, and Ejaz mourned them. His land is bordered by a stream among reeds which becomes a raging flow during the monsoon.

Back on the plush edge of Pindi, we stopped off at the barber shop. It's worth coming to Pakistan just to experience this treatment: to be trimmed, shaved, to have your hair oiled, then your head, neck, shoulders, back and arms massaged.

Another day we went to play golf at the twenty-seven-hole Rawalpindi club, or rather Ejaz played his friend Ahmad while I tagged along. The weather was perfect, brisk and sunny, and Ejaz, quietly despairing of the country he lived in, made brisk commentary. 'It was one of the worst days of my life,' he said, 'when Mr Zardari became our president... Could they find no one else than Mr Zardari? Could not ten of them, or even one, stand up and say what is obvious to all of us?'

Elegant little grey squirrels made mighty chirpings in the trees. Clouds of brown hawks reared and tunnelled above. Sometimes, I was told, they swoop down and steal the ball. But here was the rough, the green, the trusty caddy... What was incongruous were the bunkers bristling tin hats and rifle butts which punctuated the course. This was because General Kiyani's official residence abutted. About an hour into our game a couple of camouflaged personnel-carrier helicopters loomed close, tousled our hair, and landed in the general's compound.

'What's this about?' I asked.

Ejaz sniffed. 'One of his wife's friends must have left her handbag in Lahore.'

Out on the expressway patriotic road signs counselled against my friend's attitude. 'Be A Proud Pakistani!' one said. Each of the ninety-nine names of God had its own sign. The bridges were adorned with images of Presidents Zardari, Karzai and Ahmadinejad, for the three were meeting. Pakistan announced the construction of an oil pipeline to link with Iran. Hillary Clinton announced America's imperial displeasure. Our car passed a cemetery whose grave slabs were draped in flags and tinsel. An entirely naked madman (or perhaps a holy fool) strode with great purpose along the hard shoulder.

Islamabad's monumental buildings and residential quarters are inter-spersed with plenty of jangal – not the tropical jungle summoned by the English appropriation of the word, but scrub and forest: bamboo and pop-lars, peepuls and acacias, eucalyptus and neem. The mountains glow blue through a slight mist.

Up close, from the upscale areas, the Margalla Hills tower greenly alpine. Just through the trees Saidpur village, including its deserted Hindu temple, has been restored and preserved. Cars slide smoothly around Kohsar Mar-ket, its cafes, restaurants, boutiques, a book shop.

I was thinking that Islamabad must be one of the best places in the world to be a rich man, with his drivers, cooks, housemaids and secretaries, in a fine unpolluted situation, with sporting and hunting possibilities close at hand, in a fine climate, with fine restaurants, and plenty of whisky and charas if you like that kind of thing. Then Mahvish appeared and immedi-ately reminded me – this market forecourt was where Salman Taseer was murdered. Taseer, Chief Minister of the Punjab and certainly a rich man, was shot by one of his own bodyguards while the others stood and watched. The minister's offence had been to criticise General Zia's 'black law', the blasphemy law which has been used to victimise members of the minorities. Christians have been charged with blasphemy on the flimsiest of pretexts – often in the context of local disputes which have nothing to do with religion. And whatever the courts decide, the accusation usually counts as a death sentence. There are enough people ready to take vigilante action in 'defence of Islam', people like Taseer's killer, and enough people ready to condone such action, like the lawyers who showered the criminal in rice.

Mahvish Ahmad is a Danish-Pakistani journalist based in Islamabad and teaching at Qaid-e-Azam University. We ate an Afghan lunch and discussed Balochistan.

I spent some of that evening at the home of Masud Alam, another free-lance journalist. There's a deer park on an extended traffic island near his house. Masud told me about the time when the Marriott Hotel was bombed and a friend called up to ask if he was ok. 'O don't worry,' Masud assured him. 'The Marriott is two kilometres away.' Afterwards he laughed at what he'd said. Isn't a burning hotel at two kilometres distance a legitimate cause for concern?

I couldn't stay long because I was meeting Ejaz and his family for dinner at a restaurant called Chinatown. But Ejaz was almost an hour late because a protest had closed a bridge causing a traffic jam to clog the surrounding roads. The protest had been called by the Imamia Students Organisation and concerned a suicide bombing in Parachinar the day before which had killed thirty-six Shia. The attack was claimed by a Pakistani Taliban splinter group.

Lahore

Ejaz took off for Qatar and I embarked on the first stage of my gradual descent back to Karachi. My seat on the VIP Daewoo coach service was how I imagine a first-class plane seat, and the motorway was first class too as it rolled widely down through hills and off the plateau onto the river-crossed plain. Here the soil was red and planted with wheat, mustard, orange trees, firs. Egrets poked about between the crops. Our road crossed the Chenab. Then the Ravi.

In four and a half hours I was in Lahore. I noted my first impressions: if Pindi is brown brick, Lahore is red; there are even more pictures of Imran Khan; look! there's a *hijra*.

I was staying in another kind of gated community: the Cantonment, home of the military. I discovered at the end of my stay that I shouldn't have been in the Cantt. Or perhaps I should, it wasn't entirely clear. Returning late one night I was stopped at two checkpoints. The soldiers checked my passport, asked if I was a Muslim, if I had children, if I had brothers, if I liked Pakistan, and then, grinning at the encounter, they sent me on my way. The next evening the same thing happened, but this time the soldier informed me that my visa didn't allow me to enter the Cantonment. 'But your address is not actually in the Cantonment. You must enter by a different route.' The address seemed to me to be in the Cantonment. I told this confusing story to a friend. He responded: 'To the extent that this is a police state, it's a very inefficient police state, which is surely a good thing.'

My host in the Cantt (or not) was Munim Khan, a Punjabi of Pathan origin. He was an excellent host, attentive and amusing, and his hospitality was typically Pakistani, which means warm and effortless. Over the next week I became part of the family – Munim plus wife and sister-in-law, and his two young sons Hassan and Saad, and the patriarch his father-in-law, a bed-ridden Brigadier of kind eyes and considered words, another supporter of Imran Khan.

That first night Munim took me to meet his friend Imran Shaikh, a businessman from a political family allied to Nawaz Sharif's Muslim League. We talked politics and then went out to eat. A glimpse of the city by night: couples and groups strolling around the racetrack; Pathan trucks and plush four-wheel drives and motorbikes and horse-drawn carriages competing in broad streets deprived of streetlight for hours on end; smoke and shadows and the arc of headlights.

Next morning Munim and Sarah took me for a daylight tour. First to the Wazir Khan mosque, whose distinction, other than its fading but still sparkling beauty, is its location in the heart of things, with densely-populated brick tenements peering over its walls. Then on to inspect the friendly bustle and fake brands in Anarkali: mobile phones, leather jackets, designer sunglasses. Next into the Old City markets where wood and stone buildings elegantly decay, their balconies overhanging narrow streets, and open sewers line both sides of the path. I was astounded by the flop-eared sheep I saw tethered to a post mid-market. How could I have forgotten such prodigiously long ears? Munim smiled at my surprise.

The city's walls, where they weren't draped with political messaging, boasted dramatic film posters, each a variety on two themes: big guns and big girls. One poster added a large bottle of J and B whisky to the mix. I called Masud Alam to remark on this, and he told me about a poster he'd seen which also used the whisky bottle, but in this case dramatically positioned between one of the big girls' legs. 'Welcome to the Islamic Republic of Pakistan,' said Masud.

We drove along 'the Mall' towards 'Charing Cross', past the 'Mughal Gothic' monuments of the British period. We drove past a wedding procession. 'Another funeral,' quipped Munim. 'Very sad.' The bridegroom's face was hidden by bank notes to protect him from the evil eye. At dusk we strolled through the baobabs, *peepuls*, magnolias and the thick and ropey banyans of Lawrence Garden. The sky overhead was a storm of hawks and crows. There was a small shrine inside the park, and a man distributing sweets in response to an answered prayer.

Munim disapproves of shrines. He thinks that to visit them and believe in their power is *shirk* – the sin of associating others with God – and a grim signal of lingering Hindu influence; Sarah, on the other hand, likes the peace she finds in shrines, and thinks they're fine so long as the visitor remembers that God, not the buried saint, is the one who answers prayers. Later in the evening we visited the shrine of Shah Jamal, and the dispute gently unfolded, husband and wife taking opposing sides in a burning contemporary debate – Deobandi clerics with Munim and the Barelvis with Sarah. Amongst some of those politicised by the war on the frontier, this argument has reached such a pitch of fury that shrines have been bombed and their visitors dismembered.

This is why I wasn't allowed into the shrine of Data Ganj Baksh (bombed July 2010, forty-two killed) until I'd relinquished my mobile phone and camera. There were three separate checks on the way in. It's why there are so many night checkpoints in the Cantt, why gates in general have become so popular.

In Lawrence Garden we heard the roaring of lions from the zoo just over the railings. The zoo's peacocks and bears died from fear when a nearby ISI building was blown up. Children from a neighbouring school were also blown up.

Attacks on the cities in the plains had been in abeyance for some months. People debated the cause of the lull – whether the militants were pleased by Pakistan's slightly stronger tone with the Americans, the closing of an American air base and the suspension of NATO convoys through Pakistani territory, or whether the army had scored successes in eliminating the bomb makers. Whatever the reason, people feared that the lull was temporary.

'How do you keep going?' I asked Sarah. I was thinking of Hassan and Saad.

'You ignore it,' she said. 'Otherwise you cannot live.'

Life is certainly continuing in Lahore. Pull up at the lights and there's a deformed child (probably deliberately deformed) begging, or a boy washing the windscreen, or a man making a monkey clap for a few rupees, or a man banging a drum. Alternatively park at some shopfronts, wind down the window, order some samosas or juice, and watch the people buying and selling, joking and fighting, singing and praying, smoking and snoring. And playing cricket, for Pakistanis are playing cricket wherever you cast your gaze, in empty spaces and full spaces, on the busy main road. There's a ball whizzing under the wheels of the rickshaw...

What else? A Marxist reading group was meeting at Cafe Bol. This week Foucault was up for discussion. Qalandar was worrying about the next issue of his leftist magazine *Naked Punch*. My old friend Mazhar Zaidi, then a journalist now a film producer, was waiting for the famous Indian actor Naseeruddin Shah to arrive. This was a tightly-kept secret at the time – Shah had asked for no paparazzi – but it won't be now.

Dr Zaheda Durrani, a friend of my mother's since their student years at the Royal College of Obstetricians and Gynaecologists, was still working hard, practising and teaching, despite creeping arthritis. Never married, Dr Durrani is reputed throughout Lahore. Munim and I met her in the Fatima Memorial Hospital where she'd just supervised a procedure, then had lunch at her home in Icchra. Her old neighbours moved to newer suburbs as Icchra was swallowed into the central zone, but Dr Zaheda stayed because she loves the house, roomy enough to house any number of relatives (two nieces were visiting from the United States), and shielded by a wall and a beautiful garden from the clanking and fuming outside.

Munim was reluctant to allow me to wander about alone. The way I saw it, the worst that could happen was I'd be taken for a *gora sahib*, leading some people to say 'hello hello' and gently try to fleece me. 'That's not the problem,' he said. 'Kidnapping for ransom is the problem. It's a big business. If you look alone and wealthy you could become a target.'

I can't have looked wealthy. Either that or Pakistan's gangsters are as inefficient as its police state. I roamed around on foot or by taxi or rickshaw, and I always felt safe and was never bothered.

Preferably by rickshaw. That way you experience the ride. The drivers tend to be lively and the machines themselves are versatile beasts – if there's a back seat too, up to twelve people can be crammed on board. It's a bumpy ride, not to be done with a full bladder. You breathe a lot of dust and diesel, but it's still better than Tehran.

My first independent trip was to the Badshahi Masjid, which is a wonder of the world and something to see before you die. During my afternoon there and in the neighbouring historic Fort I saw not a single tourist. There were family groups and clusters of friends and a couple of gay men cruising, but I was the only foreigner.

Outside on the grass a tournament of kabadi, the wrestling and running game, was being held. The players had oiled themselves to make slippery targets and their bodies glistened under the sun.

To my right on the approach to the Mughal monuments lay the golden-domed gurdwara of Sikhism's fifth guru, Arjan Dev, and a shrine commemorating Ranjit Singh, the conqueror who established the Sikh empire in the Punjab which preceded the British Raj. I tried to get in but the gurdwara was closed to the public. I had that feeling I'd had a couple of days before when I'd glimpsed Devnagari script on buildings in the Old City, or a distinctively Hindu tower unlabelled and hidden behind blocks, a feeling of tantalising and slightly terrible absence, of an eery silence amidst the noise. At a later dinner Ahmad Rafay Alam told me about the non-Muslim Shah Alam Gate area which was razed by arsonists between August and September 1947. Five thousand residential buildings were destroyed. As Rafay pointed out, the Luftwaffe bombings of British cities rarely did such damage.

Very much present, Allama Iqbal's tomb is prestigiously located in the garden between mosque and fort. It's slightly austere compared with the Sufi shrines, and guarded by decorative soldiers, but simple and peaceful. A man sat cross-legged at the head of the slab singing a beautiful nasheed. Iqbal is Pakistan's national poet and an originator of the Pakistan Movement, but poets in general are highly respected in Pakistan as they are throughout the Muslim world, at least once they're dead, even Marxist poets like Faiz Ahmad Faiz.

Then up the steps, through the astounding portal, and into the Badshahi compound. As monumental mosques go, I don't think this one can be bettered. It's a construction (not a building, because most of it is space) which reconciles contrasts; vast but gentle, minimalist but ornamental. It's certainly solid, yet it floats like a gauzy curtain. On its walls white marble is laid in pink sandstone in the same way that mother-of-pearl is laid into wood. Three onion domes hover over the roof. The ceilings wear floral and geometric decoration in soft oranges, reds and greens. Although it's most similar to other Mughal work in India (the Jamaa Mosque at Delhi, the Taj Mahal at Agra), the Badshahi refers too to the architecture of the western Islamic heartland. The trees and flowers recall the Umawi Mosque in

Damascus, the entrance gate Isfahan, the enormous courtyard the mosque at Kufa.

'Pakistanis can't do anything right,' Munim had said, so when I talked about the Badshahi Mosque that evening I pointed to it as an example of something Pakistanis had once done entirely right. 'But was it Pakistanis who built it?' he asked.

The question of who owns the mosque sparked discussion in a journalists' club the following night. On the one hand its construction was undertaken by Mongol, Turkic, Persian and Afghan invaders and craftsmen as well as by local workers. On the other hand, that mixture of blood and culture was what modern Pakistan has inherited, just as the Urdu language – Urdu means army in Turkish (and 'horde' in English) – had coalesced from Hindi, Farsi, Arabic, Punjabi and Turkish.

This principle was generally accepted. But could the resulting polyculture be accurately named 'Pakistani'? That was the controversy. Shiraz Raj, an Urdu poet, thought not. 'This is the Indus valley civilisation. Pakistan has been in its present form only since 1971. It was half Bengali before then. Who can tell what its form will be tomorrow?'

Which brought the conversation round to Balochistan, and America's machinations therein, and what China would and wouldn't allow. Several Chitrali cigarettes were smoked. Ahmad Nur of BBC Urdu passed me some US army issue caffeine gum, issued to patrolling infantrymen to keep them alert in Afghanistan but in this instance looted from a NATO supply convoy in Khyber Pakhtoonkhwa and sold on the streets of Lahore. Also contributing to the discussion were Shafqat Ullah, the long-haired, pensive, eloquent editor of Ham Shehri magazine; and Amir, a crime scene forensics investigator, one of 200 in Lahore. His biggest obstacle is the untrained ordinary policemen who like to mop away the blood and bundle up the corpses before he arrives. He spoke about a judicial execution he'd observed a few days previously. A hanging.

After a couple of hours we crammed into a car and drove to Shah Jamal.

One of the shrine keepers recognised me from my previous visit with Munim and Sarah. His welcome was warm and genuine. It would have made me feel at home if I hadn't already been feeling very much at home. Last time I came was also at night. The smell of jasmine and roses hung around the green dome. The walls and floor were white. There were visitors but no crowds, and a lone man singing in the attached mosque.

This time, as on every Thursday night, the shrine itself, as well as the street outside and the surrounding compound, was drunk with happy crowds. Once we'd paid our respects to the saint we followed our ears to the drums.

They played on two levels.

Upstairs Pappu Saeen, Pakistan's premier *dhol* player, was drumming. He's played in studios and with a roster of international musicians, but Shah Jamal is his home ground. He was accompanied by his deaf and dumb brother Gonga Saeen who drums as Beethoven composed, by vibration not sound. Pappu Saeen was ringletted and wore a long black shirt. His brother was heavily bearded, and wore red.

Other drummers, the students of the Saeens, drummed in the courtyard downstairs. The two levels made no attempt to play in synch but they did play in concert, frequently suggesting rhythms one to the other. The drums continued for hours – rising and falling, intensifying and declining.

Upstairs there were many more tombs to house the disciples of Shah Jamal. Men sat between gravestones and branches and red and green streamers. Rice cakes and *jellabee* were distributed, and Chitrali cigarettes and cups of tea. A vat of something was bubbling in an alcove surrounded by swinging heads. Closer to the drumbeat the men sat cross-legged in a layered circle. Some shook their heads smoothly in response to the rhythm, some shook violently, some watched and smiled. One man had covered his head with a blanket and was convulsing beneath it.

On both levels, dancing *daraweesh* spun within the circle, bouncing, gyrating, jerking; and banging their heads, swirling their hair, waving their arms; spinning through the peaks and troughs of their ecstasy. Some wore red or green turbans. A wild *malang* swung his staff and amulets and conversed with things unseen.

The *haal* had taken them. They were lost in the unity of all, possessed by the spirit of God. Take that as you will.

In the calms which arrived after the peaks a *malang* ran round the circle reviving the crowd. 'Must Qalandar!' he shouted – referring to Lal Shahbaz Qalandar, the saint buried at Sehwan Sharif – and the crowd responded: 'Joolay Lal!'

This was not the considered, orthodox Sufism of Ejaz's shaikh but another tradition entirely: the 'drunken' Sufism of unrestrained gesture. It offends the straitlaced and the literalist. But whether the modernist orthodox like it or not, this is the original Muslim culture of Pakistan, or one of them. These shrines are where Sunni/Shia distinctions, and even Muslim/Hindu distinctions, dissolve. Shafqat Ullah said so when we were standing outside Shah Jamal's tomb, and then he quoted the Punjabi poet Bulleh Shah:

'If you know the truth, you'll know the distance between Ram and Rahim is nothing.'

I preferred Shafqat's version to the one I found on the internet later:

'If you can understand, then why all this commotion?

What's this fuss about calling Him Ram, Rahim or Moula?'

Without these travelling saints, without the cultural blurring and reforming that occurred around them, this part of the world would not now be Muslim. The conquerors conquered, but the itinerant mystics converted the people. Islam's adaptability allowed it to survive.

'These are the graves of men,' said Ahmad Nur, 'who taught the true Islam, the religion of peace. This is real Islam here.'

Again, purists would dispute this. Certainly aspects of the tradition are pre-Islamic, but some are pre-Hindu too. The urge to worship through dance is ancient and universal. In those cultures which repress it, it eventually returns. The music-based subcultures among the formerly Protestant natives of the West, the raves and rock festivals, are an obvious recent case.

The Pakistani version compares favourably to the Western. The shamble-dancing of northern counterculturalists, though energised by similar urges, seems sometimes naive or contrived because it doesn't exist within a tradition, at least not a deeply-rooted tradition. But the malangs at Shah Jamal spin within a tradition of centuries' maturation, in a culture of poetry, music and prayer. Rather than showy indiscipline, there's order in their dance. 'Drunk' as they are, they spin for hours but don't lose their footing.

Somewhere at any Western rave there's an undercurrent of aggression, and an element of flashiness emanating from the people who've come to see and be seen. But not here. This was an entirely respectable, friendly, relaxed crowd reflecting a happy mix of backgrounds. Even the toilets were clean, not smeared with alcoholic piss and vomit. Half way through I realised a white woman was present – the only foreigner I saw in Lahore. No-one was even looking at her.

Apart from her there were no women at Shah Jamal, but at Sehwan Sharif in Sindh, where a million gather for Lal Shahbaz Qalandar's death anniversary, men and women (and transexuals) dance all together.

It would be foolishly Blairite to expect Pakistan's easygoing Sufism to provide any political 'answers' to local or global crises. As soon as political organisation is grafted on top, the shrine culture becomes as corrupt as any other. The 'Sufi' Barelvi clerics rejoiced in the murder of Salman Taseer as much as their Deobandi counterparts. But in social terms what I saw at Shah Jamal is one kind of already-existing answer, as well as a reminder of more tolerant times and a pointer to a possible future.

Bahawalpur

I travelled south for eight hours on a Daewoo bus. On this route there was no VIP service. I wore my neck brace and tried to relax. Faisalabad, called 'Pakistan's Manchester' for its textile industry, lay somewhere to the west. The site of Harappa, a great city five thousand years ago, was also westward.

Southern Punjab made me think of Mesopotamia, a similarly ancient river culture with similar clay bricks and kilns, canals and irrigation channels, and the desert sensed, hiding somewhere beyond the fields. Firewood was piled at the side of the road and groves of squat date and tall coconut palms grew. Down into the Seraiki belt – named after the language spoken here, a variant form of Punjabi – many more of the men wore fat white turbans.

Shortly before Bahawalpur the bus crossed the empty Sutlej. India dammed the river on its side of the Punjab according to the terms of the Indus Waters Treaty signed in 1960 by India's Nehru and Pakistan's General Ayub Khan. This is a bone of contention in Bahawalpur. 'Two new canals were to be constructed here. They never were. The result is a shortage of clean drinking water.' I was told this over a restaurant table by a group of local journalists who unanimously supported reviving Bahawalpur's provincial status, gained in 1952 when the Nawab's princely state became part of Pakistan and lost in 1954 when the provinces were absorbed into 'one unit' in an attempt to offset East Pakistan's electoral majority. In 1970 Yahya

Khan restored the provinces, but Bahawalpur was amalgamated into the Punjab. Local elections in that year were swept by the restorationist Bahawalpur United Front.

The desired province would include Bahawalnagar and Rahim Yar Khan. The journalists assured me that 95 per cent of people living in these areas wanted their province back, and that their dream was economically viable. 'We have cash crops. Wheat, cotton, sugar. All the livestock in the Cholistan desert.'

The province could be restored by executive order, they told me. Wasn't this the manner by which the Chief Justice was reinstated after General Musharraf sacked him? All the political parties support the idea, even the People's Party local leadership, but the PPP government has floated the idea of a Seraiki province instead. My journalist interlocutors were sure this was designed simply as a spanner in the works of the Bahawalpur province, and for PPP electoral gain. Unfortunately the Seraiki province is a popular concept in Multan, a large city to the north which would become the Seraiki provincial capital and overshadow Bahawalpur.

I stayed with Munim's brother. I didn't become part of the family as I had in Lahore because Bahawalpur is a much more conservative place, but Wajid's hospitality was unstinting nevertheless. He arranged a schedule of sightseeing and meetings to fill every moment of my brief two-day stay.

Everywhere we went I heard Nawab-nostalgia. Some of this is common or garden nostalgia as witnessed everywhere; some was rooted very firmly in the tangible failures of the Pakistani state. The last Nawab built Bahawalpur a library, a hospital, a university, a zoo and a cricket ground which once hosted international matches. He also established the Sadiq Public School – public in the English sense, with blazers and ties, lawns and swimming pools, tuck shops and playing fields. 'Faith, Unity, Discipline', Pakistan's motto, flutters from a post. Within these well-guarded walls a Pakistan flourishes that Jinnah would have approved of, a kind of Eton.

In the dustier parts of the city, and in the villages and farms outside, the contrast with the Abbassi family state appears very pronounced indeed.

At Uch Sharif, a centre of Qadiri and Suhrawardiya Sufism in the thirteenth century, the ruins of tower tombs are steadily crumbling. Shoeless boys tried to sell me one of the fallen blue tiles. The poverty in the nearby village was grim, and incongruously juxtaposed with the green richness of the surrounding groves of mango and date palm.

The mighty walls of Derawar Fort, out on the edge of the Cholistan desert which extends into Rajasthan, are also slowly collapsing. (In Bahawalpur, the far less interesting Nur Mahal, a nineteenth-century home of the Nawabs, has been caringly maintained – because it's used as a mess by the army.) The sand and scrub wilderness around the fort is what much of southern Punjab and Sindh looked like before wide-scale irrigation, and what they may look like again if the apocalyptic predictions of climate change theory come true and the Indus runs out of water.

In Uch Sharif's village centre women and old men and boys were begging. Some of the boys were begging on behalf of traditional or Wahhabi madrasas. I noted the glaring divergence between this scene and the Sadiq Public School. As in so many fields of Pakistani life, there are two systems. Here it's one for the poor and one for the rich; more generally there are the two political dispensations, the state bequeathed by the imperial shapers, and the other system, of strong men and kinship networks.

Muhammad Baligh-ur-Rehman, Muslim League (N) Member of the National Assembly for Bahawalpur and special adviser to the Punjab's Chief Minister, gave a balanced account of madrasa education. They cannot be despised, he said, because they provide a service to the poor which no-one else provides. Some teach very backward versions of Islam and are in effect recruiting pools for militant outfits. These madrasas must be watched and further regulated. Some madrasas, on the other hand, not only teach a more tolerant Islam but have also extended their curricula to include maths, science and modern languages.

Amongst the political class, so the MNA told me, there is finally some recognition of the centrality of education to development. He felt this would bear fruit in the future.

Baligh-ur-Rehman is a full-bearded, intelligent, apparently principled man. The people I was with assured me that he was indeed principled. He's partly responsible for a scheme which has awarded 2,000 laptops to Punjabi students according to merit. He questioned my host Wajid, who is a professor of journalism at the Islamia University, to check that the laptops distributed there had indeed been awarded to the most hardworking and highly achieving students, not to those with connections. He fed us tea and sandwiches, and then he turned his attention to the next of his many visitors and supplicants.

It's a simplification to say there are two education systems. In reality there are many – the good madrasas and the bad, the good and bad 'secular' schools, the public and private universities.

Bahawalpur's Islamia University serves the region's middle classes. Once a pioneering institution, its quality slipped for most of the Pakistan years, but now – according to Baligh-ur-Rehman and to my own observations – it is recouping some of its former reputation. I visited the Baghdad al-Jadeed campus, so named in recognition of the founding Nawab's Iraqi origins, and met students whose articulacy would put British students to shame. I was introduced to the Dean of Islamic Studies, who told me that, in a welcome bridging of worlds, his faculty recruits outstanding students from the madrasa system. I met one, a friendly man who was finishing a dictionary of Bukhari's Arabic.

Everywhere there's a hunger for education. On the hoardings above the heads of Uch Sharif's begging boys a hustle of posters advertised a range of local private schools claiming to teach everything from O levels to MBAs. In Karachi, in a cafe and arts centre called the Second Floor, I met curious middle-class high school students who had very specific opinions on the Arab Spring and nuanced understandings of feminism.

The most remarkable institution I came across in Pakistan was the world-class Lahore University of Management Sciences, where I met writer Bilal Tanweer's students (and read some of their remarkable writing). Red-brick LUMS, funded by a group of wealthy businessmen, is entirely free of the political violence which has sometimes bedevilled other universities. It also enjoys freedom of speech. Bilal Tanweer remembers his Islamic Studies tutor declaring (for Bilal was a student here before he became a teacher) that there was no such thing as blasphemy in his class, that all serious questions and comments would be welcome. Bilal calls it 'an oasis'. We talked in a campus coffee shop owned by Omar Khan, director of Hell's Ground, Pakistan's first blood-and-gore film. Horror movie posters graced the walls.

Asad Farrouqi, a British Pakistani academic relocated to LUMS, was optimistic. 'There's an intellectual community here,' he said, 'people doing good work, on a far greater scale than even ten years ago.'

This was my own overwhelming impression, that there's great cause for celebration in Pakistan. But of course the old ossifications remain to be broken. A poster in Karachi assured its viewers that the politician depicted intended to uphold 'Pakistan's ideology'. People who use this phrase undertake no examination of what it might mean. The assumption that 180 million people could share in one ideology reminds me of those audience participants on American talk shows who stand up and squawk 'This is America!', and receive resounding, unthinking applause.

Back in Bahawalpur, a collage at the petrol station depicted atrocities from Palestine, Iraq, Afghanistan and Guantanamo Bay, with a cross in the centre as if it were the motivating factor. Another collage, of past conquerors, played up Islam's martial element. As many will tell you this is the 'real' and 'true' Islam as will attach authenticity to the Sufi versions.

On our trip to Uch Sharif and Derawar we were accompanied by the father of one of Wajid's students, an ex-headmaster and very much a martial Muslim. I shared the car's back seat with him, and he talked non-stop for ten hours. At first boredom made my jaws ache, but soon I marvelled at the man's relentless energy, and I finally grew to like him. He was certainly a man of opinions – including the opinion that the 'two-nation theory' which established Pakistan can be found in the Qur'an. He talked a lot of the 'supremacy of Islam' and also, in his English redolent of a bygone age, of 'nefarious plots'. Imran Khan's failed marriage to a Jew, for instance, was a sure sign of global anti-Pakistan conspiracy.

I'd been warned in Lahore about the sectarian and terrorist reputation of the Bahawalpur region, home to the 'Punjabi Taliban'. The restorationist journalists dismissed the charge as unfair. Yes, there was extremism – Wajid's student Mohammad Zunair showed me a documentary he'd helped to make about an attack on a Bahawalpur church in 2001 – but there was extremism all over the country.

Christians, already suffering from their class and caste image (many work as cleaners and domestic servants), have suffered in recent years from illogical association with the 'Christian' West and its War on Terror. The driver who picked me up at Karachi airport was a Christian called Steven. 'How is it to be a Christian here?' I asked him. 'Worse and worse,' he said. 'If you rise up, there's always someone to put you back down.' When Irfan, the Christian servant who looked after the Brigadier in Lahore, heard I was going to give a talk at LUMS, he said, 'Tell them, Sir, to follow the example of their Prophet, and love and respect the Christians. That will be good for them and their families and for our country.'

While I was in Rawalpindi a demonstration threatened blood if an Ahmadi mosque were not shut down (perhaps we should say 'place of worship' instead of 'mosque' – Ahmadi Muslims are forbidden by a Zia-era law from using Islamic vocabulary). In Indus Kohistan 16 Shia were taken off a bus by men wearing uniforms and summarily murdered.

None of this is inevitable. There are still two million Hindus in Sindh. There are still places like Sehwan Sharif where people of all self-definitions dance together. In Karachi my Muslim friend Mazhar was recently invited to a baptism. In Karachi Mohammad Hanif and Bina Shah have both written novels featuring ballsy Christian heroines. Sarah says that in Moinuddinpur, her ancestral village, Sunni and Shia intermarry more often than not. The son adopts the father's faith, the daughter the mother's. Or the children are offered the choice once they reach maturity, having learnt about both. 'This is unusual, I think,' she says.

It's certainly more unusual than it used to be. 'I remember extremely peaceful times,' her father, Brigadier Asadullah, says, in reference to Muslim-Christian relations.

The times have changed. General Zia and the 'jihads' in Afghanistan and Kashmir have something to do with it. So, obviously, do US drone strikes and Pakistani double dealing on the tribal frontier.

More generally, rightist religious nationalism has burgeoned in South Asia since the supposed death of the left (India, unlike Pakistan, has actually been ruled by a religious-nationalist administration – that of the BJP), as well as throughout a mostly directionless and often brutalised Muslim world in which the needs of the mass of the population have been left unattended.

Waqar Ashraf, who works for BBC Urdu in Karachi, hit the obvious nail on the head. 'Just give these people justice,' he said, referring to the followers of obscurantist mullahs. 'Just give them equal law, basic health and education.'

That we tend to frame our inquiries in simplistically religious terms reveals our ignorance of Pakistan. In the West, when we hear 'Pakistan' we think of the Talibs, as if all 180 million people in the country, women included, have long beards, big guns, and bad attitudes. This despite the fact that Islamists have never come even near to winning national elections. If we pay slightly more attention we know the Talibs share Pakistan with an upper class liberal fringe. We don't know much of the diversity of the place, of ethnic and class struggles, nor of the enormous educated middle class. For me it was most illuminating to learn that there are angry poor people in Pakistan who are expressing their anger not through extremist Deobandi or Wahhabi versions of Islam, but through grass roots leftism: the Okara peasants' movement, engaged in a three-way fight with the army and the Punjab administration over the right to be tenant farmers rather than share-croppers; fishermen in the southern Punjab who express their demands at workers' councils; and the Maoist villagers of Hashtnagar in Khyber Pakhtoonkhwa who drove their landlords out. These stories are absent from our media.

Which brings me to the American ambassador's bad speech on the Karachi Literature Festival's opening night. First he made statements – like 'We are listening' – to make the most pro-American of Pakistanis cringe. Then he made a bad premise. Events like the KLF, he suggested, were an answer to obscurantism. By obscurantism he probably meant the Pakistani Taliban. But I didn't notice many tribesmen in the glamorous setting. I didn't see any refugee from a blood-drenched village nodding his head to the ambassador's speech and muttering 'Well, you know, that's right. The Vikram Seth session has indeed assuaged my anger.' Those who wish to fight America would doubtless tell us that it's the drones which must stop, not the festivals which must increase. But America isn't really listening.

The north west of the country is a war zone. A separatist movement meets savage repression in Balochistan. All over the country there are dizzying gulfs between rich and poor. Yet Pakistan as a whole seems to be flourishing. Why? Why isn't it exploding?

It didn't look to be exploding when I took the bus through Sindh back to Karachi. For parts of the fourteen-hour bus ride (Daewoo again, and not VIP) my head was exploding, but not the country beyond. Sindh – the great unexplored, as far as I was concerned. My three weeks, full as they were, had consisted of Punjab-centric glimpses. I hadn't been to the vastnesses of Balochistan, or to Khyber Pakhtoon Khwa. Nor to the Northern Areas, which I remember from nineteen years ago as the most beautiful and fascinating landscapes I'd ever experienced. But from the window I judged what

I could of Sindh. Except where flooded, it was drier, more open, and some-how softer than the Punjab, the clothes more colourful. I passed a camel market, and tractors loaded with raw sugarcane backed up in their hundreds outside a refinery.

In *Pakistan – A Hard Country*, Anatole Lieven argues firstly that Pakistan is no more a failed state than India, and secondly, that even were it in a greater mess than it is presently, Pakistan will not collapse into revolution. This is because the country is too diverse, split by region, language, class and kinship networks, by sect, ethnicity and caste.

Masud Alam was dismissive of this latter argument. 'Only someone who doesn't really know this country would say that.' Masud asked why no equivalent of the Arab Spring had happened in Pakistan, and then partially answered his question: 'We have a simulacrum of democracy, that's the problem. The democracy label is attached to the People's Party, and look at the People's Party. It's supposed to be a mass party. It's a parody of itself.'

I remarked that I'd heard many people describe Imran Khan as 'Pakistan's last hope'. So what happens if Imran comes to power and fails? What lies after the last hope? Masud shrugged and smiled a despairing smile. 'Another last hope,' he said.

Sparks flew at the literature festival when Ayesha Siddiqa, author of the fiercely anti-military book *Military Inc, Inside Pakistan's Military Economy*, accused Anatol Lieven of being too enamoured of the army. MNA Baligh-ur-Rehman, like everyone I asked, was enraged by Pakistan's surrender of its sovereignty on the frontier, and he blamed the unaccountable military high command. Pakistan's self-destructive policies would continue, he argued, until civilian democracy is strong enough to hold every decision before public scrutiny.

From his very different perspective, Mazhar Zaidi agreed. 'I am fully supportive of civilian corruption,' he wryly asserted. 'You can gradually confront civilian corruption, but you can't confront a man with a gun.'

Sindh Rangers checked ID cards on my bus as we entered the province. As we entered Karachi the Rangers got on again. This time they videoed our faces.

Security. Security. Who to blame? Corrupt politicians or wicked generals? Dastardly feudals or the nefarious plots of foreign powers?

Renowned novelist Mohsin Hamid noted that almost every Pakistani had his or her favourite bugbear to blame. He had a simple answer: 'Blame us'

We met for lunch at a high-class Italian place in Lahore. Mohsin talked effusively about Lahore. He's more optimistic about his city's future than he is about Pakistan's, but he's optimistic about Pakistan too. One in six Pakistanis lives in Karachi or Lahore, in the business/media or cultural/intellectual capitals. 'This is having an effect. It will have a larger effect.'

With its new energies released, Pakistan may be heading for a revolutionary movement, but it won't be a similar moment to the Arab Spring. This for the simple reason that Pakistan is far more developed politically than almost anywhere in the Arab world. No dictator has ever been able to completely smother Pakistan's civil society, and least of all now. Even if one group of lawyers shamed themselves by anointing Salman Taseer's murderer with rice, the judiciary is now independent. Even if much of it is bubble-gum for the eyes, and rehearses religio-nationalist rubbish, the media is independent and thriving. Even if it's presided over by a kleptomaniac, the civilian government this time is set to complete its term. The country is overflowing with the bright and the beautiful. Despite everything.

The pertinent question may not be who to blame, but who to praise. And the pertinent answer is Mohsin Hamid's 'us' – the people of Pakistan.

KARACHI IN FRAGMENTS

Taimur Khan

Shahid kept his pigeons in a coop on the roof of his home, nested some-where in the anthill labyrinth of Karachi's oldest neighbourhood, Lyari. The building was crumbling in places, but the coop was of the modern variety, replete with receding ledges and fluorescent lighting, and the birds' white feathers and painted bodies were plump from a luxurious diet of wheat, black chickpeas and almonds. 'Salman,' 'Govinda,' 'Katrina,' thirty or forty Bollywood-named birds resided here, cajoled and trained for competition, groomed to be 'flyers' or 'leaders'. A young, speckled Afghan pigeon can cost tens of thousands of rupees, sometimes payable in instalments. Upon arrival it is completely plucked. Helpless and flightless, the newly born bird is carefully fed and cared for. Forty days later its loyalty is measured in its consistent return from heights and distances difficult to discern with the naked eye.

Shahid often spent his evenings lying on his back, watching these birds, listening to their barely audible evening coo. Twenty-five nearby pigeon racers had organised a tournament for later that month. Shahid and the others had paid 4,000 rupees to enter; the owner of the bird that stayed in the air the longest would be declared the winner. First prize was a motor-cycle, but Shahid hoped to win the third prize, a television. His friends and neighbours were all lovingly grooming their birds on nearby rooftops, ten-derly feeding them 'motor-on' pills, his name for the amphetamine that would ensure the birds' high flights. The pigeons were his most prized pos-session; every evening he initiated his eight-year-old son into the craft, as Mir Nihal did for Asghar in Ahmed Ali's *Twilight in Delhi*. But the pigeon racers of today aren't the crumbling oligarchy of old. In fact they are new subjects, with unprecedented desires and novel political affiliations. On the cusp of an amorphous and ill-defined middle class, these are the new actors in the story of modern Karachi.

The deceptively capacious rooftop sat three storeys above the capillary lanes below. Drying laundry hung over the chest-high boundary wall; a baby goat tethered to the leg of a sagging *charpoy* nipped at a pile of hay. Under the adulterated purple night sky, an accretion of uneven city spread in all directions. It seemed possible to skip along the top of Lyari, roof to roof, all the way to the sea.

From the ports and beaches on the Arabian Sea to the south, Karachi crawls haphazardly north over green mangrove swamps and along the Lyari and Malir rivers, west to the lunar mountains of Baluchistan, and northeast into the flat scrubland of Sindh. Each year, the city colonises a little more of the desert to make space for thousands upon thousands of new residents.

Here, there is room for everyone; Karachi is now a Pakistan in miniature, with all of its ethnic and linguistic DNA in competition and combination. The broad strokes are familiar: Muhajir and Pashtun, Sindhi and Punjabi and Baloch. But these labels fail to contain the multitudes of sub-groups who defy the taxonomy. What of the Kashmiris, Seraikis, Swatis, Biharis, Bengalis, Goans, Parsis, Hindu banyas?

The cacophonous roadside bus depots near Cantt Station or out in Sohrab Goth are in perpetual motion. Long modern coaches inhale and exhale passengers twenty-four hours a day, the bus's front windows displaying the names of their far-flung destinations in Khyber-Pakhtunkhwa (formerly North West Frontier), Punjab, Sindh and beyond. The air-conditioned conveyors drop passengers at countless near-anonymous villages and towns along the way, a service the atrophying train network can't deliver.

The state, in fact, doesn't do much in Karachi. In its absence ethnic bonds were the grids along which neighbourhoods developed and the voice in which demands were articulated. The narrow potentialities of patronage politics pushed out other possible configurations. The Muttahida Qaumi Movement (MQM) party dominates Karachi and pioneered the city's brand of ethnic politics. The MQM claims to represent the interests of the Partition refugees from northern India, Muhajirs, who make up the largest single 'ethnic' group in the city but whose proportionate size is shrinking. Without a demographic reservoir in the provinces, many Muhajirs perceive 'their' city to be besieged by the legions of Pashtun newcomers who have imitated the MQM's politics to, among other things, organise against the MQM.

Neighbourhoods contract their ethnic political party to provide every imaginable service, from supplying water to accessing affordable housing to securing jobs and education. And sometimes, in the battle for the dwindling resources, things get ugly. It is from this conflict that modern Karachi has been born. But the city is one that runs on commerce, and everyone needs everyone else. Memon developers rely on the Lyari gangsters; the Muhajir businesses rely on Pashtun labour.

It's difficult for me not to find sympathy for the MQM's story, for it is partly my family's own. More importantly, it has produced modern Karachi. Separated from their homes, without the vertebrae of kinship in a country where such biological connections are crucial, Muhajirs were excluded from jobs and resources, from the country they paid for with their blood and sacrifice. What began as a student movement turned a culturally disparate group of immigrants of a similar class into a single, invented 'ethnic' group, Karachi's largest.

Under democracy, they won local elections and then enforced their will ruthlessly on the streets. Soon, the ruling party, the military establishment and many inhabitants of Karachi had all had enough, and an operation was launched in 1992 to put the party 'in its place'. Thousands of MQM activists were killed and tortured. The favour was returned in kind. After seven years of raids and disappearances and fresh corpses in gunny bags, the operation was declared a success.

Then in 1999, the military took over government yet again, and wanting to join the end of history, its technocrats opened Pakistan to the revolutionising flow of global capital. A thousand new economies and new desires bloomed. The MQM found its opportunity for rehabilitation in the 2002 local elections when it allied itself with the regime and became the party of the future, of the expanding middle classes with globalised aspirations. Without the constraints of democratic compromise, the party dreamed of creating a smoothed-out new city of malls and corporate high rises and flyovers. If whole communities of the working poor were smashed apart in the process, so be it. But during this revolution, the ranks of the city's already large Pashtun population swelled, as war displaced millions from the northwest. Eventually, the military regime began to crack and a return to democracy looked inevitable. 12 May, 2007 was the tipping point.

The chief justice of Pakistan, the nemesis of former dictator Pervez Musharraf, scheduled a rally of his supporters in Karachi. MQM leaders said they would not allow him to leave the airport, and its armed cadres fanned out through the city in a show of force. But the unexpected happened. The parties that supported the restoration of democracy, the previously minor Awami National Party (ANP), a party of Pashtuns, and the Pakistan Peoples Party (PPP), fought the MQM in pitched battles throughout the city. More MQM men died than anyone else. Over sixty of their sector offices were burned to the ground. The chief justice never made it out of the airport, but the ANP accomplished something far more momentous: they showed that the MQM's hegemony could be successfully challenged.

Karachi is a city of the poor. Under the new economy, with its 'flexible labour' and privatisation of state-run corporations and all the rest of the structural adjustments of capitalist modernity, the great majority of its citizens are suffering from economic insecurity and ruthless competition. They are also in danger of being physically dispossessed by the developmental plastic surgery reshaping the city's physiognomy. The ANP's (and to a lesser extent the PPP's) street power made credible its claim that it represented a new political force in the city, and many in the working classes threw their support behind the parties, Pashtuns with the ANP and Baloch, Punjabis and others with the PPP. Whether the party elites have the interests of the poor in mind is less and less certain.

In response to its inevitable loss of electoral dominance, the MQM has catered to the varying strata of the Muhajir middle classes in Karachi, and more recently the elites, who are diverse and live more or less outside of the city's ethnic and political logic, ensconced in luxurious high-walled villas in exclusive neighbourhoods by the sea. For the middle classes they have continued to construct 'luxury' apartment blocks and gated communities, modern shopping malls, for-pay parks and public spaces. And for the elite, the flyovers and signal-free thoroughfares that can take them with ease from the upmarket area of Defence to their factories in Korangi or the airport.

But this is not their story.

Saddar

A column of brown hawks circled slowly overhead. I had come to consider the local raptors, ever-present in Karachi, as the unbiased guardians of the city: the only residents with the wisdom to see all, coldly and without prejudice. In a city hissing and steaming with inexorable change, to pause and look up at the birds provided some sense of certainty and comfort, and I had projected on to them this role of guardian observer. If you look around, wherever you might be in the city, the ragged predators are ceaselessly turning against the sky or tussling with crows or swooping down to snatch food from the ground in front of you.

On that late January day as the birds gathered like flies over carrion, I was standing on the footpath in front of the Karachi Press Club with a reporter for 'Metro One', a local Urdu-language news channel, and another young man from 'Khyber News', a Pashto-language channel based in Peshawar. We were waiting for the latest episode in a long-running drama pitting the unionised workers of the Karachi Electric Supply Company (KESC) against the latest private company to try its hand at running the city's beleaguered power utility. Seven years ago the public power company was privatised as part of Pakistan's push to sell off what were called inefficient public companies. In 2009 when KESC attempted to fire around 4,000 employees whose jobs it said had become superfluous, the workers struck back. Substations were burned, non-union employees were attacked, and KESC's headquarters besieged.

The company responded by offering a golden handshake, which most of the striking workers accepted. A handful were rehired on low wage contract salaries with no benefits. The remaining workers have done their best to 'disrupt business and poison the minds of our workers', as a KESC spokesman put it. Two weeks after the rally, I attended another of these disruptions in front of the gleaming new KESC offices. There I saw a striking worker set himself on fire. Nearly every day for a week after this I received calls from the leader of the union, Ikhlaq Khan, who asked me to attend the next decisive, all-important protest. But public sympathies dwindled, the press gave fewer column inches and airtime. The octagenarian KESC union was limping towards the grave.

With or without the union, you can still set your watch to the daily black-outs in most parts of Karachi. Electricity prices have nearly tripled since 2004, even with continuing subsidies, while the new corporate managers are paid indecently generous salaries. In upmarket neighbourhoods like Clifton, where theft is supposedly less frequent, residents suffer fewer blackouts and there are even call centre hot-lines to report disruptions. But in middle-class areas, blackouts can last half the day. The same is true for industrial zones, compounding the misery of increasingly insecure labourers who can't work when factories go limp during load-shedding. In the poorest neighbourhoods, where the parasitic kunda power theft system of wires, metal hooks and bamboo poles is necessary and bills go unpaid, power is simply shut off.

A couple of dozen of the striking workers arrived to commandeer the street. Middle-aged and strong, the KESC workers were a multi-ethnic lot, no small feat for a political organisation in Karachi. Some carried black flags, some red, some wore salwar kameez, some sweat-stained shirts and pants. The leaders of the workers union climbed on to the bed of the truck, flanked by a young boy who looked about ten standing with them. 'We will be victorious, even if it means waging war on these sister fuckers!' one screamed into the microphone. 'Your voice will even reach the ears of the Zardari!' In between speakers a random member of the crowd broke through the hum of chatter with a chant that was then taken up by every-one: 'Mazdoor, Mazdoor - Bhai, Bhai!' (labourers, labourers, brothers, brothers). Another speaker took the microphone, 'In Musharraf's time we ate *lathis* and *dandas* (sticks) and now in Zardari's time we're eating bullets. But nothing can stop us!' The boy punched his fist into the air.

While the workers posed for the line of cameramen standing between themselves and the speakers, I noticed a group of men, four or five, stand-ing to my right near the press club gate. They were religious men, wearing fist-length beards, prayer caps and salwar kameez, and they all appeared to be in their twenties. Crisp clothes, clean appearances and cool counte-nances. Youths with wispy beards arrived holding the black and white striped flags of the right-wing religious party Jamiat Ulema-e-Islam-Fazlur (JUI-F). They wore salwar kameez but with a modern flair: designer glasses and expensive looking leather loafers. I immediately understood in some phenomenological way the charismatic appeal of these Islamists, their seductive pheromone of purpose and power. The religious men watched amusedly as a dark, grey-haired worker at the rally recited an Urdu poem over the truck's PA system. The crumpled Baloch and Pathan and Bihari workers looked tired on their feet, attention waning, shoulders drooping.

As the man transitioned from poem into song, another flatbed truck slowly turned the corner at the far end of the street and inched towards us. Young men hung off of its sides waving the black and white stripped flag of the JUI-F. Hundreds of young acolytes followed on motorcycles, many with three or four men and boys riding sandwiched together. They were at the head of a procession that had been winding through the city, with a stop at the press club, to drum up support for a rally the party was holding later that week. The cleric's proclamations and the growl of the engines combined to drown out the union leader, his poem ground to bits. As the truck rolled closer at a snail's pace, the first phalanx of motorcycles began to pass the KESC truck, JUI-F flags fluttering passed the red ones, barely touching.

De Silva Town

The JUI-F rally a few days later drew hundreds of thousands of Karachi's Pashtuns. It was at least as big as cricket-star-turned-politician Imran Khan's heralded rally a month earlier and seemed to indicate that whatever monopoly the ANP had enjoyed over Karachi's Pashtun communities was now in question. Abdullah, a Pashtun man from Karachi, chuckled when I asked him if the ANP would be replaced by the JUI-F or Khan's Pakistan Tehreek-e-Insaaf (PTI). 'Those were all jobless madrassa students with nothing better to do,' he said. 'But many Pashtuns are very tired of the ANP.' He said they were corrupt, and moreover, had failed to protect average Pashtuns from political violence.

I had met Abdullah in 2010 while reporting on the endless scourge of drive-by assassinations between Muhajir and Pashtun political activists. At that time, the ANP had Abdullah's support, though he said he would rather focus on making money than become a card-holding party worker. Now, less than eighteen months later, Abdullah said he would vote for the PTI. We were chatting in front of the car rental shop his cousin owned in Liaqatabad. Abdullah, twenty-eight, was born and raised in a Karachi neighbourhood called De Silva Town. He was a bit self-conscious of his relatively dark complexion, and once explained that he wasn't as 'beautiful' as the members of his extended family in Manshera, in Pakistan's northwest, because of Karachi. 'They put chemicals in the milk here. And if you go to a hotel run by Muhajirs they don't even put buffalo milk in the tea, they use powder,' he had said. 'In my village the milk is fresh and the weather is cold, unlike Karachi. So I have black skin.'

Abdullah has a wife and two young sons, one three and one six. They live with his parents and one of his brothers and his family in a two-story house that he proudly tells me the family owns. Abdullah began working as a driver when he was twelve, and it seems like he knows every lane and gully in Karachi. Along with driving, he also makes money as an ace cricket batsman, a ringer in neighbourhood leagues. Abdullah exists at the upwardly mobile end of the Pashtun working class. He saved enough to put himself through English language courses and he hopes to invest in a transport company with his brothers one day. But he still lives hand to mouth, earning around Rs20,000 every month.

Although household expenses are split between him and his brother, Abdullah manages to save very little after paying private school fees for both of his sons as well as the rising electricity bills. If there is a strike, an increasingly common occurrence, or another round of violent political skirmishing, of which ordinary Pashtuns are the most common victims, he loses his wages for the day. During the Ramadan violence in the summer of 2011, he didn't work for a week straight as one of the worst bouts of political violence in a decade bloodied the streets around his house. With his Gold Leaf cigarette smoking between his fingers he points to the charred wisps above the doorway behind us, the result of Molotov cocktails.

Abdullah offered to introduce me to his friends, and that night we drove towards De Silva Town to meet them. We cut through North Nazimabad on a main street, past the big gated houses and the dozens of checkpoint style gates that close off the inner streets from the thoroughfares. De Silva Town shares with Katti Pahari, an ANP stronghold, the rocky ridge that separates Muhajir North Nazimabad from Pashtun Qasba Colony and multi-ethnic Orangi Town. This small triangle has been a violent flashpoint in the recent political violence.

As we turned on to the road at the base of the ridge, the tricolour stripes of MQM flags gave way to the red flags of the ANP. In the midst were the crescented green and white of the PTI, as well as the black and white flags of the Sipah-e-Sahaba Pakistan, a banned extremist anti-Shia party. The clouds had dissipated to reveal a large jaundiced moon, which hung over the ridge as we drove. Lights from the rows of shops and stalls illuminated bullet holes pockmarking a school. Further along, walls daubed with graffiti lionising 'Bollu', an infamous local ANP gunman.

We parked the car in front of a 'Quetta hotel' tea shop. Quetta hotels, run by Pashtuns from Balochistan, are all over Karachi and serve the city's best tea, kept on the boil and made with fresh buffalo's milk. Anyone, of any ethnicity, will concede to its superiority. As we walked toward one of the gulleys leading into the heart of the neighbourhood I asked Abdullah if we needed to take the necessary precaution of having someone watch the car. He wrinkled his brow and smiled, as if it should have been clear: 'I don't even need to lock it here. This is my area.'

Nearby was a pool hall with no door, its gulley-facing side open, but we had to squeeze by the big carom board, set atop precarious stacks of cinder-block and scrapwood, to get inside. 'What's going on, you motherless pimp?' Abdullah said to Ronny, the proprietor, as he feinted a jab at his stomach. The locals looked up from their games and chuckled. Ronny was tall with a gaunt face, hair parted on the side. He cut a comical figure, in a zip up Notre Dame hooded sweatshirt with a winter scarf wrapped several times around his neck and white woollen gloves. He circled from station to station, collecting money, chiding the players, asking for cigarettes. After each round, he would kneel beneath the pool table hammering at a creaky leg. The hall was about 25 by 10 feet, its walls originally painted a pleasing eggshell blue. But in that oft-described Sub-Continental aesthetic, the black grime and *paan* spit had crept a good four feet up the walls, decorated with a gold 'Allah' in Arabic as well as a silver cross, and a poster of Bollywood star John Abraham. One could play foosball here, or Pac-Man, as well as carom and billiards, but the real drama was in politics.

The pool hall was full of local Christian teenagers. They looked a lot like the young middle and upper middle class Muhajir kids you might see in the Allahwali Chowrangi McDonald's or the Millennium mall in Gulshan-e-Iqbal, except a bit more frayed around the edges. Globally hip, with hyper-stylised asymmetrical haircuts, tight jeans, Che Guevara t-shirts. They all seemed to know Abdullah and his friends and would come over to us at the carom table and sledge us before we took our turns.

I lined up what looked to be an easy shot, and flicked the donut shaped striker, which knocked my piece away from the hole. One of the kids, named Yousaf, with bleached blonde hair, asked me in a whispered deadpan, 'Oh ho, are you feeling cold?' They had assumed I was a local Pashtun but when I told them I was an American journalist they crowded around, eager that I take their pictures. All of them were in secondary school, and some could speak English. Most of their parents were 'sweepers' but none of the kids were willing to do to the same work. The older ones all said they hoped to become nurses.

A twenty year old named Johnson said that the neighbourhood used to be controlled by the MQM. But even then, De Silva Town had been dominated, demographically, by Pashtuns. After the irruptions of 12 May, ANP fighters threw out the MQM leader in charge of the sector, effectively bringing De Silva Town under ANP sovereignty. The ANP gave the Christian community a choice: drop its support for the MQM and live in peace, or else. Johnson thought that by and large the Christians still notionally supported the MQM but in practice go to the local ANP functionaries when they need something taken care of. This kind of double (and triple) bind was in some way emblematic of the complexity of Karachi's politics.

I asked Abdullah and his friends about how life was for them, as Pashtuns, in Karachi as they navigated political violence and ethnic suspicion. Abdullah said that he had been trapped in his house for days during the bouts of violence, his children frightened that every time a loved one's phone rings and rings with no answer the spectre of death appears. He has Muhajir friends, from cricket, from his English classes, even from the neighbourhood. But after the ultra-violent summer of 2011, they have all moved away, to safer, homogenous spaces. The same is true of his relatives who lived in mixed areas. Slowly, almost imperceptibly, the prevailing state of nature has put into motion a self-cleansing. It's not about hatred or being scared of one's neighbours, it is the result of fear of being caught in the crossfire, on the wrong bus, when the parties decide it's time to play the game.

Abdullah himself was almost killed in that summer of 2011, on the night the former home minister Zulfikar Mirza gave an incendiary speech in which he said Muhajirs had come to Sindh 'naked and starving'. Abdullah was taking a Muhajir man from Malir to a family wedding. The rental Corolla was decorated with flowers; it was meant to be the couple's honeymoon car. But the speech aired and the backlash began on the streets immediately. The man asked Abdullah to turn around; the wedding was cancelled. He took the man back to his house, expecting to be invited in until the city stabilised. But the man closed his front gate, and that was that. 'I didn't know what I was going to do,' Abdullah said. He thought the decorated car would save him. It's a Muhajir thing, not a Pashtun custom. But he was wrong. When he drove out of the man's lane onto a main road, four motorbikes, each with a gunman riding pillion holding a pistol or AK-47, cut him off, men pointing guns at him from three sides. One of them reached through the rolled down window and punched him. 'Aap kaun?' the man asked. Who are you? More to the point: what are you?

Abdullah thought that they would shoot him. But he had an idea. He told them that he was Hazarawal, from a region of Khyber Pakhtunkhwa agitating for autonomy. They asked him to speak Hindko to prove it. He couldn't. He told them a partial lie and said he couldn't speak it because he was born and raised in Karachi. They threatened to kill him. They would surely kill him. But he told them to call his friend, a Hazarawal, who was in the MQM. They did and the friend vouched. The men let him go. Abdullah sped home on deserted streets, faster than he'd ever driven in the city, doubling back when he saw men with guns burning tires at intersections.

In some ways, the narrow escape routes of Abdullah and many of his friends explain the anxious rise of the ANP. The story of Jehangir, who was walking in just in time to witness my demise on the carom board, was a case in point. Jehangir was tall and muscular, handsome in his long hair and *pakul*. An activist for the party hoping to draw recruits, and something of a playboy interested in luring other kinds of admirers, it was an 'authentic' Pashtun look that he cultivated. When I took his photo later, he looked at the image on the camera's screen and said with a wink, 'Wow, John Abraham of the Pakhtun.' But Jehangir also carried a pistol, which he kept sheathed in a neoprene holster and, on this night, wrapped in his brown shawl. He came inside and put the shawl-wrapped pistol on the blue metal stool next to me, and stood around waiting for us to finish.

Abdullah and another friend, Rehmat, were arguing with each other in Pashto after the former cleaned up the board with a series of laser-precise shots. 'You should have let Taimur *bhai* win!' Abdullah was scolding him. Everyone was hungry. I had been looking forward to trying a local Pashtun roadside restaurant as part of my mission to conquer and know Karachi's culinary universe. I had eaten at the most famous *nihari* (spicy meat curry cooked slowly) joints in Malir, had kebab fry and *gola* kebab on Burnes Road, *cutacut* (offal curry) at Noorani in Mehmoodabad. But I still had not eaten at an authentic Pushtun spot. They tried to sway my hand towards a nearby Pizza Hut. But I persisted and they settled on a place in Patel Para, a busy commercial area lined with repair shops and small restaurants catering to the drivers and mechanics and working people nearby.

Jehangir asked if I wanted to ride with him, on the motorcycle, and I climbed on unsteadily, unsure about riding pillion with an armed ANP activist, along a road through an MQM stronghold. I didn't ask him what would happen if his enemies saw us, but I did ask him about the police. Yelling over the whooshing air and traffic, Jehangir casually allayed my fears: 'Don't worry, boss. The police are too scared to arrest party men.'

He told me with great pride that he was shot at from the overpasses on Sharah-e-Faisal as they tried to greet the chief justice at Karachi airport on 12 May. He didn't do much fighting that day, but it prepared him for what was to come. 'We are forced to fight by the MQM; we don't want to fight,' he said. 'They want to kill as many Pashtuns as they can, so that we get scared and leave. But this city is ours too, we have the right to be here, just as much as they do. They are immigrants just as much as we are!'

This noble self-conception is true in a sense, but as with all ethnic politics in the city, it's been hollowed out; the empty shell of rhetoric eclipses what is a closer approximation of the truth: all political actors in Karachi use violence, or the threat of it, against their rivals. That members of their own group will be targeted is an afterthought. The mantra: get rich, get rich; kill, kill, kill. But even working-class Pashtuns are starting to see through the lie. Illusions die in Karachi. Bodies fall, blood flows, deals are cut, money is counted. The party leaders are growing rich, as are many Pashtuns. But most still toil, more worried about making it through the day with their lives.

Federal B: Haji Club

Not far away, in the Federal B neighbourhood, is Haji Club, the biggest gym in Karachi. Its slogan, written on its website in English, is, 'Come as you are... leave as you want to be!' The club is symptomatic of the desires -- and unsettling frustrations -- produced by the new economies of consumption that have accompanied Pakistan's incorporation into the global economy. The mushrooming of private media, the liberalisation of finance and banking, and the boom in local and multinational telecom companies have created over the past decade an important, growing middle class in the city. It has also created the potential for upward mobility, for everyone, no matter how unlikely, adding to the confusions and contradictions of urban Pakistani life.

Haji Club started as a one-story house in 1968 and has grown since then into a massive three stories sitting on two large plots. Its Muhajir neighbourhood is solidly upper middle class, well maintained, and green. The main intersections have big hoardings with photoshopped pictures of Altaf Hussain, the leader of MQM, smiling benevolently through aviator glasses or raising an index finger, mouth bent in righteous anger. Underneath there are slogans in Urdu or English and the area's 'sector number'. 'GA Altaf [Brought to you by] Sector 187.' Outside of its red brick gate and pretty bougainvillea hedge there was a long line of at least three dozen motorbikes. One had the phrase 'Silent Lover' painted in green on its side.

The young men who make up the majority of the club's members can only be described as a breed of hipster, native to certain sections of Muhajir Karachi. Much like the poorer Christian kids in the pool hall, they had unorthodox haircuts, pomade-assisted spikes and slicks. They wore tight jeans and tighter t-shirts from which protruded the muscles of film stars. The second floor is a full gym for the 600-plus female members, and by the early evening the post-work rush had already begun. Young and middle-aged women streamed up the staircase at the front of the club that led directly to the women's portion.

Inside, Zaid, the owner, and Muhammad Akhtar, the director, took me on a tour. Zaid, who wore a track suit and slippers, had a large belly that didn't distract from the fact of his powerful arms. Akhtar was older and exceedingly kind, with dark circles under his eyes and a melancholy air. Zaid was directly related, on his mother's side, to Bolu Pehlwan, the famous wrestler who migrated from India during Partition. Zaid's father founded the gym as a place where the local youth could 'stop smoking cigarettes and chewing pan on the side of the road and do something productive'. They proudly showed me a picture of Mohammad Ali, the boxer, when they say he visited the gym during a trip to Pakistan in 1989.

The machines all looked familiar, but there was something rough and odd about them. They were all made from scrap metal, replicas of machines that Zaid had seen in stores or looked up online. The contraptions ingeniously bypassed the need for electricity. The stair climbers and treadmills ran on a system of gears. There was an indoor children's pool and another full-size pool on a second plot, next to a workshop area filled with rusting bits of beds and furniture that Zaid would transform into workout equipment. 'Each machine costs me about Rs25,000 to make,' he said. 'At the store they would be at least Rs60,000 new.' The pool was empty through the winter but Akhtar assured me that the club's swim lessons would be packed in the summer, though, 'it's a much more selective membership,' he told me. 'Before, people were always spitting *paan* in the water, disgusting.'

Fixing the self seems to be the new trick to getting ahead. A new focus on the body, articulating masculinity designed for a new world: self-improvement, individual effort, meritocratic gain. All over the gym, the teenagers and twenty-somethings finished their sets and then unselfconsciously posed and flexed in front of one of the mirrors that lined the walls, dressed in their most stylish clothes. A young boy in white Ray-Ban frames with no lenses and an immaculately tended hairstyle stood before a mirror, flexing his arms, turning from side to side.

Kamran, twenty six, was one of the happier young men I talked to in the gym. He had an enviable job as an engineer for the Sindh department of finance. He graduated from Karachi University and his father's friend who worked in the department gave him the job. Kamran had very big muscles. 'Everyone is inspired by me. "Kamran *bhai*, I want to look like you." And a lot of them started coming to Haji Club. A lot of guys. This is why they come: every hero in Indian movies has a build now. Before none of them did, but now, you have to have a big build,' he told me. I ask him about life in Karachi. 'Life is very good in Karachi. You can enjoy it here to the fullest, to the point where you don't even feel like you're in Karachi,' he said.

'Every Saturday night we have fun. We organise parties at the beach, we go to Hawkes Bay. Sometimes it's just boys, sometimes boys and girls.' Without lowering his voice he asked, 'Do you like beer? I love Millennium,' referring to the Pakistani beer sold at 'wine' shops all over the city.

Zahid Zaki, who was toning-up his calf muscles when I approached him, told me that he was an engineering student at a local university and had been working out for nearly half a year. 'I am going to be Mr Pakistan,' was the first thing he said to me, referring to the national body building competition. He had only been in one competition, a local one, but did take fifth place. He looked fit but wasn't exactly of Arnold Schwarzenegger proportions. 'I will take steroids. Without them it will be impossible,' he said, without hesitation. Akhtar had told me that steroid use is rampant in Pakistan's body-building world and that suppliers routinely come by the gym and ask if they can set up a booth to give out free samples. I tell him that the drugs are not safe, at least that's what they say in America. 'No, no, there are no side effects,' he assured me. 'If you're under professional guidance they'll tell you how to use them correctly.'

Guru Mandir

Somewhere near Guru Mandir, one evening, I found myself sitting on the red floral print carpet of a bookie's safe house. The naked edge of the boarded-over window allowed an orange blade of sunset to cut through a widening waft of smoke. Its source was a man sitting cross-legged and smoking a large joint. His beard and the dark prayer indentation on his forehead seemed at ease with his blood-shot eyes. The apartment was one of a handful the bookie maintained for his small operation, rotating between them every few days. He and his crew worked in shifts of varying length, depending on how busy a sports day it happened to be. The bookie handled bets on many sports, but mostly cricket, as well as wagers on a range of mundane events. T20 matches were the busiest time, and the crew had to work quickly and precisely, like a production line, to keep track of all the sets of numbers.

A burly Pashtun man in a blue salwar kameez, with a kalashnikov dangling upside down from his shoulder, had let me and my guide into the small fourth-floor apartment in a nondescript residential building. We squeezed down a narrow corridor into the sitting room, which had been converted into the 'office', and sat against the far wall. The bookie was listening intently, the phone next to him on speaker. The man on the other end updated the odds on the Bangladesh Premier League T20 match after what seemed like every ball. The bookie wore a brown leather motorcycle jacket and sweat poured down his forehead. A crescent of balled-up damp tissues in front of him grew as he dabbed his brow every minute.

The mechanics of betting in Karachi are well-established. The man on the phone was based in Ghaas Mandi in Lyari, the neighbourhood that is a world unto itself within the city. He set the odds for a number of bookmakers in Karachi. Bigger operations were affiliated with the big-time betting rings based in Bombay or Lahore, and their odds came from across the border. The bookie was a Gujarati-speaking Memon, and he said that the bookies he has dealt with in Bombay were Gujarati as well, so they got along. One of his workers manned the row of ten land-line telephones and also a computer. He logged the bets into a spreadsheet programmeme. What happened if they botched a number? I asked. 'This never happens because we record every single call,' he replied.

The bookie said he was always looking to get out of this line of work; the tension, the paranoia, was exhausting. The intensity of human relations, of having to deal like a psychologist with bettors who couldn't pay, cajoling them to give their cars or wife's jewellery. In the last instance there's the violence, which the bookie said he very much disdained but, when it becomes inevitable, he hires the right people for the job, usually thugs from Lyari. I ask if he has to pay *bhatta* – the slang for extortion money – to these same gangsters. He says he doesn't. But of the Rs7 to 10,000 he makes every month, he pays two to the police.

Earlier in the day I was sitting on a sofa across from Arshad, the man who would later take me to the betting operation. We were in the offices of a wealthy Memon property developer named Yusuf. Yusuf, a large rotund man with hands big enough to hold three cricket balls, holds court on his couch as business partners and Memon friends circulate through to talk money or swap the day's news and stories. Yusuf speaks his Memoni Gujarati very loudly, in comical up and down tones. I had an hour to kill before Arshad and I were scheduled to visit the bookie. He was showing me the wallet-size fold-out sports schedule that his bookie distributes to clients and an SMS that the bookie sent to him that morning: 'BPL second match. Main *kaam hoga* (the main work will be done) 5pm'. Arshad went back to watching the BPL match on the flat-screen TV hanging on the wall. He had a small amount, Rs3,000 he said, riding on the first inning's score and he kept a dialogue with the TV as the run rate accelerated. Talk in the developers' salon moved on to a discussion more generally about the underworld; the land developers worked in a particularly dirty and violent sector.

Pakistan's IMF-administered economic liberalisation integrated Karachi into the global property boom at around the same time that some classes grew tumescent with cash. The richer oligarchy, the new rich, the growing middle classes, the army flush with post-9/11 'aid' money – they all used real estate to sop up their anxious surpluses. Demands for new kinds of spaces of leisure and consumption also made land very profitable. The poor began to be dispossessed, and with a martial law regime and one political party holding all the cards, there was little they could do.

Someone described what happened next as a process of primitive accumulation by the elites, transmuting public goods into private wealth. If one had the muscle, connections, and wherewithal, one could fence off the commons or throw out the inhabitants of the goths, the original villages that the ever-expanding Karachi has since absorbed. On that public park or village, one could build a mall, an apartment complex, a bank. Others would claim it, as was their right in this Hobbesian state, and armed minions would fight it out.

The democratic government of the PPP has slowed down the rate of this accumulation to a degree by passing laws that regularised some unofficial settlements, and protected the goths. But with the scale of the profits, and natural demand, it inevitably persists; officials can be bought off, or brought in as partners in land deals. Zoning laws are ubiquitously ignored. Under democratic rule, poor Karachiites, the majority, with the help of urban land use groups, have successfully fought back in some cases to land grabbing that would otherwise dispossess them.

One of the Memon developers told me a story, as we sat drinking tea and eating fried snacks of the Gujarati variety. 'In this business, you have to be ready to show your strength, at any time,' Tariq began. He said that when he starts a project, depending on which part of the city it is in, the local political or criminal power will approach him and ask for *bhatta*, protection money, 'Rs50 to 100,000 per month' during construction. Sometimes a representative will ask him directly, sometimes they leave a *parchi*, a note, and sometimes they send a letter to his home. These letters usually give personal details of daily routines and children's names and urge the recipient to pay up. He received one recently that listed details about his son. He said he always has.

But he also described how he formed a productive relationship with Rehman Dakait, one of the biggest gangsters of Lyari, after he began paying *bhatta*. Whenever he needed to show his strength, Tariq called on Rehman to flex. In the story he told, he said that he had arranged to buy an old apartment building in 2006 and planned to put up a more up-scale building in its place. Tariq first had to buy the flats from their individual owners, but one tenant wouldn't budge and kept asking for more and more money in exchange for selling the property. Tariq decided it was time to be strong. Rehman and his thugs kidnapped the holdout and took him to one of Tariq's unfinished buildings. A band saw stood in the middle of the room, over it the man was held as the saw's blade spun to life. The man was given a simple choice: sell the flat or else. Today, the upscale apartment building is full of happy residents.

Lyari

Even as they fall victim to it, land developers like Tariq need Lyari's muscle to operate in Karachi's law-of-the-concrete-jungle property market, where the potential profits dwarf the fees paid for services and extorted as 'protection'. In fact, Lyari gets used in many ways by the powerful. It has provided a loyal vote bank to the PPP since Zulfikar Ali Bhutto's populist government in the 1970s. Lyari was a stronghold of the Left opposition to Zia ul-Haq's martial law rule of the 1980s, and Lyari's gangs evolved out of the militant anti-Zia movement in much the same way that Los Angeles' Bloods and Crips were the post-ideological bastard children of the Black Panthers.

Lyari is the only significant area of Karachi that votes for the PPP, and the party uses it to launch the careers of its politicians. It's likely that Bilawal Bhutto, President Asif Zardari's son, will run from Lyari when his time comes to inherit the party, even though he has barely spent time in Karachi, let alone Lyari. But while the party takes Lyari for granted in its electoral strategies, Lyari's fortunes have changed very little. After Benazir Bhutto's return to Pakistan in 2007, the gangster Rehman Dakait more or less extinguished the endless gang war that had torn Lyari apart. He brought the neighbourhood factions that had been fighting each other over the control of turf, drug markets, smuggling routes, and extortion together under the umbrella of an organisation he called the People's Amn Committee – *amn* meaning 'peace'. With most of the gangs united behind him, and the fires of daily violence doused, Rehman wanted a place in the PPP power structure; one of Lyari's own was determined to control its destiny. Rehman was killed in a police encounter in 2009. Many say the PPP was responsible: it wanted Lyari back in its place. But as everywhere else in Karachi, Lyarians aren't willing to walk backwards in time and accept the old reality; it's not even possible.

A friend of mine who reports for local television had become personally familiar with Lyari over the years. He offered to introduce me to the men who had inherited Rehman's mandate. They're all heart, he said: 'They want Lyari to stand on its own.' And in a way this is true: they want to be the patrons of Lyari and provide leadership that responds to immediate needs. But they are also undoubtedly still neck-deep in crime and violence and while they are officially banned, Amn Committee leaders appear in television interviews and at political rallies. With the MQM on a back foot, they have now entered the fray of Karachi's patronage politics.

My friend hadn't been able to get through to the Amn Committee leaders beforehand so we had to rely on an alternative network of communication. We pulled over near Lea Market in the heart of Lyari and he approached two grease-stained mechanics working on an old black and yellow taxi. 'We're looking for Uzair *bhai*, of the Amn Committee. Do you know where he is tonight?', my friend asked. One of the Baloch mechanics wiped his hands on his kameez and gave us a suspicious look: 'I don't know who you're talking about.' My friend explained that we were journalists and that he knew brother Uzair but that he couldn't get through on his mobile phone. The mechanic reached into his pocket and used his mobile to make a call. Then he hung up and said: 'Drive two lanes down and take a right. They're at the old hospital.'

If you drive through Lyari, your immediate sense is that this is a world apart from the Karachi that Pakistan knows. The people look different and speak languages that, for an outsider, are difficult to place. It's dominated by the Baloch, and many of them came long ago from the Makran coast and are of black African descent. Kids in Lyari don't play cricket, they prefer football and boxing, and many will swear to you that Lyari has more football clubs than Rio. There's a bit of favela flavour to the place. You see boys wearing Ronaldinho jerseys with their salwars. 'FC Barcelona Messi' was spray painted in black on a wall. Lyari has its own pop singers and rappers, unheard of outside its remit. Lyari's identity, it seems, is constructed on an anti-identity, on its difference from mainstream Karachi culture. Lyarians speak in terms of being black, *sheedi*, as they call it, not Pakistani or Muslim in the first instance.

My friend parked the car in front of the Amn Committee headquarters. It looked like an abandoned municipal building, but one that someone had begun to renovate before giving up halfway. There was scaffolding over the front gate and planks of wood ran through it, over unpaved dirt. The area's electricity was cut and the shadows cast by the empty-looking building obscured the faces of those hanging around out front.

The young *sheedi* men perched on the boundary like hawks stared us down as we walked by them into the courtyard but they didn't stop us or ask about our business there. I tossed my friend a look. He replied, 'Don't worry, they knew we were here before we even asked those guys for directions.' Lyari, perhaps as a result of its insularity and impenetrability, particularly during times of conflict, radiates a feeling of surveillance. You always have the sense that you are being watched by many eyes.

Uzair Baloch and his lieutenant Zafar Baloch sat at the far end of the courtyard, under a neem tree. A group of men hovered around the pair, talking with each other and smoking cigarettes. There were no guns in sight. Zafar was bearlike, with drooping, doleful eyes. He was holding an infant girl in a purple frock and pigtails who laughed and squealed. 'Come, come, we've been waiting for you,' he said with a big smile and a tinge of lisp, and we sat in the white plastic chairs arrayed in a circle. His unusually baggy salwar caught awkwardly on the metal rods screwed into his right leg where shrapnel from a hand grenade had nearly killed him last year. Uzair was a smaller man, but through his economy of expression and speech exuded cold power rather than Zafar's avuncular warmth.

I asked them how the Amn Committee had tried to raise the status quo in Lyari. Uzair, the leader, stared intently into the glow of his smartphone, letting Zafar articulate the Committee's narrative of redemption and perse-cution. 'We made one voice so that no one can ignore Lyari anymore,' Zafar began, tapping the ground with his cane for emphasis.

We want to break the mindset of Lyari, that is the biggest problem. If we go to Gulshan or Nazimabad (Muhajir neighbourhoods) and we see all of the schools and the businesses and the clean roads, we realise, where are we living? But just as Muttahida [the MQM] did it for themselves, it's for us to worry about how to change ourselves. I will surely not leave things this way for my children. We cannot leave here – what, go back to Balochistan? My great-great grandfather was born in Karachi. So I am not going to let my children be destroyed by the gun culture and drug culture that has been imposed on us by those who want to take over Lyari, that has destroyed so many people here.

They said they were tired of sacrificing for the PPP and then discarded when the party has no use for Lyari.

That is what we wanted to change. Three times they [PPP] came in to power and didn't do anything for us. The fourth time, it is only because Uzair *bhai* is screaming all the time that Lyari gets any money for development. The MQM gets jobs in the police and appointments. We are PPP, its backbone in Karachi, and we don't get anything. They are better off that they think about this before we do. If Lyari is Bila-wal's constituency, then develop it, prove that it's yours. We will make him prove it.

Lyari and the PAC are interchangeable terms with Zafar and Uzair, a trait common to all of the political groups in Karachi, who conflate parties, peoples and neighbourhoods in a self-serving abstraction.

Zafar's mobile rang and interrupted our conversation. He spoke in a hurried Balochi, briefly, and hung up. 'Commando!' he yelled, and a sheedi man wearing a kaffiyeh stepped out of the building behind us. Zafar said something to him and the man walked across the courtyard into the old hospital-cum-headquarters. A few moments later, another man walked out carrying a holster with two pistols. He put it on underneath his jacket, got on a motorbike that was parked next to the boundary wall, and rode out into the street. There are so many anecdotes of violence that pepper the narrative of the Amn Committee. I thought of the massacre at Sher Shah during the violent summer and the extortion letter that one of the Memon businessmen had received that had been signed 'Uzair *bhai*'.

I asked Zafar about the violence of the previous summer and what the PAC's role in it had been. He told the stories of two grenade attacks, within the span of a month, the second one nearly taking his life. He had been having tea at nearby Lea Market just before midnight when he walked into the street to talk to a boy who was having trouble at work. Suddenly, the electricity went out, and the night swallowed everything, he said. The would-be assassins had found their moment, and they shot at Zafar and then threw a grenade, which nearly ripped off his leg. Who did it, I asked. He claimed that they had found cells of terrorists hiding out on the outskirts of Lyari, killers he alleged worked for the MQM. 'If you use fire against us, you will get fire in return,' he said.

An attendant signalled a visitor, interrupting our conversation again. A group of women approached, one older, holding an infant, the others carrying plastic folders, dressed in brown niqabs. The older woman talked to Uzair in Balochi and then the girls introduced themselves to him, each shaking his hand in turn. I could make out the words 'CV' and 'medical college'. They were asking for the PAC's help finding placement in a Karachi college.

My friend and I got back in our car and drove past Cheel Chowk toward the port, and then out into the city. As we sped over the new curving flyover, the yellow lights of Karachi Port illuminated the serene mechanical off loaders, their Chinese operators sitting high up in the cabins, guiding the steel dinosaurs slowly to and fro along the silent dock. I had visited the port a few weeks earlier and saw the blockaded American Humvees and shipping containers of material, sent for the NATO troops in Afghanistan, gathering a veil of brown dust.

My mobile rang. There had been another grenade attack in Lyari. Or was it a bomb? People from the Amn Committee had died. The caller, another friend, wanted to know if we were alright. We were out of harm's way, I told him. But things would only get worse for Zafar and Uzair. Their vision for Lyari wouldn't be able to survive the reality of their on-going connections to the gangs of Lyari, and their weak political position. Through the late winter and spring of 2012, demands for protection money from Muhajir traders and businessmen, the *parchis* delivered in Uzair's name, piled up voluminously. The MQM demanded the PPP provincial government, who controls the city police, carry out an operation in Lyari to cleanse it of the criminal menace. Eventually, the government assented, and the police moved in. Local press reported that the police were guided through Lyari's serpentine lanes by masked members of the Arshad Pappu gang, sworn enemies of the PAC dating back to the days of Rehman and, many say, proxies for the MQM. At first, aggrieved Lyarians fought back with stones and Molotov cocktails, then, day after day, police fought pitched battles with PAC members, who fired machine guns and rocket propelled grenades from windows and rooftops. Bounties of Rs1 million and Rs300,000 were placed on Uzair's and Zafar's heads, respectively. Word on the street was that Uzair was hiding out in Baluchistan.

A newspaper editorialised that, 'While Lyari is in the throes of violence, the rest of Karachi remains relatively unaffected, indicating there is a disconnect between what goes on in that forsaken corner of the city and the rest of the metropolis.' But this, I thought, was wrong. Lyari is not some rotting limb hanging limply at Karachi's side. Lyari is like an organ vital to the health of the body, but one that has been neglected.

Next Decades

In less than fifteen years the waves of migration to Karachi are expected to subside. When they do, the city will be even more diverse than it is today. No ethnic group will have sufficient numbers to dominate, and the illusion that any party can rule alone, or that any party can be completely sidelined, will disappear. In order to maintain a competitive electoral advantage, Karachi's rulers, one hopes, will be forced to transcend their myopic communal vision and appeal to the interests of its poor inhabitants. The ethnic nationalist parties, the MQM and ANP, and the PPP, all have similar long-term political goals and talk about providing basic amenities and security for the city. They all advocate greater provincial autonomy, for example, and more equal distribution of national resources. Crucially, none of them cloak their interests in the vestments of religion. Karachi's future thus need not repeat the mistakes of its past.

Karachi is a young city. The average age of the inhabitants is about twenty five. It is this young generation that will shape the future of the city. In Qasba Colony, a Pashtun-majority neighbourhood that has seen more than its share of target killing, I met Imran, a high school student who lived with his family. Imran's mother was Muhajir and father Pashtun; both were Karachi natives. When the violence begins, Imran makes sure to call his friends and relatives, of many ethnicities, who live in other parts of town, and they do the same. Sitting on the cool concrete floor of his home, I asked Imran if he felt as torn as the city itself, between allegiances, even within his own family. 'Not at all,' he replied. 'I understand both sides. But the truth is that it is not a war of languages, it is a war of the parties.' He admitted that fear had become ingrained in the city's psyche, and said that his friends tell rickshaw drivers to take routes that avoid specific ethnic neighbourhoods. 'But I have been all over Pakistan and even to India, and I can say this: I never want to live anywhere else but here.'

PESHAWAR BLUES

Muhammad Idrees Ahmad

On the Kuwait Airways flight from London to Islamabad, the unusually boorish flight crew handed us disembarkation cards that the government of Pakistan requires all international arrivals to fill. Besides our passport numbers, addresses and reasons for visiting, the form also asked if we had been to Africa or Latin America in the past week. The purpose of this question was unclear except perhaps as a means to boost national self-esteem by implying that Pakistan is healthier than those two continents. With the only pen in my row, I helped five other passengers fill their forms.

At Islamabad's decrepit Benazir Bhutto International Airport, I was pleasantly surprised to find the immigration staff making no undue effort to inconvenience new arrivals. Former president Pervez Musharraf's successful effort at gender-balancing has markedly improved the behaviour of male airport staff. After sailing through immigration and customs, I became conscious of the disembarkation card still in my hand. Not inclined to take chances, I asked an officer where to deposit it. He hadn't a clue — nor did anyone else. Finally, a customs official took the card from my hand and threw it into a waste basket. I wasn't asked for it again.

What is still known internationally as the Islamabad Airport is actually based in the city of Rawalpindi. As the historic Grand Trunk Road passes through its crowded precincts, its name changes twice — to Peshawar Road and The Mall. We drove North-West on the Peshawar Road, past the General Head Quarters (GHQ) of the Pakistan Army which in 1895 had served as the launching pad for the Malakand Field Force, the British colonial army's counter-insurgency campaign against the recalcitrant frontier. The sanguine details of this campaign were preserved in vivid detail by a young Winston Churchill who was also serving as a correspondent for the *Times*. More recently, on 10 October 2009, the GHQ was the site of a bloody raid by a group of ten militants who breached its defences and triggered a hostage crisis which ended with nine soldiers, two civilians, and nine of the assailants dead.

On Peshawar road we encountered a scene which would be unusual anywhere else: bearing down on us on both sides of the road was a procession of cars, lorries, carts, *tongas*, motorbikes and SUVs, with passengers hanging out of windows, standing on roofs, dancing and chanting. The merry crowd carried no banners, signs or placards to broadcast the cause of their jubilation. It was six am.

Soon we were on the M1 highway, heading west. If traffic in Pakistan thrives in a permanent state of exception, then the new six-lane highways might be another country. The drive is smooth and uninterrupted, the traffic is light and rules are abided by. Should anyone fail to observe the rules, an honest and efficient police force is always at hand to enforce them. The mystery of the motorway police's incorruptibility lies in higher salaries and an independent inspectorate general which places greater emphasis on training and accountability.

On entering the Peshawar valley the hills far north and the Khattak hills in the south were visible. But on approaching the city, the Khyber hills beyond Peshawar were obscured by a sky smudged with thick smog. Peshawar, according to a 2011 Word Health Organisation survey, has the world's seventh highest levels of outdoor air pollution — twenty times higher than the WHO standard, nearly twice as high as Beijing. It has no thriving industry or Chinese-level development to show for it. The noise level is also significantly above the WHO limit of 85 decibels. Rickshaws have been blamed as one of the main causes. But as transport for the less well-off, they are easy to scapegoat. The city is congested with traffic and emission tests are still an alien concept. The air is further poisoned by the brick kilns that dot Pakistan's landscape. The city is more crowded and less green than it was when I was growing up here.

Palimpsest

Like the cinema billboards that adorn Pakistan's busy streets, painted over with garish images of large women and furious men, the city is a palimpsest whose façade has been drawn and redrawn since its birth in the sixth century BCE. As a gateway to India, the valley has played host to conquerors throughout history who came through Khyber or Bajaur, lured by the riches of the

Indus and the splendours of the Ganges further east. The Persian Achaemenids led by Darius; the Greeks, led by Alexander; the Mughals, led by Babar; the Afghans, led by Mahmud-e-Ghaznawi. Some conquerors also approached from the east; first the Hindus, later the Sikhs, and eventually the British. The city has been sacked many times and destroyed twice — by the Huns in the fifth century and the Sikhs in the nineteenth century.

It was under the Kushan monarch Kanishka, in the second century, that Purushapura — literally the 'City of Man' — replaced Pushkalavati (modern day Charsadda) as the capital of Gandhara. The name eventually mutated into Peshawar. The Gandhara kingdom, which thrived for over two millennia, was eventually conquered by Mahmud of Ghazni in 1021.

Peshawar, the oldest living city in South Asia, has developed in four phases which correspond to the city's major settlements. The inner city — *ander shehr* — has been inhabited constantly since at least 539 BCE. People here mostly speak Hindko, which after Pashto is the region's most widely spoken language — a language that also attests to the city's Indo-Aryan origin. Hindko-speakers from the inner city have supplied some of Bollywood's most celebrated screen talent. Dilip Kumar, Raj Kapur, Vinod Khanna: they were all born here. Shahrukh Khan, arguably India's biggest film sensation, was born to Taj Mohammed Khan, an independence activist from Peshawar's historic *Qissa Khani* (Story Teller) bazaar. The whole Kapur family, which has a long history in Bollywood cinema, traces its origins to the inner city. Peshawar also gave India one of its greatest English language novelists in Mulk Raj Anand.

Ander shehr is also home to Gorkathri, the most significant reminder of its Buddhist past. It once housed Buddha's giant bowl and was pilgrimage site for both Hindus and Buddhists. Under the Mughals, who ushered in the city's next golden age, the site was turned into a caravanserai by the princess Jehan Ara, who also built a mosque inside the compound. The Mughals extended the Grand Trunk Road right up to Jamrud and built several magnificent gardens, including the Shalimar, Shahi, and Wazir Baghs (gardens), whose splendour left an impression on all visitors to the city. These gardens, alas, became a casualty of the city's haphazard expansion. Images of Mughal grandeur today survive only in the distinct architecture and ornate interior of the Mahabat Khan mosque, named after the much-loved Afghan governor who built it.

The city was later sacked and rebuilt by the Sikhs. Paolo Avitabile, the Italian mercenary whom the Sikhs appointed governor, made Gorkhatri his residence. Avitabile enclosed the city in a wall overseen by the citadel of Balahisar. The sturdy fort survives today as the headquarters of the Frontier Corps, a federal paramilitary force recruited mostly from tribal Pashtuns; but the wall has since been overlaid by new construction. In recent years the local government has made an effort to rebuild some of the sixteen gates that once punctuated the wall. Despite their absence, however, the gates remained firmly as geographical references in the city's memory. As kids growing up, we would buy crickets bats near Kohati gate, have iced molasses near Sarki gate, walk past the Kabuli gate for the famous sweetmeats of Qissa Khani without ever wondering where the actual gates were.

The city's second settlement and its first major expansion came with the arrival of the British, who built a cantonment on a plain to the west to house their garrisons. This is the only part of the city that shows signs of planning. The roads here are wide and the single-storied houses are elegantly built; there is plenty of greenery and very little of the ubiquitous litter that defiles the rest of Peshawar. It is a sad comment on post-colonial rule in Pakistan that some of city's most enduring institutions and infrastructure — the Edwardes College; the Lady Reading hospital; the Karachi-to-Khyber railway; the extensive irrigation canals — were all built under British colonial rule, some over a century ago. But as in other places, His Majesty's government also left a sanguine legacy of repression and massacres, the most infamous of which happened when a gathering of Bacha Khan's Gandhian red-shirts was gunned down at Qissa Khani in 1930.

The third phase of development began after partition with the founding of the Peshawar University in 1950. The university rose around the nucleus of the Islamia College, an institution which was built by the frontier's conservative elements with the help of the British authorities in part to countervail the anti-colonial influence of the Aligarh University. According to its founding Committee, the aim of its Oriental faculty was 'to turn out mullahs...with their whole nature permeated with devotion and loyalty to the British crown, a duty which is ordained by our religion in its true spirit and light.'

In 1953, authorities began developing the University Town, a residential area to the east of the university campus, in a location separated from the cantonment by the city's main airport. The Town is a leafy neighbourhood whose handsome, single-storied homes line wide and well-maintained streets. It was conceived as an abode for the intellectual elite of the city, an aim which has fallen by the wayside. During the 1980s, it came close to resembling Kipling's fantastic image of Peshawar, with international aid organisations, Afghan mujahideen factions, Western intelligence agencies, and arms and drugs smugglers often living in close proximity. Al Qa'ida leader Usama Bin Laden had his abode at 61 Jamaluddin Afghani Road. It was near what is now called Iqra Chowk that in 1989 his mentor Abdullah Azzam was assassinated. A one-time professor at a Saudi University, the Palestinian Azzam had devoted his life to the cause of jihad, inspiring many to join the Afghan resistance with his impassioned sermons. With his moderating influence gone, Bin Laden would come under the influence of the ruthless Egyptian ideologues, led by Ayman al Zawahiri, who persuaded him of the *takfiri* justifications for mass murder.

Peshawar's most recent development is the suburb of Hayatabad, a township built to the west of the city abutting the semi-autonomous Khyber agency. Over the past two decades, the suburb has developed in seven phases, creeping closer and closer to the tribal region. The remoter regions of the township are today frequent targets of retaliatory rocket fire from the adjoining conflict zone. Phase 6, the neighbourhood closest to the Khyber hills, was attacked almost daily during the month I was there. Even Phase 1, which is nearer the city, is often hit by rockets. The insecurity has also created a law and order vacuum which is frequently exploited by kidnappers. Kidnapping for ransom is now widespread and has turned into a key source of funding for militants operating in tribal battle zones. Minorities, particularly the region's remaining Sikhs, are most vulnerable; but even the vice chancellor of the Islamia College University, Professor Ajmal Khan, a grandson of the iconic Pashtun nationalist Bacha Khan, could not escape abduction.

The violence that once besieged the city has declined somewhat in the past three years, especially since Pakistan banned NATO supplies through its territory. But a low-intensity conflict still continues in and around the edges of the city. Bombings and assassinations continued apace throughout my stay. Just in the first six days of my arrival on 13 May, there were two roadside bombs, two assassinations, several rocket attacks, an attempt to shoot down a passenger plane, and two car bombings. And so it went.

Being and Nothingness

In Peshawar no one walks as a potential victim. It must be part of human nature to never imagine oneself in the day's plane crash or car wreck. Death always seems escapable. Not so the burden of existence. The astronomical rise in the cost of living is putting a visible strain on most people. Inflation has remained in double digits since 2008, second only to Vietnam in Asia. Prices of some commodities are comparable to those in Britain. Bananas are cheaper at Sainsbury's in Leicester.

The free flow of dollars in Afghanistan has created a further distortion, raising prices and emptying markets of commodities which are flowing freely across the border. Smuggling is rife. According to Sayad Waqar Husain of the Institute of Management Sciences, with 141 transit points along the Durand Line, and with dysfunctional customs regulation, there are now 133 illegal markets in Khyber Pakhtunkhwa and the Federally Administered Tribal Areas (FATA) alone, where trade in non-custom paid goods is booming. Property prices have also risen and rents are high. Real estate prices amplified by inflation are making people invest in the only commodity which is likely to keep its price. With an exploding population, accommodation is always scarce and buyers always at hand.

Although Pakistan's cumulative birth rate has declined in recent years, the fertility rate in Khyber Pakhtunkhwa is still the country's highest. In 1809, when the first British envoy to Kabul Monstuart Elphinstone visited the city, it had a population of about 100,000. Following the Sikh conquest in 1832, the number fell to 80,000, dwindling further to 63,079 by 1891. After independence, however, the population began to increase steadily, reaching 109,715 in 1951, and 166,273 by 1961. But by 2010, the number had shot up to 3,625,000. This figure very likely excludes the large number of unregistered Afghan refugees who at one time numbered in the millions. All of this places an enormous strain on the city's resources. Water, which had always been abundant, is now scarce. The city's sanitation system is overwhelmed — it is impossible to escape the vague odour of raw sewage in most parts of the city. Where once Peshawar dazzled visitors with its verdure, today it is permanently covered by a coat of dust; the varieties of flowers which were eulogised by everyone from Babar to Elphinstone have today receded into private enclosures.

But unlike others in adverse circumstances, Pashtuns never reconcile themselves to what fate has assigned them. Pride is both their blessing and their curse. It keeps them from being overwhelmed by adversity, but it often also impedes their progress out of it. It gives the society an irreverence that disposes it to egalitarianism, but it also instils a vanity that consumes it with maintaining appearances. People in the region are given to grandiose gestures. These impulsive attempts at gaining the respect of peers often drive people of modest means into penury. Like the impoverished protagonist of Gabriel Garcia Marquez's *No One Writes to the Colonel*, determined to uphold his dignity amid dwindling means, the burden of a man's pride is inevitably borne by the wife and children.

Possession marks the distance between being and nothingness as far as life opportunities go. Amid a crumbling economy, and without a social security net, there are those whose lives are so diminished that survival is their only concern. These shards of human debris crawl along streets, lurk about the bazaars, go door to door, rummage through refuse, and rely on the generosity of strangers to see them through another day. Henry Byroade, the US ambassador to Pakistan from 1973–77, once described these shiftless ambulators as 'bipeds'. The inheritors of this attitude today regard this tableau of misery with equal disdain as they zoom past in their imported SUVs. You can't be a person of any consequence and be seen on foot.

The quickest way to lose peoples' interest in Peshawar, in effect to become invisible, is to walk. This could sometimes be a blessing. Traditional cultures can be notoriously claustrophobic. Less due to physical space — though space is often a factor— than to the oppressive presence of a society which is forever disciplining, restraining, and confining individuals in its mind-forged manacles. You are assigned a role and your life is reduced to a performance. To be yourself, to escape its onerous expectation, you have to be anonymous. Like Baudelaire's poet, the only place you can find solitude is often in crowds. Peshawar is too big for the comfort and security of community, but not big enough for the freedom and opportunity of anonymity. Anonymity has to be manufactured. And one way of doing it is by walking. So I walk.

Eros and Thanatos

On Shama Chowk, at the western limit of the old British cantonment, the GT Road veers right toward the Khyber hills in the west and assumes the name Jamrud Road. The roundabout was once decorated with a life-sized model of a Shaheen medium-range ballistic missile, since replaced by a modest memorial to those who fell defending the American consulate nearby. The heavily fortified consulate sits on a street which approaches the roundabout from the left. In 2009, when I was last here, the compound was protected by three layers of security, including concrete barriers, two armoured personnel carriers, and a sandbagged guard post. Through the aperture you could see the anxious faces of young soldiers whose notion of duty did not include serving as human shields for the representatives of an overbearing ally. Across the front of the post was draped a black banner emblazoned with the *shahada* — the Muslim affirmation of faith. It was a pathetic attempt to signal to would be assailants that their attack would only kill co-religionists. All of this proved insufficient when in 5 April 2010, the consulate came under a ferocious coordinated attack which killed many, none of them Americans.

Turning into the Circular Lane at Iqra Chowk, heading towards University Town, you pass a building on your right that once housed the Alliance Francaise. Turning left at the first intersection, a couple of hundred metres along Park Road, you arrive at Coffee Pot, a new establishment. There have been western-style fast food joints, restaurants and takeaways in Peshawar, but never a café. I am there to meet a friend: a young woman. When we were at the Peshawar University, it was possible to visit the more traditional university cafeteria with female classmates. Meeting an unaccompanied girl in public however was quite uncommon and would invite assumptions of an amorous tryst. But my friend assures me that times have changed: the best way to avoid undue suspicion, she tells me, is to meet openly in a very public place. Hence the location.

The café follows a standard western layout, featuring a coffee bar, an espresso machine, and liveried barristas behind the counter. There is a variety of seating options. The menu could have come from Costa or Starbucks. Prices are only marginally lower. This is not a place for the average Peshawari. But what strikes you most is the curious location of the café. It sits almost in the middle of what used to be the old Ladies Club tennis courts. My friend mentions in passing some litigation over the location, but the conversation moves on.

Later I learn that one of the ministers in the provincial government has used his authority to lease out the Ladies Club premises for thirty three years for an absurdly low price (less than £4,000). Inevitably, the beneficiary is a close relative. But in doing so, the minister has also sparked a historic development: he has spawned a militant women's movement which has braved threats and defamation to hold frequent public demonstrations against the usurpation. The campaign to save the Ladies Club has since been joined by environmental NGOs and a host of civil society groups. The press is sympathetic; so are the denizens of University Town.

The expropriation of the Ladies Club is not an isolated event. The historic Shahi Bagh — the King's Garden — had also been built over in a similar fashion. The ruling Awami National Party, unlike the Islamists who preceded them, are treating their five years in power as an extended opportunity to seize patronage from the state and distribute it to their supporters. The Bilour clan, an old Hindko-speaking merchant family, which is allegedly implicated in this scam, also has the distinction of being the sole manager of Peshawar's repressed libidos. They own the Shama Cinema, the only theatre which has tended to the city's need for onanistic satisfaction with a steady diet of hard-core porn.

Peshawar's highly segregated society presents few opportunities for romance. Young people as a result develop highly charged notions of love long before they find objects to project them on. Love is over-determined by years of reverie — the object of love becomes secondary. The value of a romance is affirmed by the number of barriers society places in its way. First encounters in this respect prove fateful. In most instances love never suffers contacts with reality. But a premature experience of romance which goes awry could leave lasting scars. Perfidy has wrecked more than a few lives in Peshawar. One young woman, whose first experience of romance resulted in pregnancy and abortion before she suffered the further indignity of abandonment, turned to lechery. A man, whose first encounter also ended in betrayal, went the other way, and adopted a life of celibate seclusion. There were more than a few suicides. Some found solace in drugs.

Many young men adopt a personal posture of celibacy against temptations that aren't there while hawkishly guarding others against pleasures they are themselves denied. But stories of the moral police relenting on virtue to submit to occasional temptation are legion. One militant of the Jamiat-e-

Talaba (the fascistic youth wing of the Jamaat-e-Islami party), who used to terrorise the co-ed Peshawar University campus in an attempt to enforce segregation, shaved his beard and eased into a pair of jeans at the first flutter of a wayward maiden's lashes. His example was followed by many others in the virtue police.

A significant minority sees no reason to let its public performance of modesty determine private behaviour. Dating in Peshawar is a dangerous business — you can lose your life. When the usual pleasures of dating are combined with the added thrill of adventure, the temptation to transgress is high. The young man who vaults over walls and braves guard-dogs to make a tryst expects, or is often rewarded by, an equally daring leap over the walls of traditional morality by his partner. Repression is successful for the most part in tempering desires, but it also has the adverse effect of launching some into perversity. Love in Peshawar exists in a purely ideal or a highly eroticised form. With the arrival of satellite television and increasing Western influence, the trend is increasingly toward the latter.

For many youths repressed desires only find expression in ribald homo-erotic banter. Homosexuality, as in all traditional cultures, is disdained. But the attitude toward pederasty is curiously relaxed in some places. What separates the two is the obvious power relation: homosexuality compromises masculinity in a manner that pederasty, with its clearer distinction of paramount and subordinate actors, does not. It is therefore not uncommon for a Khan or a man of stature to keep a boy without suffering the kind of social sanction that would attend a sexual relation with someone his own age. Instances of child abuse are frightfully high — children of the poor and vulnerable are often easy prey.

Marriage in Peshawar, in most instances, is a transaction. Of all the considerations that go into traditional matchmaking, love isn't one. The instances of romantic unions are still rare enough to carry a separate, hyphenated label: 'love-marriage'. The union is as much between families as it is between individuals. The families are usually a closer match than the couple. Perfectly matched individuals on the other hand are denied union because of differences between families. Families, for understandable reasons, like to go with the familiar. For all their radical pretension, men for the most part are curiously conformist when it comes to domestic convention. Libertine lifestyles are quickly abandoned once the boy is called on by parents to man up and marry a cousin.

It is still uncommon for individuals to marry outside the clan. But as the old landed aristocracy is eclipsed by the urban bourgeoisie, marriages between them are becoming more common. The transactional purpose of these unions is made more explicit as one trades its wealth for the other's prestige. Marriages between classes, however, are still rare and inevitably lead to conflict. Between ethnic groups they are rarer still. Rivalries often turn murderous. Two young men from my home town, Chitral — a place known for the gentleness and good looks of its people — were brutally killed in Peshawar over the past year by jealous rivals and outraged clansmen.

Marriages also place onerous demands on families who have to conduct them with sufficient pomp and ceremony or risk losing face. Burdened with its class anxieties, the middle class is particularly vulnerable to pressure. People are forever stretching their means in an unrewarding quest for respectability in a society grown ever more materialist. In the 1990s, the then prime minister Nawaz Sharif placed a ban on excessive spending at weddings, which for many was a welcome relief. It gave cover to those with the means for only a modest ceremony. Invoking the Islamic tradition of austerity is another way out for respectable families with limited means to avoid extravagant expenses. Dowries, thankfully, were never as big an issue in the North West as they are in the regions where Hindu influence is greater.

Hope and Despair

On the Mall, inside the cantonment, I see a curious sight one morning. People are queuing up for a chance to secure a work visa to Afghanistan. With Pakistan's economic doldrums, prospects look better next door where foreign aid dollars are circulating freely. The *dihari* — day-wage — for a labourer in Pakistan currently stands at Rs300. In Afghanistan a labourer can earn up to Rs600. Rustam Shah Mohmand, Pakistan's former ambassador to Kabul, later told me that there were over 70,000 Pakistanis registered to work in Afghanistan. The actual number is likely higher. In the queue I meet people who have come from as far afield as Punjab.

In a country where most people have to rely on an informal economy for survival, if you have the means to get yourself a job you are also able to maintain it. The social capital which ensures Pakistan's survival also impedes its progress. Except for the more dynamic sections of the private sector, all institutions prioritise relationships over qualification. In hiring, you are who you know — more so in Peshawar than anywhere else in Pakistan. This naturally leads to a brain drain which pushes the country's best minds into seeking employment elsewhere. It also accounts for the low premium that the country places on educational attainment. Intellectual achievements give you far less of a cache than your possessions.

Pakistan has very few public intellectuals. Peshawar's last one, the great archaeologist, historian and linguist Ahmed Hasan Dani, passed away in 2009. This void has generally been filled by poets who, unlike in the West, where poetry has retreated into the academy, still have an audience. The illustrious tradition that began in the seventeenth century with the subversive versifying of the warrior-poet Khushal Khan Khattak and the mystical reveries of Rahman Baba has been carried into the present day by the likes of Ameer Hamza Shinwari, Ghani Khan, Qalandar Momand and Sherzaman Taizi. Pashtun nationalism is a common theme running through all their works. The contradictions between romantic tenderness and masculine assertion, between the parochial and universal; the balance between pastoral motifs and a warrior ethos, between spiritual ruminations and a pagan literalism, give to this poetry a character that make it the frontier analogue of what has been called 'Caldedonian Antisyzygy', the duelling contradictions of Scottish literature.

The popular tradition of poetry notwithstanding, Peshawar, like the rest of Pakistan, lacks a reading culture. The literate are not always educated. Libraries are few and far between. Book events are rare; the only one I attended was at the Khana-e-Farhang-e-Iran — the Iranian Cultural Centre. The British Council Library scaled down its operations immediately after the Cold War; the American Cultural Centre first closed its library and later its whole operation. Bookshops, to the extent that they existed, are vanishing. Other than the many sellers of used books, there were only two that sold a wide enough range of material, including both foreign and domestic titles. The bigger — Saeed Book Bank — closed down and moved to Islamabad. Even when it was around, it charged cover prices in British or American currency, putting most of its books beyond the reach of the average reader. Books, as a result, were reduced to a mark of status; they could be seen neatly arranged behind glass panels in the homes of educated arrivistes, showing little signs of wear. Their content would rarely make it into a dinnertime conversation. The once strong oral tradition of story-telling has also receded into the margins.

The confinement mandated by a highly segregated society means, however, that women have more opportunities to read then men. As a result, the degree of literacy among women has always been higher. Men are not confined to homes, but are oppressed all the same by the realisation of how little there is to do with their freedom. Many have sought escape in drugs, some in sports, a few in the arts. Others have left.

Soil and Soul

In the early hours of 27 May, I arrived back at the crumbling edifice that is the Benazir Bhutto International Airport. As I waited in the gloomy departure lounge, the place went pitch dark. The country's main international airport wasn't spared a blackout.

Power outages are plunging much of the country into darkness each night but the cuts aren't indiscriminate. In the military enclave of Peshawar's cantonment where I stayed for two weeks, power cuts were rare. Areas of major cities not under military control on the other hand are experiencing up to eighteen-hour blackouts. Dams, clogged with silt, are operating below capacity. Electricity theft is alarmingly high and revenue collection very poor. The state is even unable to provide basic safety gear. One line man was electrocuted across the street from where I was staying, his body hanging from the pylon for over an hour. Pakistan's rulers suffer from a perennial failure of imagination. Places which have given up on the state are actually faring better. In Chitral, for example, people on their own initiative have started small hydropower projects which provide reliable electricity at a fraction of the usual cost.

Peshawar is Pakistan in a microcosm. The public infrastructure is crumbling as more and more wealth is squirrelled away into gated communities of extraordinary opulence. Notions of civic responsibility are hard to cultivate when the state is dysfunctional and services poor. This absence of civic consciousness is particularly evident in people's liberal attitude toward littering: there are few streets which aren't strewn with plastic bags, soda cans, empty bottles, pizza boxes, food wrappings, and other filth. It is also evident in the crumbling public transport system. Railway tracks are frequently stripped by thieves for scrap metal. The Khyber Steam Safari — a train which crossed 34 tunnels and 92 bridges on its short scenic journey from Peshawar to Landi Kotal — was once a major tourist attraction. Today the two 1920-vintage steam engines have little track to roll on. A recent visitor to Dara Adam Khel's famous weapons market told me that after he purchased a hand gun, the seller congratulated him on his choice. The gun, he said, was made from 'hundred per cent track metal'.

But Peshawar is not all pain. It has a grace and nobility which lend it an enduring magnetism.

One day a friend and I were walking down Peshawar's Saddar Bazaar when we were approached by a little girl, no more than eight years of age. She was offering to sell us balloons. My friend bought one and gave her money for two. The girl refused to take the extra money. My friend insisted and we walked on. We had barely gone a few steps when we heard the child shouting after us. We turned around to find the girl running away. Before leaving she had tied a second balloon to a railing near us.

Underneath Peshawar's rigid structures, amid the tyrannical traditions, despite the social disintegration, there exist traces of a community whose dignity, hospitality, generosity, irreverence, humour, compassion and grace under pressure remain matchless. In Peshawar, friendships are real and courtesies backed by genuine sentiment. Its culture prizes self-sacrifice and community service — qualities that have given the city resilience despite decades of neglect. Had there been a government interested in genuine nation-building, it would have tapped into this as a civic resource. But until now, Peshawar has lacked a civil society, or elective affinities based around issues and ideas rather than class, clan, or party affiliation. The space for political engagement was limited, monopolised by Pakistan's visionless political parties. There were no causes to join, no forums for meeting like-minded people. But this is gradually changing. Pakistan's rambunctious new satellite channels, for all their flaws, are broadening the scope of political activity. Blowback from an unpopular war in Afghanistan has further shaken people out of political torpor. People are more politically aware and a civil society is finally emerging. The women's movement around the Ladies Club is serving as a nucleus. The city is being reclaimed. Peshawar is in poor shape, but it is a city in transition. It will rise again.

QUETTA DIVISIONS

Mahvish Ahmad

'It's too dangerous. I'll have to send a driver.' The voice on the other end of the mobile takes a breath. 'I hope you don't mind.'

The caller is Ali Ahmad Kohzad, leader of the Hazara Democratic Party, whom I had arranged to meet. As a prominent politician, Kohzad is constantly under threat, particularly from the Sunni-militant group Lashkar-e-Jhangvi, that has been targeting Hazara-Shias since 2001. At Kohzad's request I park my white Suzuki van in front of a dull sand-swept petrol pump just outside Hazara Town. The town isn't really a town, but more a settlement, one of two, where Quetta's 500,000-strong Shia Hazaras live. I wait to be picked up by his driver, whose name is Arif. When Arif pulls up in a white Toyota Corolla, he is easy to recognise; that's because Hazaras rarely marry outside their ethnicity and their distinct central Asian features have survived since the 1800s, when they first settled in Quetta. Their distinctiveness also makes them easy for militant groups to spot, and kill. Arif comes armed. I walk up to him and introduce myself; he unlocks the safety latch of his pistol, and says: 'Have to make sure you're ready — just in case.' He then starts the engine. 'We never venture out of our areas without being armed,' Arif says, as we begin to drive into Hazara Town.

Quetta is the hill-side capital of Balochistan, Pakistan's highly strategic western province. Bordering Iran to its east and Afghanistan to its north, it is rich in natural gas, gold, copper, and minerals. It also has the country's longest coastline and second-largest port in the southern city of Gwadar. Balochistan's land mass constitutes 40 per cent of the total land area of Pakistan, and yet paradoxically its population is among the country's most impoverished.

At the same time Quetta today is a crossroads for several overlapping and violent conflicts. They include a six-year-long separatist uprising being led by the province's ethnic Baloch peoples, which is taking place at the same time as the Taliban insurgency across the border. Quetta is home to the Taliban Leadership Council and also their Pakistani allies, Lashkar-e-Jhangvi. If that wasn't complicated enough the city is also a vital supply-line for NATO-bound food and weapons.

I have come to Quetta to get underneath the patchwork that is Balochistan. I want to know why Hazaras are being killed. I want to know if it is true that the Pakistani state is tacitly backing the Sunni extremist Lashkar-e-Jhangvi group and if so, why; and I want to understand the love-hate relationship between Quetta's two main nationalities: the Pakhtuns and the Baloch. And perhaps above all I want to know what is driving Baloch nationalism, the very longstanding desire of many in the predominantly left-wing Baloch leadership to escape from Islamic Pakistan.

With such a rich and deep history, and with so many conflicts in play, few know whom to trust and, understandably, the atmosphere on the heavily militarised streets is palpably tense. Khaki-clad soldiers, mostly young, are everywhere; standing awkwardly at checkpoints, leaning against graffiti-marked walls, or in the middle of busy markets, surrounded by sandbags, and steel fences; all the while locking, loading and re-loading their weapons. A tiny blue rickshaw is stopped for yet-another random search. A 'suspicious-looking' student leaving his campus is pulled aside. Some checks are routine, requiring little more than a flash of an ID card. Others though are more intrusive, such as when drivers are told to open-up the bonnets of cars in case of hidden bombs. If a soldier isn't satisfied with what he sees, a driver can expect a lengthy grilling, sometimes lasting hours at a time.

Hazara Town is in the western outskirts of the city. There are only a handful of Baloch and Pakhtuns here, concentrated in the settlement's southern parts. Hazara Town itself came into existence in 1986, when Haji Nisar Ali, an ethnic Hazara, bought the land from a Baloch family and began to build and sell houses to those Hazaras who wanted to move out of Alamdar Road, the older and increasingly over-populated Hazara settlement at the other end of the city. 'We'll make sure to take you to Alamdar Road later today,' Kohzad says after Arif drops me off at the Hazara Democratic Party office. Here I meet Asmatullah Yaari, President of the Hazara Student Federation, who will be my guide for the day. As seems to be the norm, guns are clicked and unlocked, as we get into a white corolla and drive off to our first stop: a cemetery.

The choice of a cemetery is no accident. More than 700 Hazaras have died in the past decade, mostly killed at the hands of Lashkar-e-Jhangvi. We park the car next to a small cottage high near a cliff overlooking the graveyard. The road is over-shadowed by Quetta's sand-coloured mountains and it isn't hard to imagine militants of any variety sneaking down from the mountains to attack soldiers and minorities alike.

'One of our attacks happened right here,' Asmatullah explains, referring to a 6 May 2011 attack when eight people were killed and fifteen wounded. 'Some people were playing cricket and football down there', he says pointing to a large empty area of land next to a grey patch of gravestones. 'Ten men showed up from the mountains behind us. Two of them were carrying rocket launchers and the rest of them had automatic assault rifles. The attack went on for almost twenty minutes, but no one showed up. Army checkpoints are only a five-minute drive from here'.

We continue our drive to the graveyard, inching our way down a steep slope leading to the gravestones. It is here that I see bodies buried in straight lines and each of the headstones carries the same date. 'You'll find that a lot of the people here got killed all at once,' Asmatullah says. Remarkably, the killers have yet to be caught. Remarkably because, as Asmatullah observes: 'This is a small city, compared to Karachi, Lahore or Peshawar. But you'll see a check post on every corner. There are a thousand [paramilitary] forces in this town, and 50,000 in Quetta. So it is hard to fathom why our security forces have been unable to track down and stop Lashkar-e-Jhangvi for carrying out these killings,' he says ruefully.

We leave the graveyard for lunch with Ali Akbar, the Hazara Democratic Party's Deputy Secretary and its oldest living member. The *baithak* – or sitting room – in Akbar's house is unusually pink. Pink carpets and pink cushions line the large room's four corners; airbrushed pictures of Akbar's large family are arranged side by side, next to plastic flowers and flowery teacups. At one end sits an old Kalashnikov rifle, with bullets, displayed in a large frame. 'It's quite old, nothing to worry about,' Akbar says as he greets me.

Kohzad also joins us as we sit down to eat. 'You need to be here, and talk to locals to understand the dynamics of this place,' he says. 'Ask any member of the HDP and they will tell you that Pakistan is letting Hazaras be killed because of its alliance with Islamist militant groups,' he says. 'The militant groups have historically been an asset for the security state.'

'That's not all,' Asmatullah intervenes. 'There is no doubt that we are getting killed because of our Shia beliefs; and that we're more vulnerable because of how we look. I'm not saying that the state is killing us with its own hands. But you need to look a little deeper to understand what's actually going on here. This doesn't have to happen if the state lived up to its promise of protecting us as Pakistani citizens. Lashkar-e-Jhangvi is being tolerated for a reason. We're just collateral damage.'

Akbar explains that the Hazaras have typically been told that the perpetrators are Baloch. 'They are deliberately trying to turn us against our neighbours. Of course we know that some of the members of Lashkar-e-Jhangvi are ethnically Baloch. But all ethnic groups have ideological differences. The vast majority of Baloch are engaged in a nationalist struggle, not in Islamist militancy. And these nationalists are not interested in murdering us,' Akbar says. 'Ask them yourself,' Kohzad adds.

Histories are always contested and the story of how Balochistan came to be is no exception. Ask the Pakhtuns and they will tell you that according to the earliest eleventh-century accounts of Quetta, taken down when Sultan Mahmud Ghaznavi invaded South Asia, the area was inhabited by the Pakhtun Qasi tribe. And Pakhtun representatives today claim that the Baloch did not really inhabit this city until Quetta was made the provincial capital by the British of a transboundary region, which straddled modern day Afghanistan, Iran and Pakistan. According to the Baloch, however, Quetta was given as a *shal* or gift in the eighteenth century by Ahmed Shah Durrani, the Emir of the Afghan Empire and the founder of modern Afghanistan. The gift was for a powerful leader, who called himself the Khan of Kalat, the leader of the Baloch-Brahui kingdom known until the 1950s as Kalat.

The Khan and his successors, however, were no firebrand nationalists and latterly seem to have found themselves in the role of Imperial pawn. The British saw Balochistan as a buffer between India, the 'jewel in the crown', and the Russian Tsardom that was eager to gain access to the Indian Ocean. A series of treaties from 1839 onwards solidified the Sardari or tribal leader system, culminating with the occupation of Quetta in 1875, when the British bought the loyalty of the sitting Khan of Kalat, and the Sardars that surrounded him. The Sardars positioned themselves as the key mediators in all internal issues of Balochistan and their influence continues today as they occupy positions of power within Pakistani provincial and federal governments.

The Baloch peoples of today comprise two linguistic groups: those who speak Baloch and those who speak Brahui. The Pakistani state tries to portray the two groups as distinct, which is deeply ironic given that the state merged Balochi and Brahui-speakers into the same ethnic category in a 1998 census.

Ever since Nawab Akbar Khan Bugti, one of Balochistan's Sardars or tribal leaders, was killed in 2006, the Baloch have been up in arms against a state that they have long accused of neglecting their needs. More than that, many of the Baloch peoples believe that the state is now at war with them and hundreds of bodies, mutilated, bullet-ridden, or charred beyond recognition, have been discovered.

When I go to a Baloch *abadi* (settlement) in the south of the city, Pakistan's paramilitary Frontier Corps patrol the streets in search of what they regard as 'suspicious-looking Baloch'. The locals tell me they get stopped randomly and asked to recite the *kalima* –Islam's article of faith – to prove their Islamic credentials. 'They think we're *kufrs* (unbelievers) funded by India or Israel,' they say. 'But we're Baloch, tired of how we are treated, and the tortured and mutilated bodies that they dump of our sons.'

I decide to take up Kohzad's suggestion and find out for myself why it is that the Baloch want *azaadi*, or freedom from Pakistan.

A party fighting a war of independence cannot advertise itself on the Internet, nor can it operate freely in public. Most Baloch nationalists live in an underground world; a world that I am able to enter via Agha Ashraf Dilsoz, a young and leading nationalist who is part of a group that calls itself the Baloch Fikri (*fikri* meaning 'thought') Council, and a former member of the Baloch National Movement (BNM). I find Dilsoz sitting cross-legged in a garden, under the shadow of a tree. 'I can move around a little bit, but I generally have to stay put. You never know when the paramilitaries decide to pick you up,' he says. 'I've prepared my wife and my kids, just in case.'

The Baloch Fikri Council and the Baloch National Movement are part of a long tradition of separatist political groups in the province. The Baloch have risen up against the Pakistani state four times in each decade since 1947, led by popular Sardars from the well-known Murree and Bugti tribes in eastern

Balochistan. The Sardars still lead parts of today's independence movement. However, a growing, if not a dominant core is now led by the middle classes. The uprising has also moved south-west, to an area called Makran a more urbanised and relatively affluent area close to Pakistan's strategic Gwadar port, where the National Movement is particularly strong and where residents are well- connected to Karachi and to the Gulf states of Dubai, Abu Dhabi and Sharjah. The shift indicates not just the entrance of the Baloch middle class in separatist politics but also a broader united front for independence.

Although Pakistan is officially an Islamic republic, Baloch nationalism is avowedly secular and left-wing. Moreover, 'Baloch nationalists have always been secular and progressive,' Dilsoz tells me as we sip *kaava* (green tea) in his garden. 'We are not split across religious divides or identity. But the establishment feels threatened by us.' The 'establishment', a term frequently used by activists, describes an alliance between Pakistan's commercial, security, and political elite. Dilsoz also confirms what I was told by the Hazaras: that it is nonsense to say that Baloch are killing Hazaras. Being largely secular, the Baloch are not too concerned with the fact that the Hazaras are Shia. These accusations are designed to 'create divisions between Quetta's locals. People who have been neighbours for a long time,' he adds. 'Those critical of our movement also try to create divisions between us. Between our linguistic groups, our religious traditions, and our class,' Dilsoz says.

Some of the separatist Sardars, like Khair Bakhsh Marri, were known to be highly critical of the very structures they were born into; and many were Marxist. Members of organisations like the Balochistan National Movement and the Baloch Student Organisation-Azaad know their Che Guevera, Paulo Freire and Lenin – and do not hesitate to cite them. The Baloch are critical not just of conservative Islam but also of the security state and the federal Pakistani framework that promotes inequality and treats them unjustly. 'This sort of progressive politics makes Pakistan feel threatened,' Dilsoz says. The state uses the particular and peculiar formation of 'the Muslim' in the 'Islamic Republic of Pakistan' as an instrument to sideline, divide and suppress the Baloch nationalist identity. Ethnic nationalism threatens the fabric that constitutes the Pakistani self, a peculiar mix of conservative middle-class Islamism with a moralising and capitalist logic, where some people need to be sacrificed for the abstract notion of 'the greater national good'. Dilsoz suggests that the Baloch usually constitute 'the sacrificed'. 'We live on top of resources, but they get exported to the rest of Pakistan.'

After meeting Dilsoz, I make my way to Balochistan University to listen to the Pakhtun perspective. The University serves the entire province, which means it attracts every member of Quetta's ethnic communities. You would be mistaken in thinking that this makes the university a cultural melting pot. Instead, it serves as a mini-arena for Quetta's larger battles. The campus has broad pavements and giant trees arranged in straight lines, and Pakistani paramilitary rangers are stationed outside the gates. I have already heard stories of security forces following and picking up Baloch students on the campus. A student called Khalid, I was told, 'was asked to exit a school bus on his way home, and then chased through the campus and picked up. He was too scared to go back to the university, so he has dropped out now and gone back home.' Some ninety-five students with nationalist sympathies have been kidnapped and killed since 2006. However, it is not just the Baloch students who are threatened by violence. Several Punjabi and Urdu-speaking professors are also believed to have been murdered by sections of the Baloch nationalist movement because they were seen as establishment puppets. Pakhtun professors, too, have been targeted.

Like much of the rest of the university, the history department feels hollow. I arrive to find the head of department, Professor Kalimullah, sitting behind a large mahogany desk in a sparsely furnished office, dressed in white short-sleeved shirt and red tie. Kalimullah is both an academic and Pakhtun-supporting politician: a leading authority on the history of Quetta, Kalimullah is a member of the Pakhtunkhwa Milli Awami Party (PKMAP). The party was formed in the 1970s by Abdul Samad Khan Achakzai to agitate for the division of Balochistan so that the Pakhtun and the Baloch could live in separate provinces. In common with Baloch nationalists, Achakzai is not only a stalwart of nationalism, but he, too, is a champion of progressive politics. A pacifist, he was a member of the Congress party of India (before Pakistan was created) and argued for Pakhtun autonomy within a united and secular India.

The nationalist cause is dominating news about Balochistan. But there is a much longer history in this city,' Kalimullah tells me. 'Quetta was the capital of Pashtun territory under the old British colonial administration, where the province was split up into two parts – Kalat State and what came to be called British Balochistan.

The latter – in the north of the province — was our home. But despite their distinct ethnic make-ups, the two parts were merged forty years ago, and now we are politically dominated by the Baloch even though we (the Pakhtuns) are a majority in Quetta.

Kalimullah gets off his chair, walks over to a bookshelf, and pulls out a cardboard-bound book recording the 'historical claim of the Pakhtuns' over Quetta. He starts narrating a story that I was to hear a few times, speaking of the fundamental rift between the city's two dominant groups, the Baloch and the Pakhtuns. Alongside the state's attempts to pit the Hazaras against the Baloch, and the Baloch against each other, Kalimullah's tale hints at how the state – both directly through specific policies, and covertly – pits the Pakhtuns against the Baloch.

On my way out of the university, I notice that the walls of various buildings on the campus are covered with graffiti declaring student support for one ethnic group or the other. One can detect the unease and lack of trust between Pakhtun and Baloch students, who huddle together in separate groups. The students ask me not to mention their names.

On the way back we pass Quetta Rail Station, where thousands live in slum-like dwellings around the tracks. I ask the driver, Nabeel, which ethnic group they belong to. 'They are settlers,' he replies. Nabeel, a Baloch, sees many Punjabi and Urdu-speaking locals as an embodiment of state rule. Despite having lived there for decades, to him they are still outsiders. In fact, the 'settlers' were originally brought in by the British during colonial rule to run the city, and various Pakistani administrations have added to their numbers since them. They too have been frequently attacked, mostly by the Baloch. 'We lived peacefully together before,' he says. 'But it seems like a very, very long time ago.'

That 'long time' was the 1950s. In 1954, Pakistan's then Prime Minister Muhammad Ali Bogra announced what he called the One Unit Province policy in which then West Pakistan's provinces were merged into one. Any attempts to acknowledge the diversity and complexity of different ethnic groups that made the state of Pakistan were swept aside in a single, sweeping move. Ethnic communities throughout Pakistan saw the policy as an unacceptable affront to their identities, and their right to self-rule. They came together to form a broad coalition of progressive and leftist groups to fight the policy. It resulted in the formation of the National Awami/Peoples' Party (NAP), established in Dhaka in erstwhile East Pakistan, in July 1957.

The new party advocated provincial autonomy, recognition of different ethnic groups as 'nations', demanded certain rights on the basis of ethnicity, rejected the Islamist foundations of the Pakistani state and advocated a secular politics. Virtually all the leaders of the ethnically-based groups in Balochistan joined the NAP and Quetta became a magnet for the progressive left and those critical of a dominant, Islamic and centralist Pakistan.

One sixty-year-old resident told me that he 'came to Quetta forty-five years ago because it was the home of an inspiring and alternative form of politics'. Another, who preferred to remain anonymous and described himself as neither Baloch or Pakhtun, said Quetta was a peaceful, united city, 'a place for a progressive politics. NAP was its greatest manifestation.' Even after NAP-days, and during the fourth Baloch uprising, a group of left students from London are said to have joined the Baloch in their resistance against the Pakistan government. The 'London Group' consisted of some of the biggest names in Pakistani journalism including Rashid Rehman and Najam Sethi.

NAP split into two factions in 1969. One faction remained in the newly formed Bangladesh, while the other became the main opposition party to the rule of the then Prime Minister Zulfiqar Ali Bhutto. It won a decisive victory in the Balochistan provincial elections in 1970. But the Party was outlawed in 1975, after Bhutto accused the NAP of working for the secession of Balochistan and the northern Pakhtun province. NAP leaders were accused of importing arms to fight a war against the central government. The party's leaders were imprisoned, in what later came to be known as the 'Hyderabad Conspiracy Case'.

Two grand old men of the NAP are still active in politics, albeit from different sides of the fence; Dr Hakeem Lehri and Abdul Rahim Khan Mandokhel agree to meet with me to tell me more.

Lehri, a senior member of the Baloch Republican (nationalist) Party who believes in secession, lives under a self-imposed curfew. He is fearful that he will be kidnapped or arrested if he leaves, so like the Baloch Dilsoz, prefers to stay indoors. We discuss his time in NAP. 'Back then,' he says, 'I would share a dorm with a Pakhtun friend, and we would read leftist thinkers and translate those we thought were crucial. He would translate it into Pashto; I into Baloch. They were fantastic times.' He pauses and takes a deep breath. 'I used to believe in our ability to change the situation through elected rule. But in 1975 our government was dismissed. We were accused of importing arms. Our leaders were tried on trumped-up charges.'

Later the same day, I meet Mandokhel, one of the most senior members of Pakhtunkhwa Milli Awami Party. He sits in an office under a white and beige painting of his party's founder, Abdul Samad Khan Achakzai. 'We all believed in NAP once upon a time,' he tells me. 'It was an incredible exercise in unity. But we, the Pakhtuns, were ignored and marginalised.' His politics, he says, is not set in stone; but he is suspicious of the Baloch. 'Achakzai left NAP because he felt that the Pakhtuns in Balochistan were not being heard.' Nothing much has changed, Mandokhel laments.

Lehri and Mandokhel do not seem to talk anymore. One is a separatist fighting for independence; the other agitating for Balochistan to be divided into separate provinces. One seeks to break away from Pakistan, the other to become a more integral part of Pakistan and have a greater share of its resources. Their dedication to their separate ethnic groups, it seems, keeps them apart, busy in their own issues and battles. Neither is very successful. Lehri and his co-fighters are overwhelmed by the firepower of the Pakistan military; and Mandokhel is overlooked in a national debate where the issues of his party are largely ignored.

Any meaningful resolution to the problems of Quetta can only come when local ethnic groups are united, and able to articulate an inclusive politics that both recognises the particularities of culture and ethnicity and takes a critical stand towards the state. Balochistan needs a new alliance, modelled on the old NAP. It's a sentiment I heard many times during my conversations with Quetta's residents on the street. 'Perhaps there is a small chance that the rupture and violence can push us back in the same direction, and open up a little bit of space for something new just as it did so many years ago', the sixty-year-old who remembered Quetta's glory days in the 70s told me. If ancient history is being used to divide Quetta, then perhaps modern history is a potential way forward. But first, as Mandokhel admitted, we 'need to be willing to sit around the table once again'.

BREAKING NEWS

Ehsan Masood

'This is your daughter, isn't she?' The voice was direct; the question unambiguous. 'Is this your daughter; have you tried to sell your child?' An impoverished young mother had opened the door of her house to what she thought were visitors. The visitors were actually a TV crew from ARY TV, one of Pakistan's popular private television channels. She stared in stunned silence through the gap between the wooden door and frame. Standing on the other side was a reporter cradling a baby. Like a volley, the question came again. 'Is this your daughter; have you tried to sell your child?'

'No, it isn't,' she replied, barely audible. 'It isn't my child.'

'Swear on the Qur'an that it isn't.'

More silence followed, before she begged the crew to turn off the cameras and she promised to let him inside. A few seconds later viewers to this incident, broadcast in January 2012, were led inside a one-room shack, the cameras still rolling.

Babies and young children are traded all over the world, but in Pakistan child trafficking is believed to be of epidemic proportions. The demand is from a spectrum of society, from leaders of professional begging syndicates, an industry of Bill Sykes in need of their Oliver Twists; to wealthy couples who want to avoid the lengthy process of a formal adoption.

Pretending to be an interested buyer, the ARY reporter had managed to trace one such child back to its mother. Having gained access to the inside of her house the cameras were back on. Speaking slowly, the mother explained that she had given birth to five children and that her husband, a security guard, earned a paltry £40 a month. The family were in debt and on most days there wasn't enough food to go round: she felt she had no choice but to sell one of her children, which she did for £60. 'Which mother could ever sell one of her children,' she said, breaking down. 'Believe me; believe me,' she begged. 'I had no choice.' At this point the camera zoomed out so that more of the sparse room was visible; except that it wasn't that sparse. Seated on the bed and on the floor were members of the woman's wider family, including all of her children.

On that same January day, ARY TV, along with practically every Pakistani news channel, was broadcasting a most unlikely news-flash; unlikely that is for a country officially an Islamic republic. Wars, natural disasters, political events were of no consequence on that morning. Instead, the news ticker at the top of every ARY's viewer's screen was carrying breaking news in the life of Lahore-based actress and model Veena Malik. No ordinary model, Malik is in fact Pakistan's first ever topless celebrity. She posed nude for the December 2011 cover of the India edition of the British men's magazine FHM. The cover shows Malik sans clothes with the letters 'ISI' stencilled, or tattooed, in large lettering on her arm. ISI, or Inter Services Intelligence, the country's all-powerful spy agency run by the military, in which Malik's father once served.

Reporters follow her every move and on that day had traced Malik's whereabouts to the front desk of a Lahore police station. Her reason for going was to apply for a 'police character certificate', a peculiarly Pakistani piece of bureaucracy and a requirement for a citizen who needs a visa to travel abroad. A character certificate is not, as the name suggests, a certificate confirming the strength of the holder's moral fibre. It is, in fact, a piece of paper confirming more mundane details such as their name, date of birth and home address. Pakistan's police service holds the right to issue one of these certificates, without which citizens are forbidden to travel. The TV networks of course knew this, but no matter: why let the facts get in the way of a good story. 'Veena Malik seeks character certificate' is the kind of headline that any editor would find almost impossible to turn down and so, tongues firmly in cheeks, ARY along with many other networks continued to give plenty of airtime to this event.

Television in Pakistan has come a long way during the last decade. It is light years from its origins as a single channel owned and operated by the state-owned Pakistan Television Corporation when programming would begin in the late afternoon with Qur'anic recitals and end with Qur'anic recitals at half an hour before midnight. Back then, each half-day schedule would include no fewer than four news bulletins (in Urdu, English, Arabic and one in a regional language). The evening's TV news would be dominated by the activities of federal and provincial leaders, rounding off with a report on the day's sport, meaning cricket and hockey. Product advertising would consist of the luxuries of the day such as batteries, soap, and agricultural fertiliser. There would be plenty of footage of politicians and world leaders sitting in sumptuous lounges, sipping tea; or footage of politicians and world leaders disembarking from airplanes and walking purposefully towards the next guard of honour. An outside broadcast involved giving a reporter a microphone with an impossibly long lead and getting him to do a piece to camera while standing outside the main PTV headquarters.

But all of this is history. Today no politician of any party can expect an easy ride from journalists. A plethora of talk shows, such as Capital Talk and 'Aaj Kamran Khan Kay Saath' (Today with Kamran Khan) on Geo TV, 'Pakistan Tonight' and 'Off the Record with Kashif Abbasi' on ARY, and 'Tonight with Jasmeen' on Samaa, exist for the sole purpose of grilling members of the government and the main opposition parties. Only one politician can expect a relatively safe passage, and that is the cricketer-turned-politician Imran Khan. This is largely because the incumbent Mr Clean of Pakistani politics is building a formidable base of support, especially among young city dwellers, including many senior and junior media folk. When he launched a series of what he called 'Tsunami' mass rallies earlier this year, broadcasters generously gave Khan and his supporters plenty of relatively uncritical coverage.

There are changes elsewhere too. Pakistani television channels are full of investigative programmes, like 'Geo F.I.R.', where criminal activity is fearlessly exposed. Comedy and satirical shows, such as Geo's 'Um Sab Umeed Say Hain' (We Are All Hopeful) and 'Butt Tameezian' (Bad Manners) on Dunya TV, mercilessly lampoon politicians and feudalists. Equally popular is 'Late Night with Begum Nawazish Ali', where a drag queen probes influential people with searching questions. Pakistan TV has in addition helped to unleash a minor revolution in music, providing airtime and sponsorship for numerous new (and old) bands. And television soaps, for decades the medium's main staple, continue to be a major strength. When the last episode of the critically acclaimed 'Hamsafar' was aired on Hum TV, the streets of Karachi were deserted.

Hit TV soaps are just about all that survives from TV of old, when viewers would gather in the house of a relative wealthy enough to afford a black-and-white set, which would often be encased in a stylish wooden concertina cabinet; or covered in an embroidered dust-sheet, to be taken off minutes before the start of the evening's transmission. Most weeks, however, there would be at least one programme imported from the UK or America (which are now conspicuous by their absence). For many years, Pakistan's state-controlled TV bosses broadcast episodes of the 1970s British comedy *Yes, Minister* and its successor *Yes, Prime Minister*. One reason why *Yes Minister* was so popular is because it was broadcast at a time when the country was in the grip of its then latest military dictator, General Zia ul Haq, and viewers could identify with the programme writers' portrayal of a supine minister and member of parliament vainly trying to exert control on an all-powerful civil service.

The Zia years, 1977 to 1988, were particularly challenging for programme makers. New ways to make innovative content without falling foul of the censor had to be constantly invented and things came to a head in 1979 when the General decided he had had enough and cracked down hard on the media as part of a broader programme to enact new laws enshrining Islamic principles in the public sector. These laws included the infamous Hudood Ordinance in which a woman subjected to rape could stand accused of committing adultery; and the Press and Publications Ordinance in which print media articles had to go through a state censor before being published. In retaliation, editors, while not defying the ban, printed empty columns on their front pages in place of articles that had fallen foul of the censor's spike.

Less extreme, but no less intrusive were enforced 'guidelines' for public sector employees such as one in which 'Western-style' clothes were to be replaced with eastern styles to work. Ties, open-necked jackets, shirts and trousers were out; loose-fitting salwar kameez tunic and trousers, and if appropriate, a long jacket with a Nehru collar, known as a *shirwani,* were in. Tailors and dressmakers couldn't believe their luck as overnight, schools, colleges, post offices, nationalized banks, essentially any public institution, became a sea of flowing salwars.

As public employees, TV newscasters had no alternative but to follow suit. Women on TV (both newsreaders and actors) were required to cover their hair with a thin scarf known as a *dupatta*. Not surprisingly, comedy shows, such as the popular 50:50 programme, had a field-day, and in one particular sketch broadcast in 1979, newscasters are shown reading the news wearing string-vests and shorts, as studio bosses had not bought enough *shirwanis* to cover all four of the evening's news bulletins. In another sketch, a send-up of a popular TV soap, husband and wife characters are filmed sitting and talking alone in a bedroom while the wife struggles to keep her *dupatta* from slipping off.

Military dictators come in all shapes, sizes, and opinions. General Zia ul Haq was short in stature, wore his faith on his sleeve, and took satisfaction in watching his male newscasters exchange ties and shirts for baggier clothing. Pervez Musharraf on the other hand is a well-known liberal and clearly not averse to a bit of flesh. In 2000, Musharraf finally agreed to lift five decades of military-style control over the media. In the space of a decade, Pakistan's viewing public has progressed from having access to a handful of state and private TV channels, to literally hundreds.

Musharraf had the confidence to open up the airwaves because he was popular to begin with, and foolishly thought that this popularity would last. These were the months before the 9/11 attacks changed everything for him, and when he still believed that a free media would broadcast to the world all the great things that a military dictatorship can do for a country. That view changed more quickly than many could have imagined and led to a series of standoffs between Musharraf and the media. He later tried to close channels down when they became too critical.

No media institution has been pushing at the boundaries of state censorship more than the Jang group, publisher of the largest-circulation Urdu daily of the same name and its more recent English language daily *The News*. Battle-hardened from its encounters with censors during the Zia years, Jang and its editors have their pulse on the nation thanks in part to a national network of bureaus and correspondents. When TV licenses were offered, the group had the journalistic capacity and money to set up a nationwide news channel. Geo TV was launched in 2002 and overnight brought its viewers the horrors of the wave upon wave of terror attacks that followed Musharraf's decision to back the War on Terror. Its live reporting from the

aftermath of natural disasters such as earthquakes showed up the incompe-
tence and corruption of state officials and landowners. Its talk shows on
religion, such as 'Ghaimdi', which presents the analysis on the well-known
liberal theologian Javed Ahmad Ghamidi, opened up viewers to the idea that
Islam could be debated, and that differences of opinion can be discussed. Its
extensive social affairs programming has uncovered hidden stories of one-
parent families, child trafficking, the plight of the large trans-gender community, and drug and alcohol abuse among the poorest in a country that is
officialy dry.

Geo and other TV channels are relentless in their coverage of corruption,
and in their dogged questioning of officials, including the army. Many television journalists have paid a heavy price for their bravery. In the most benign
cases they have been roughed up by police and intelligence; in other
instances the penalties have been harsher. Geo has become, rather like Al
Jazeera soon after its own birth, a window on a world that many in official-
dom and some in society would like to hide. Indeed Musharraf himself, five
years after letting the genie out, tried to bottle it again by ordering Geo and
other channels to close. This followed his decision to sack the country's
chief justice Iftikhar Chaudhry. The media had been documenting and
largely supporting a nationwide campaign to have Chaudhry reinstated, and
Musharraf told TV bosses bluntly that unless they agreed to new rules of
engagement they would remain closed. But most eventually returned to the
airwaves, including Geo.

Countless media outlets, broadcasting twenty-four-hour news, have their
own demands. There is an insatiable hunger for news stories; and not infre-
quently ethical and journalistic standards are compromised. Veena Malik,
Imran Khan, angry talk-shows and biting satire are emblematic of several
new strands in Pakistan's new broadcasting landscape: the rise of celebrity
broadcasting coupled with the fearlessness of broadcasters who believe that
anything is now possible. Programme makers crossed the threshold of fear
a decade ago and are happy not only to take on the rich and the powerful,
but also to broadcast culturally risqué material.

One former breakfast TV presenter represents another and quite different strand. Maya Khan is a household name and her show 'Subha Savayray
Maya Kay Saath' (Breakfast with Maya) on Samaa TV was a popular morning
programme, mixing studio chat with hard-hitting interviews on the day's

big themes, which was abruptly taken off air in January 2012. Herself a liberal, Maya Khan's following was dominated by society's conservative core, and her programme would return again and again to the subject of immorality. One early January morning in 2012, Maya Khan's viewers tuned in to find their favourite presenter striding out of doors with trademark sunglasses perched high above her forehead, leading a posse of some twenty women. The group was a mix of young and old, marching through the gates of a public park near the centre of Karachi. 'Viewers, if you've just joined us, we are broadcasting to you live from Bin Qasim park,' she proclaimed breathlessly before shouting to her cameraman: 'Let's go.'

Khan and her crew were mounting what amounted to a post-dawn-raid on the many married and unmarried couples who use Bin Qasim and many other parks as a way to meet. As public intimacy is almost impossible, the small hours of the morning or night represent the best time that couples, whether married or not, can get to go out on their own, without the 'protection' of brothers, dads, grannies, chaperones or even entire extended families. Samaa TV's camera began scanning the park and then stopped, fixing its gaze on a hazy image of a man and a woman. As it zoomed in closer, the lens focused on a man walking next to a woman in a black burqa.

'Catch them. She's in a burqa,' Maya Khan shouted to her cameraman, before breaking into a run.

'Sister,' she called out to the woman.

'Hello, hello, hello. Assamalamu Alaykum.'

'Please. What's your name? Don't lie to your parents.'

But the presenter and her crew were too late. The couple beat a hasty exit.

The camera continued to scan the park and this time Maya had a better plan. 'I'm going to go and talk to them, you watch from a distance,' she instructed the cameraman, and began to walk towards a park bench occupied by a second hapless couple.

'Assalamu Alaykum. My microphone is turned off, don't worry. How are you?'

The couple looked shocked.

'Are you engaged to marry?'

'Yes, but please turn off the camera. Please leave us alone'.

'Do your parents know you are here?'

'Yes'.

'Then don't be so scared. Are you engaged?'

'Yes. Please leave us alone.'

The couple quickly got up and looked for the park exit. Maya Khan let them go and turned to the camera confirming to viewers that they were indeed engaged to marry. Members of her aunty posse, however, did not agree and took turns with the microphone to vent some much-suppressed spleen. 'If she is engaged, then [her fiancé] should visit her at home,' proclaimed one indignant young student wearing all black, before deciding that: 'If they are here, it's impossible that they are engaged.' An older woman was angrier. 'Even if they were engaged, they shouldn't be allowed to meet. A lot of families don't allow it because being engaged is not a legal contract.'

At this point, the camera cut back to Maya Khan who informed viewers of an impending commercial break. When the programme returns, she said, the group will continue to hunt for dating couples in different parks. Her support team joked that parks were probably emptying of couples (they weren't wrong). Maya Khan then issued the following call to action: 'If you happen to see an unmarried couple in a park or a public place, then do call.'

This episode, dubbed vigil-aunties by the media, made headlines around the world and ultimately cost Maya Khan her job. She was forced to apologise by Samaa TV bosses and went underground for a time. It confirmed (if such confirmation were needed) that Pakistani society is deeply polarised. A liberally-minded minority were outraged, but easily the majority of viewers couldn't see what was wrong with TV exposing what they regard as immoral behaviour. This, in the opinion of many, is what TV is supposed to do.

That Musharraf believed a free media could be kind to a dictator is mostly down to Javed Jabbar, a canny and strategic advertising mogul and conservationist who Musharraf picked as his first minister for information and broadcasting. No sooner had Jabbar been handed the keys to his desk in Islamabad, he set about organising the sell-off of broadcast licenses. Anticipating that this brave new digital world would need a strong regulatory framework, Jabbar created a new body called PEMRA, or Pakistan Electronic Media Regulatory Authority, which has the power both to issue and to revoke broadcasting licenses.

Jabbar is urbane and well-travelled and PEMRA is modelled on the regulatory practices of countries with a longer history of media freedom. The regulator sits in a shiny glass building in Islamabad, the capital city, and has fifteen regional and city offices. Unlike the rest of the public sector, PEMRA seems to be not short of money, and yet it is hard not to feel sorry for those charged with carrying out its mandate. Even with all the resources at its disposal, trying to regulate Pakistan's new electronic media is like trying to be the sheriff in a cowboy movie.

PEMRA's inabilities were well exposed in the coverage of the country's latest air tragedy. In April 2012, an aircraft operated by a small private airline called Bhoja Airways crashed during a flight from Islamabad to Karachi. Reporters from most of the new networks (public and private) rushed to Karachi airport and besieged relatives and friends, some clearly traumatised, waiting in the arrivals hall for news. Requests for privacy were flatly ignored. In one case, a relative kept asking on camera to be left alone, only to be greeted with yet more intrusive questions about a missing passenger.

As one group of journalists ringed Karachi airport, a separate set of their colleagues sped off to hunt for the plane's wreckage. In retracing the aircraft's final minutes camera teams stumbled upon more than just debris; they also found dead and mutilated bodies, footage of which was broadcast continuously on the night of the crash, and then again afterwards. PEMRA issued a warning to seventeen channels that if such behaviour continued then action would be taken. Like previous such warnings, it had little effect.

Quite possibly the worst case of lax media regulation (extending beyond the reach of PEMRA) is the coverage over two years devoted to Shamsul Anwar, a con artist who fooled all the newspapers and news channels. In 2010, a tearful Anwar presented himself at the offices of the *Express and Tribune* newspaper with a tale that had all the makings of a Bollywood movie. Clutching a battered plastic file, Anwar, a retired solider, explained that the Taliban had kidnapped two of his teenage sons and were demanding £100,000 in ransom. If he didn't pay, he wailed, they would chop the boys alive and send back body parts in a cloth bag. He said he had no money and nothing to eat at home except some sugar and half a carton of milk. His wife, looking equally forlorn, was with him.

Anwar was also holding a page from a yellowing newspaper from a decade before. It contained an article praising him for saving a Rawalpindi mosque from being blown up in 2001. In the article, Anwar had claimed to have been washing himself in the mosque, preparing to pray when he saw a man try and connect wires to a box of explosives. 'I started shouting for help but no one listened to my cries as the *khutba* (sermon) was being recited on the loudspeaker,' he told a journalist later. He claimed to have tried to restrain the bomber who promptly shot him in the legs.

Five years later the Taliban came calling, and kidnapped his two sons to avenge their failed mosque bombing. He claimed that one of his boys had been sawn alive and the Taliban sent back his body parts, together with a CD containing a video of the killing. They released his second son, but not before injecting the fourteen-year-old with toxic chemicals. His second son, Anwar said, was now dying of cancer.

It was all too much. Prominent human rights organisations took up his case and hundreds of thousands of pounds poured into Anwar's bank accounts via Facebook and Twitter (his supporters created the saveshamsulanwar hashtag). Imran Khan donated money as did thousands all over the country, and abroad, many organised collections and many more gave generously out of meagre wages.

Anwar was only rumbled when, late in 2011, he again went to the police claiming this time that his daughter had been kidnapped and that the Taliban were once more asking for a similar ransom. Again, thousands came to his aid, pouring in cash via appeals on social networking sites. But for the police it was a case of once-bitten. Senior officers felt that something wasn't quite right, and further investigation revealed Anwar to be a hoaxer of the first order. It turned out that his 'kidnapped' daughter was alive and well (she had in fact left home to marry). It also turned out that his first son did not die at the hands of the Taliban, but had in fact died soon after being born.

Anwar is now under arrest and the law presumably will take its course. But what of the media? Who will ask questions of the media? A very contrite Sehrish Wasif, the young journalist who first interviewed Anwar, apologised, but not before writing on her blog: 'It is my belief that anyone could have easily fallen for his ploy, since he was eager to show his bullet-ridden legs and reports that his surviving son had blood cancer.' But even if Wasif fell for Anwar's sobs, the story ought to have been properly vetted by her editors, as well as by editorial staff on the hundreds of other newspapers and TV channels which carried it. And where was PEMRA?

PEMRA has two fundamental obstacles to doing its job properly: it is trying to enforce laws in a country where private institutions (large and small) have almost no respect for an often corrupt and inefficient state. And it is regarded by broadcasters as little more than a censor in regulatory clothing. Many of the complaints it receives from members of the public are about the falling standard of taste and decency in programmes, and about channels that broadcast little more than continuous advertising. PEMRA allows only six ads per hour, at intervals of twelve minutes. However, a good number of complaints are from politicians and members of the ruling classes objecting to their portrayal in comedy and satirical shows, and complaining about journalists who ask tough questions.

While broadcasters wince at its name, PEMRA does have its fans, and lots of them. For arguably the majority in conservative Pakistan, PEMRA is a buffer against an unwelcome tide of liberalism, particularly from Geo TV. Notwithstanding the bravery and doggedness of its news journalism, Geo is often accused by some of its viewers of a none-too-secret Westernisation agenda, and there is no question that in addition to holding the powerful to account, Geo's editors are also continually testing - and pushing – the limits of tolerance of a highly conservative society.

In April 2012 Geo unwisely chose to broadcast yet another interview with Veena Malik at the peak-time slot of 7pm when most people with young children and extended families would have been watching. The broadcast kicked-off an almighty uproar among viewers. 'Geo TV is spreading vulgarity in society,' one complainant said. 'Geo News shocking interview with Veena Malik should be stopped,' said another. 'Block Geo and all of its channels,' yet another implored PEMRA. 'They are against Pakistan, against Islam, against culture and against Muslims.'

Broadcasters are clearly revelling in their hard-won freedoms, as they hold the powerful to account, expose corruption, and bravely hold a mirror to Pakistani society. Each day Pakistan's TV media, and Geo in particular, remind their viewers that no institution can be above scrutiny, whether public or private, religious or secular. These institutions, of course, also include the media. State (and to some extent private) institutions in Pakistan, such as the courts and the police, command little trust because they are perceived by their publics to be corrupt and unethical entities that offer low standards of service. It may surprise the broadcasters, but many Pakistani see the mass media through a similar lens.

If TV reporters continue to barge (or trick) their way into peoples' homes, TV presenters continue to harass members of the public on air, or pretend that someone isn't being filmed when the cameras are rolling, individuals and especially children are identified on TV without consent, the little trust that remains in Pakistan's TV channels will gradually erode away. TV channels such as Geo and ARY are rightly committed to opening up a largely conservative society to ideas of diversity and plural voices. But such a commendable goal has to be coupled with ethical standards and established practice of journalism. Poor standards of journalism will erode peoples' trust in their media institutions, and when that starts to happen the agenda for pluralism will be seriously threatened.

BEYOND THE IMAGINARIUM

Merryl Wyn Davies

We make a steady climb through mountainous terrain. I thought to myself, once this stretch of immaculate highway carries us over the top we'll be there. When we topped the crest, the road ran on through mile after lush green mile. These are peach orchards, I am told. No, they can't be! Ridiculous! No one ever mentioned peaches! I am on the road to the North West Frontier. On so many levels nothing is as expected. Not a single vista corresponds to the landscapes of my imagination. There is not even an inkling of the devastation I have come to see. Nowhere can I detect visible wreckage or any intimation that just a year before an immense disaster had overtaken the land.

My trip had not started this way. I was giddy with excitement as I stood within the landscape of my imagination on my first excursion around Lahore. Friends took me to the House of Wonders. There was the great gun, *zam zammah*, standing before the gates, exactly as it should. In my mind's eye I could see Kim sitting nonchalantly atop the gun. Nowadays it would be a perilous perch as the gun is marooned resplendent on a spit of grassy turf dividing a dual carriageway alive with jostling cars and motor rickshaws. The House of Wonders, however, is just as it should be — a grand edifice of red sandstone with white pointed cupolas in that incomparable Anglo Mughal style that reeks of Orient.

When I noticed the sign announcing Kim's Bookshop, a small kiosk in the forecourt of the House of Wonders, I was in paroxysms, transports of delight that are the legacy of a misspent youth. My mother had a great fondness for *Kim*, Rudyard Kipling's novel. The book opens with Kim, the irrepressible street urchin who is the friend of all the world, astride the great gun. There he meets the old lama who has come to learn the secret of his own history from the bespectacled keeper of the House of Wonders. My brother was more a fan of Kipling's *Barrack Room Ballads* and relished reading the poems to me, especially the maudlin ones, which always made me cry. While I wept for Danny Deaver my brother would troop out the 'boots, boots, boots marching up and down', especially the ones following behind the plucky Kanaharder, Bobs Bahadur. My own favourite, probably because of the lovely illustrations provided by the Keeper of the House of Wonders himself, was the Just So Stories. Having made it to the House of Wonders perhaps one day I will even get to see the grey green greasy Limpopo, beside which the elephant got its trunk.

I was aware the friends who so kindly offered to show me Lahore were looking bemused. Even I knew my prattling exuberance was not entirely appropriate, decidedly not politically correct. What exactly is the appropriate etiquette? Would it make more sense to boldly declare: 'look at me – I'm through the mirror into the imaginarium'? Was I even sure why this barely remembered idea, from a forgotten 2009 fantasy film — *The Imaginarium of Dr Parnassus* — surfaced and suddenly seemed such an appropriate description of what I was experiencing? Would it make more sense to say I found myself confronted with a profusion of jumbled alternate realities that were simultaneously disorienting?

Throughout my time in Pakistan I kept coming back to the idea of an imaginarium, the power of imagination to shape reality, to construct the worlds we wish to inhabit. I remember little detail of the film's plot, except that as it was directed by Terry Gilliam, there was a host of associations and allusions to the power, longevity and legacy of myths and stories suggesting that these are the vehicles in which the worlds we imagine are conjured, preserved and communicated. What better place to begin wrestling with this power than in front of the Lahore Museum? This building has a life of its own in story, being the House of Wonders referred to in *Kim*. The imaginative name it is given by Kipling evokes the books of wonders, the medieval genre in which all the garbled fables about the vaguely unknown wider world were imagined and given longevity in western minds. Simultaneously I am conscious that the conception, design and operation of the museum was itself an imaginary construction whose purpose was to appropriate, contain and control the exotic and subordinate it to the ends of colonial domination. The style we call Anglo Mughal is found all across the Orient in buildings of authority, the places from and through which the dominance of the British Raj was exercised. It is also found back in Britain as delightful ornament to display the nation's acquisition of power.

The Lahore Museum presents not one but multiple imaginariums, it speaks of construction and deconstruction, delight and disdain, different realities differently perceived, meaning different things at one and the same time. A museum, by definition, is where imaginary reconstructions of pasts are housed for the delight and wonder of the public. When this museum was built the British were busy establishing their invention of the history and cultures of the subcontinent fashioned out of their own needs and aesthetic sensibilities. An imagined reality becomes truly mythic because people act upon it, learn about it, react to it as if it is indeed fact.

What disturbed me as I stood before the museum was the ease with which old discredited myths and stories surfaced and claimed me as their own - with delight. The point is not the proof positive this provides that the imaginarium of the British Raj existed, we all know that. It is the realisation of the hold it retains over an imagination dedicated to seeing through and beyond its clutches. Ways of seeing the world, myths and stories spun by history are tenacious deeply embedded and cannot simply be jettisoned. The legacy of old myths remains, while one seeks to understand and reason with all that was wrong, partial and pure fantasy in their creation and operation. So perhaps the task is not to insist that only one imaginarium can be real but to acknowledge that we have to deal with a plurality of alternate realities that are always present in any time or place.

I made my way to Kim's Bookshop. It proved to be a cave of wonders. A tiny space crammed floor to ceiling with books while what little floor space there was housed more pillars of accumulated knowledge. The keeper of this cave of wonders was a venerable gentleman of advanced years. He had no need of spectacles to know the exact location of every book. More importantly, he could tell which scholarly imaginarium each book represented and the superiority of one over another for the purpose of the potential buyer. Sons were on hand to rummage among the strata and extract the specific title while the maulvi sahib sat behind his glass counter and expounded its faults or virtues. His effortless learning was elegantly combined with mercantile acumen – he instantly spotted the lack of sales resistance in an eager bibliophile. He kept his sons excavating, finding more and more wonders that had to be possessed until the entire stock of ready money was exhausted. It was a neat inversion of the relationships alluded to in the name 'Kim's Bookshop', a turning of the tables of command of knowledge and mastery over the conjuring of images of the world of Pakistan, past and present. Mutual profit ensued, and was enjoyed. I left encumbered with an armful of new realities to learn.

The museum itself was not as exciting, nor as informative as the bookshop sahib. To term him a book wallah somehow seems beneath the dignity he unquestionably deserves. Its main attraction for me, heavily supported by the treasures gathered in the cave of wonders, come from the Indus Valley civilisation. Why is it, do you suppose, that this wondrous epoch in the foundations of human history is so overlooked? It is a great enigma, a mystery if you will. And people often like mysteries. Is it just that it is in the wrong place, uncovered at the wrong time and overwhelmed by the disparity in attitudes to the modern imaginariums of Pakistan and India? India appropriates all the associations with the British Raj and Mughal India as well as all the ideas associated with being steeped in antiquity. Pakistan is a modern construction founded and entangled in the unfortunate realities of contemporary political dilemmas. Not only are the archaeological sites of the Indus Valley civilisation in Pakistan but they predate the coming of the Aryan culture to which the legacy of Indian antiquity is traced. So the civilisation that went before all that became India has been marginalised, its script remains un-deciphered. The cities of the ancient Indus Valley were contemporaneous with the great civilisations of the Fertile Crescent and equally sophisticated. Yet, unlike anything we know of Egypt or Iraq, it seems they may have been devoid of social hierarchy and with precious little evidence of martial organisation or warfare. Imaginariums are built upon the legacy of the past, how we conceive the past to have been creates a frame of reference for the influence it casts on later ages. A pity then that this civilisation is known to so few, it is an alternate reality worth contemplating and conjuring with.

As mile after lush green mile of my road trip to the North West Frontier rolled by my mind was awash with questions about the images that lived in my expectations. It is spring and Pakistan is green, fertile and flowered. So why is it that all the pictures that live in my head are of sultry high summer, with dust and fly-blown palm trees? I am taken aback by the reality of peach trees because I expect barren wastes of rocky mountain outcrops and boulders. It occurs to me this is the imaginary landscape of every film I have ever seen about the North West Frontier. It is the imagery drawn by every artist of empire. I think of the prints I acquired in the cave of wonders, a set of four reprints of Lahore 100 Years Ago. In these pictures the city's ancient Mughal monuments, the Lahore Fort, the grand mosques stand faded in sepia tones that befit the obligatory dry and dusty environment. Did no artist ever witness spring in Pakistan, the richness of the colours of the innumerable flowers, the luxuriance of the trees, and the abundant shade they offer? Gardens were the great art form of the Mughals – how do you have gardens without flowers and springtime? Why did I never gather any sense of this lushness from the works of Kipling who lived and worked in Lahore where his father was the man who designed the museum and was its first curator, the original of the Keeper of the House of Wonders? Why did the reality of spring never feature in the imaginarium they all helped to construct?

Europe beat a path to the subcontinent to lay claim to its riches. To substantiate their claim to ill-gotten gains they re-imagined the land as stultified, stalled in tradition lacking the capacity of invention, the engine of fashioning modernity. It was a potent fiction conjured to give empire a reason and it spawned its own visual imagery of backwardness. Peasants had to toil ineffectually, scratching at unrewarding soil which only the aid and guidance of a colonising power could conjure into riches. If the land was admitted to be fertile with its own potential, the industry competent and productive, what would empire be but a parasitic imposition? As I gaze on peach trees, the mental images I have absorbed, which bob to the surface as my expectations of what I should be seeing, reveal themselves as necessary disinformation. The myth of backwardness and all the imagery it trails through the mind gleaned from pictures and stories create the alternate reality of a land dependent on the aid and tutelage of western powers – it is a potent imaginarium. It irks me to find I am, in my own way, still influenced by this vision of history, an unfortunate inheritor of a mental landscape, its victim in a different but related way to those who inhabit this land.

As an antidote I turn my mind to Mohenjo Daro, the ancient city of the Indus Valley civilisation located in Sind Province, north of modern-day Karachi. I determine to add it to my itinerary. I have seen innumerable pictures of the piles of brick structures that trace out its remains. I have been reading up on the subject courtesy of my new fund of acquired wisdom. A vast city complex has been unearthed by archaeologists yet the mystery of how it met its end is a matter of much debate. Was it overwhelmed by the influx of Aryan invaders? An alternate theory to the old idea that history is a gory story of one people supplanted by subjugation to another is actively debated at present. It is argued that the abrupt end and complete abandonment of Mohenjo Daro may have been the result of a different kind of inundation. The site of Mohenjo Daro is subject to periodic flooding. Could some great flood not only have swamped the city but altered the course of the Indus river leaving the once vibrant city if not exactly high and dry then somehow redundant? It must have been some flood. I am not sure I can visualise such an event.

I was still musing on devastation in ancient times when we arrived in Pir Sabaq, a small village in the Khyber Pakhtoonkhwa region of the North West Frontier that was in the path of the great flood of 2010. The narrow alleyways of Pir Sabaq are cluttered with piles of stone and bricks. At every turn the clatter of construction work can be heard. One year on from the floods this small village is on the mend. In late spring it is surrounded by lush green fields of ripening wheat. We drove through mile after mile of wheat fields once we left the peach trees behind. It is an image at odds with the trauma that overwhelmed this village.

A short walk through the alleyways that weave their way between the mud and stone houses brings you to the river. At the most elevated point on the river bank an old shrine is still standing. It's a nineteenth-century monument to a Sikh commander in the long-departed army of Ranjit Singh. It stands in front of the most imposing building the village has to offer, a three-storey brick edifice. On the side of the building, level with the top of the second floor, a banner proclaims that the Labour Education Foundation is building a new school in the enclosure next door.

Then people explain that the banner marks the height the flood waters reached. As I stand looking up at the building I realise it would take three of me standing on each others' shoulders to have a chance of keeping my head above such waters. An unimaginable amount of water even when you give it some scale, some kind of approximate measure.

Pir Sabaq stands at the confluence of the Kabul and Swat rivers. Look upstream from the old shrine and the elegant bend where the two rivers merge is visible, about half a mile away at the far end of the village. Both rivers run from the mountains where monsoon rains gave birth to the devastation that swept down the whole course of the Indus Valley to the sea. Pir Sabaq stood in the path of a perfect storm as two walls of water converged.

Now, the river runs calmly four or five feet below the steep cut bank on which the old shrine stands. What does fourteen, or was it seventeen feet of water look like? What does it do to the places and the people inundated? What happens in the lives that come after the flood?

Natural disasters have their own imaginariums. We are familiar with the images on television. How much do they tell of the reality? How much do they evoke the trauma of the victims? The reporting has its own repertoire of practised images to engage the sympathy of audiences far removed, safe from such overwhelming devastation. And that's where our imagination gets stuck. We try to empathise with the hardship but how can we imagine the aftermath, the imperative to keep on living; how can we conceive of what it takes to rebuild and regain normal lives?

Pir Sabaq is a fortunate place. One year on and almost all the houses are rebuilt. There are now only a few reed huts with their distinctive blue plastic roofs, the temporary disaster shelters, left dotted around the edges of the village. It doesn't take long, however, to learn that the people of Pir Sabaq will be living with the nightmare and the consequences of devastation all their life long. Nothing will ever be the same. This is the first law of natural disaster and it has many complex meanings.

The villagers too are stuck, constantly reliving their memory of awful events. For them memory fosters the second law of natural disaster: insecurity, and it too is complex. The insecurity is not just material, the fact that everything the villagers ever owned has gone. The deeper insecurity is that nature and normality can never be really trusted again. The land one lives on is only seemingly solid, clouds are potential threats. One day this world could liquefy again. What comes after floods is all uncertain, fraught with fear and anxiety that abides as the rebuilding of lives goes on.

It is not hard to accumulate stories about the flood. Ask any villager what happened and their faces light up, they shake their heads, smile and then a torrent of words pours out. They cannot help reliving that night when it rained and rained. Then they tell of the sudden alert and everyone running,

running for the rocky spine of mountains beyond the village. So desperate was the scramble to get to high ground there was no time to take anything with them. 'We could not even take our holy books with us', said Abida. 'I did not even have a shawl to cover me', says Dilraj. It is an expression of the ultimate indignity, of impotence in the face of the deluge, in a village where women traditionally wear the veil as their personal badge of honour and self worth.

The alarm was raised in the early hours of the morning. When daylight came those who had made it to higher ground looked down and saw that Pir Sabaq had disappeared beneath the waters. Families were divided, not knowing if their loved ones had survived or not. They were marooned for three days on the barren rocks before any aid reached them. It took seventeen days for the waters to subside. Seventeen days to think about their old lives washed away. Not only houses but everything they contained: clothes, furniture, utensils and all personal documents including land titles was a watery mush of debris making its way to the sea.

And all the animals were gone too. It's true. As I walk around the village I realise there is a total absence of the normal agricultural sounds and smells of livestock. For a farming village it is a multiple loss: a source of transport, power to plough and work machines, milk as well as meat — it all has to be replaced or substituted from outside for money, which is in as short supply as the beasts of the fields. The sole animal I saw was a painting of one goat, bright blue, on a signboard. And there was one leg of an indeterminate animal (not entirely delectable) on the wooden slab of the butcher's stall. Only as I left this agricultural village did I see one, just one, scrawny ox hitched to a cart. When Noah began again he at least had two!

The hardship of the days the villagers endured on the mountain, days when no help was at hand, are a shared experience, a bond between survivors. Dilraj tells me that by the time she realised what was happening her house was already half submerged. She awakened everybody and they floundered through the waters before being picked up and helped to higher ground. She was separated from her mother who ended up on a different mountain peak. Dilraj found herself with her brother and his heavily pregnant wife. On the third day: 'She gave birth right there. She gave birth like an animal. We had no medical help, we didn't even have anything to wrap the baby in. No one should have to come into the world in such conditions.' Then she lifts the shoulders of her petite frame, shaking off the horrors and gives me a feisty smile as she tells me what happened next. Dilraj is a widow, her husband died after three years of marriage leaving her with one daughter, 'a special child' as villagers refer to the disabled, and caring for her aged mother. So her sister-in-law gave the little boy born in such desperation into Dilraj's care. 'I will have someone to care for me in my old age,' she says with glowing pride. How is the boy? 'Oh he's wonderful – and there's no way they're getting him back now', she adds with brisk determination, the defiance of a survivor.

Being stripped bare of everything is unimaginable, incomprehensible. Everyone I speak to in the village seems to have their share of defiance, a legacy of survival. And then, as if they cannot help it, each reminiscence ends with a backward glance as if scanning for clouds on the horizon, checking out the other legacy: abiding fear. Everyone adds the same grace note — what if it happens again? There are rumours, always rumours that the floods are coming again. 'And what will we do then?' Abida leaves the question floating in the air. Disaster diminishes the ability to cope with disaster, not just psychologically but also materially. There are no more savings, no nest eggs to rely on, no family members from whom to borrow, no credit rating, few jobs to be had and everyone is in the same boat, or rather without a boat to float.

Abida has four children and tells me that before the floods she and her husband had borrowed money and were in the process of renovating their house. So when the waters receded they had no home and debts to pay. After three days on the mountain with no food and clean water they went by boat to where some relatives were living. All of their family connections made their way to this last house standing. The strains on everyone were enormous. 'It was as if I was born once again. Nothing was possible, there was nothing in my head and I cried all the time.' To overcome the strains they borrowed again, from her husband's brother, and returned to Pir Sabaq to rebuild their house.

For weeks there was no one living in Pir Sabaq. Chaos, the flotsam of the floods, affected everyone. Relief efforts struggled against the overpowering tide of need, need for every conceivable basic necessity and utility of life. Yet Pir Sabaq emerged from the waters and found itself to be fortunate. It had the good fortune to discover it was 'aidable'. And there was another chance of good fortune. A Pakistani doctor, who had seen the news coverage in his home in Switzerland, decided to help. He turned up one day in Pir Sabaq and found a place where he could make a difference. He opened a website and collected money to get the relief process underway. And Pir Sabaq began to find it had other attributes which would help it rebuild.

Aid – now there's an imaginarium. We who live comfortable lives far from imminent danger have become attuned to the images, ideas and caveats of aid and assistance to the less fortunate. And we have come to demand our expectations be met for the money we hand over to charities and appeal funds. When disaster strikes, international aid agencies and the money they raise are confronted with chaos, like everyone else. The aid agencies have their necessary procedures and regulations. At our behest they need projects that can be assessed, quantified, justified, costed and accounted for. And they need the means to engage with the victims in their own language with due cognisance of culture and custom. This means disaster is not an equal opportunity event. Equal agony and devastation do not translate into equitable distribution of aid for a multitude of logistical and practical reasons that have nothing to do with the politics of compassion.

Pir Sabaq, however, was 'aidable' because of the antediluvian presence of a Pakistani organisation. The Labour Education Foundation, a local affiliate of the International Federation of Workers Education Associations, had for some time been running projects with the local stone cutters' union. The rocky spine of mountains beyond the village was not merely the refuge for the village as the waters rose. It is the main source of employment, producing chippings for road works and construction. 'We had workers and volunteers on hand who knew the village and its people. Our presence convinced aid agencies they could work here. They tried to poach our people and we were happy to oblige', explained Khalid Mahmood, the LEF Director.

Walking around the village, painted signs on the compound walls that surround the rebuilt houses testify to the variety of agencies which set to work here. Oxfam and UK Islamic Mission are notable among them. Some 1,700 houses in a village with a population of 6,000 were destroyed, the rest were damaged. There was plentiful work for project aid. The regulations and ideal plans of the aid agencies are a cause of some complaint. What aid donors demand and aid agencies seek to deliver is not quite what the villagers envision. The expectations are different. The villagers accept the reality that they must rebuild their lives on a more modest scale; this is the inevitable consequence of disaster. 'If you had a four room house, now you will settle for two rooms. But if your plot is 14 metres the agencies say you have to have a path around the house so you must build on 12 metres. It's a waste of space,' Zahid explained. Outside amenity is a novelty for which Pir Sabaq has neither fondness nor need.

Aid also provided the seed for re-planting. And 'it was better quality seed than they had previously. That's why the fields are so lush,' Khalid Mahmood explained. He had driven me all the way from Islamabad to Pir Sabaq. Had he noticed my confusion as he pointed out the peach orchards that confounded my expectations and been aware of my surprise at the bountiful green growing of springtime? They are testimony to the seed and the fact that the floods deposited their own small afterthought of compensation: the silt they tore from the deforested mountains has replenished the soil.

Rebuilding the houses and replanting the fields was the first priority. Now comes the challenge to sustain the future for people cut adrift from the moorings of their former lives. Job creation, generating income, and education for the children have a new urgency born of harsh necessity. Because they must, change has become possible.

As Khalid Mahmood observes, before the floods the LEF had great difficulty in reaching out to the women of the village. Now they are running classes teaching tailoring and embroidery and tending poultry. Women who previously would have resisted leaving their homes are enthusiastic recruits. The regular sessions at the LEF compound in the village are boisterous, offering companionship and mutual consolation as well as a potential route to better financial times ahead. 'I will sew for other people and this will be good', Dilraj told me. Her classmate, Abida, however, strikes the characteristic note of caution, 'Everybody lost so seller needs buyers – it won't be easy.' The future is a place of fraught calculations.

Listening to the villagers talk it is clear they are grateful for the aid received. But aid has not answered all their needs nor has it been available to everyone. Also, they subtly suggest, the aid agencies have their own agenda while the government has simply been ineffective. The answer will be to do more for themselves. Certainly the women of Pir Sabaq are gaining courage and endorse this new spirit of the times. 'It'll be my own hard work and it'll all benefit us,' Mehnaz said of her hopes for the future.

Mehnaz is a mother of four; she has a disabled brother living with her as well as her father and mother-in-law. Her husband, a labourer, injured his back helping to clear the rubble of what remained of Pir Sabaq when the waters receded and now he cannot work. The family spent five months in a relief camp before they could return to the ruined space that once had been their home. At first Mehnaz was wary of attending the sewing classes but admits now she is drawing courage from them. And in the end it is a simple equation: 'to learn I had to get out of the house. My husband agrees. We're not narrow-minded now, a lot of positive change has happened. I want my daughters to be educated so that they can be better than me.'

Disaster has been a stern taskmaster. Mastering life after the floods in Pir Sabaq seems to vindicate the old adage 'what doesn't kill you makes you stronger.' 'We are more aware that we have rights and entitlements now,' Behramand, a local businessman, explained. 'We have learnt how to get what we need and should have', he says. New schools for the children, for example, and especially a school for girls right in the village is a priority. 'Yes, we always wanted the girls to go to school', he says looking at me with a knowing smile. Clearly I am not the only one conscious of preconceived ideas and the expectations of reality they impose. Everyone is pleased that there are classes for the girls now, but there is no actual school and the one planned is a long walk outside the village. 'To have it in the village will be more suitable and effective', he explains — it's self-evident common sense that suits their expectations. In the late afternoon the alleyways and paths around the village are full of children making their way home from school, all in smart uniforms distributed by LEF. 'Education is essential if they are to have a chance of a better life', Behramand says with determined emphasis.

The buildings of Pir Sabaq are rising from the waters. But its people face a long and arduous path to a sustainable future. The animals that generated income from milk and meat, the tractors that not only worked the fields but could be hired out to transport people and goods are gone. The shop keepers lost all their stock and need capital to set up again. While some NGOs are tackling these problems they help only the few. As Behramand commented, the villagers have lost hope in their government. 'It was not able to protect us.' The arrival of aid agencies 'made people aware of their rights and started us thinking. It made us realise we have the resources and manpower and could do that work for ourselves. We are aware of the problems and the things we lack. The list of needs is extensive and affects everyone.'

Pir Sabaq has found a new spirit of enterprise washed in the waters of disaster. It has found its own voice. 'Before no one listened. Now the village demands.' It is clear the villagers are talking to each other. I attended a meeting where the stone cutters mingled with local businessmen, like Behramand, and Zahid who works for the Cereal Crop Research Institute which has a branch just beyond the village. And then there is Amarullah, a young man who has emerged as a new community leader. He took me to see his new flour mill; he posed beaming with pride beside this engine of a new future as I took a picture. A future there must be. Survivors keep on living, they have to eat, they have to work no matter how their lives are clouded by the losses they have sustained and all the complications churned up by the waters.

There is no lack of invention and daring. I realised this as I stood beside the old shrine on the river bank. Across the water I could see the much larger city of Naushera. There used to be a bridge linking the two, which of course was washed away in the flood. I turned to look up river where brightly painted fishing boats clustered at what passes for the local harbour. These few small skiffs must be about as reassuring as the number of life-boats on the Titanic if floods come again, I thought. And about as ineffectual when it comes to connecting people with Naushera. I turned back to take a last look at the shrine and out of the corner of my eye caught some move-ment over the water. I could not make out what it was. It drew nearer and got larger and to my amazement a metal cage with a full load of passengers made a stately progress across a wire rope to a stone pillar that must once have supported the bridge. A cable car! Not one I was in the least tempted to venture on. Precarious but determined: my lasting image of Pir Sabaq.

We left Pir Sabaq and made our way to Peshawar. A name to conjure with from all the stories and films lodged in my visual memory. At last we would arrive where exotic regiments had performed deeds of daring. We would be in the narrow alleyways of an ancient city where news reporters speak of the arms bazaar that sustains the still-enduring menace of the wild and turbulent tribesmen we now dub terrorists. In the fading light of evening we drove through the suburbs of a rapidly expanding city indistinguishable from any other. A reasonably well-lit dual carriageway bustling with traffic

was lined with shops and malls, government buildings, hotels and restaurants lit by neon signs. It was getting dark so we finally stopped. We pulled
into an ordered car park full of cars surrounded on three sides by busy
shops of the distinctly modern and conventional convenience kind. There
was a '7/11', open all hours of day and night, defying the mental imagery
now associated with the North West Frontier in the Taliban-obsessed aftermath of 9/11. When we got out of the car it was raining and we scurried
to meet the members of the teachers' union Khalid Mahmood had come to
see. They greeted us and hurriedly ushered us to dine. We climbed a flight
of stairs and found ourselves in the 'Thames Chickenland', a fully authentic
replication of the Colonel's famous franchise, KFC – booths, formica
tables, plastic chairs, even the orbs of plastic tomato ketchup dispensers
ready to lace the items on the typical menu, and the production line deliv-
ery. I saw the look on Khalid's face. It bears witness to the inverse reaction
to my performance outside the House of Wonders. Imaginarium; imagined
worlds and all their alternate expectations: images of Orient; dreams of
cultural authenticity; the quest for indigenous modernity. I have been and
made my visit. I have touched reality — it is chicken fried and burgered.

FOUND IN TRANSLATION

Aamer Hussein

As a boy in Karachi I was taken regularly, in the company of my sisters, to see films that starred Jerry Lewis, Bob Hope, Doris Day and Debbie Reynolds. I was, however, a fan of at least three kinds of films my sisters considered unwatchable: Westerns starring Charlton Heston; historical and biblical costume dramas starring Charlton Heston (these they would make an exception for, if they also starred Sophia Loren); and sword-and-sandal epics from Cinecitta, Rome, which Heston would have considered too lowly to star in. For the last category, my mother found me a suitable companion who was not only a distinguished classical musician but also, as it emerged, an inveterate reader of Urdu fiction. As he sat through these violent films with me, he seemed to become increasingly aware that with my '*angrezi* (English) medium' education, I only had one side of the picture. That was the *Ivanhoe* version purveyed by Europe since the Crusades. Or if I wallowed in Christian epics such as *Ben Hur* and *Quo Vadis*, he knew the Muslim equivalents would never be made available on film, as Pakistan did not allow portrayals of holy personages. So he undertook my retraining by summarising for me the stories of Abdul Halim Sharar, who at the turn of the century and the height of the Raj, had set out to tell the story from the other side. Sharar presented the Moors and Saracens as heroes and the company of all the Lionhearted Richards and their loyal Ivanhoes as dastardly crusading villains.

When he thought I was ready to graduate to reading Urdu novels, he lent me a book by another redoubtable historical novelist, Nasim Hijazi, who has followed in Sharar's footsteps. Born in 1914, Hijazi was still writing then, and very prolific. The novel was *Qaisar o Kasra* (Caesars and Chosroes); its axis was Arabia and the Persian and the Byzantine East; it did for early Muslim history exactly what *Ben Hur* and *Quo Vadis* did for the Christian era. He achieved his goal as I had never read anything with such

immersion since my time with *Gone With the Wind*, a season or so before.
The difference was that while the American South had little to do with me,
Medina wasn't too distant from my native country. Hijazi's imaginative
landscape with its deserts, palms and dunes, reminded me of my surroundings and was close to the heart and mind of the eleven-year-old I was. I
remember the name of the hero, Aasim, and the heroines (one Byzantine)
Faustina and Samira. I got through the very long book in about a month;
that, too, with my very basic Urdu reading skills. But one of the results of
this mammoth undertaking was that I acquired a certain facility with the
Urdu script. In spite of intervals and distances this literacy was never
entirely to desert me, and I always spoke the language with some ease.

I discovered another writer at about the same time through a film when,
among our trips to the cinema, there was a surprise family outing in 1965.
It was to a private showing of *Naila*, possibly the second Pakistani film I'd
ever seen. (I had often wanted to go to vernacular movies because I loved
the songs, but it was considered extremely un-chic and local cinemas were
seen as anarchic and were not even air-conditioned). It was the first Pakistani film entirely in colour, and its sets and costumes had been designed
as an eye-feast. It was a romantic melodrama about two half-brothers in
love with their eponymous cousin Naila, who finds herself marrying the
wrong boy and commits suicide on her wedding day by swallowing a diamond from her ring. (Or was it poison concealed in the the diamond?) The
brothers, Santosh and Darpan, both major stars, were portly and approaching middle age in their elegantly tailored grey western suits. The slim,
youngish heroine, Shamim Ara, also a popular actress, was rigged out in
finery that would only have been worn at traditional wedding ceremonies.
But there was an enchantment about the proceedings I can't quite recap-
ture in words; the closest analogy would be a visit to the opera, but cinemas allow you to dream in the darkness in a way live theatre does not.

I do not know quite when I discovered that *Naila* was based on a novel
of the same name by the novelist Razia Butt. At twenty, though, I certainly
recognised her name, when at Wimbledon Park Library, London, I picked
up one of her books: *Saiqa*, also made into a successful film by Shamim Ara
in the late 60s (it was remade, in 2009, as a TV serial). I brought it home
in a rush of nostalgia. I had been in London five years and had found myself
looking, with little success, for traces of belonging in novels from Nigeria,

Japan or Turkey. What my sister and I took turns to read out loud was quite unexpected. It amazed me. The prose was lushly descriptive of landscape and emotions alike, the situations lachrymose – a young Cinderella figure languishing in the kitchen for the male cousin who sweeps by her. The unintended reaction the combination elicited from a cynical young reader was laughter, and laughing at Butt became, to the chagrin of my mother, a guilty pleasure.

Yet I also knew that the novel was a bestseller in Pakistan. Today I can see that the world-behind-a-curtain Butt portrayed was far closer to the lives of most of her young readers than our 'modern' way of living or our anglicised tastes. (Years later, in my collection *Turquoise*, I would take pleasure in writing stories set in that semi-traditional world.) Butt's name was often mentioned along with that of A R Khatoon as a writer who appealed to provincial teenagers and suburban housewives, but I was to discover that these writers were born a generation apart and had very different styles and aesthetics. Khatoon had a gift for dry comedy, and Butt, who reached her peak after Khatoon's death, was to move from the heightened romanticism of her signature stories to plain tales of domestic life in small Punjabi towns and suburbs. Both, however, had experienced Partition as refugees, and made it the subject of some of their writings.

In later years, my female friends were to tell me how, as teenagers, they had read Khatoon on sleepy summer days in the homes of their grandmothers and aunts, and I would snigger. But one day I realised I too had encountered her as a child. In 1994, I was leafing through a book in SOAS library, with the attractive title of *Nurulain*. It was a 'tale of jinns and fairies'. I recognised some lines from it. My mother had read the story to us when I was about seven. A princess is married off to a dog who turns out to be an enchanted prince. They are separated, and the princess sets off on a heroic quest to rescue her lost love, in a wonderful, *dastan*-like adventure. I didn't know the writer's name then, nor did I realise that the writer of romances was also a gifted teller of wonder tales, until I was nearly forty. I have kept her generous volume of children's stories by my bedside ever since I found it.

For two years after reading those few pages of Butt, I was to think that History (of the sword-and-sandals variety I had long outgrown) and Romance were all the Pakistani fiction on offer. In my early teens, I'd read Khushwant Singh's translation of *Umrao Jan Ada*, and Aziz Ahmed's elegantly satirical portrait of life in pre-Independence Hyderabad Deccan, *The Shore and the Wave*, in a translation by Ralph Russell, but probably thought of those books as Indian. But then, at SOAS in the late 1970s, when I studied Urdu alongside Persian, and was immersed in the prosody and the poetic tradition of both languages, I was also to be introduced to the moderns and near-contemporaries: Saadat Hasan Manto, Munshi Premchand, and Ismat Chughtai, and changed my mind about Urdu writers. Far from lachrymose, I found their prose lucid and direct. But the timbre of these Progressives, whose representative stories we studied, was often too polemical or too dry. I longed for some romance to relieve their poverty and pain, but found that in the *masnavis* and *ghazals* I read by Mir Taqi Mir and Ghalib, those magnificent nineteenth-century poets of Delhi whose verses we were privileged to read.

My own quest for the house of treasures that is Urdu was to begin in my thirties. My interest encompassed all kinds of stories: from the postmodern to the populist, from the comic tales of Shafiq-ur-Rahman to the wonder tales of A R Khatoon. The quest continues to this day. I read most of the fictions I am going to discuss in the original before the translations appeared. I played godfather to more than one; often feeling (as with Hyder's work) that there were compressed passages that would never be more than approximated in English. Some stories by Hyder, Hussain and Hussein, I actually read first in English, and was then compelled to seek out the originals. I spent six years in the 1990s researching and editing *Hoops of Fire*, an anthology of short fiction that appeared in 1999. Intended originally to cover short fiction of the post-independence period, my book became, for reasons of space and demand, a book of stories by Pakistani women.

So let me invite you to discover for yourself what is available in translation. For those who can read Urdu, I urge you to seek out the originals.

Aamer Hussein's Dozen

Modern classic Urdu fiction everyone should read; and can read in translation.

Ghulam Abbas, *Hotel Moenjodaro,* Penguin India, 1996

Aziz Ahmad, *The Shore and the Wave*, George Allen and Unwin, 1971

Altaf Fatima, *The One Who Did Not Ask*, Heinemann, 1993

Intizar Hussain, *Basti*, HarperCollins India, 1995

Abdullah Hussein, *The Weary Generations*, Peter Owen, 1998; and *Downfall by Degrees*, Tsar, 1988; reprinted as *Stories of Exile and Alienation* by OUP, 1997

Qurratulain Hyder, *River of Fire, Kali for Women*, 1998; New Directions, 2000

Saadat Hasan Manto, *Kingdom's End* , Verso, 1987

Khadija Mastur, *Aangan* (The Inner Courtyard), Simorgh, 2000; and *Cold Sweet Water*, OUP, 1999

Ahmed Nadeem Qasmi, *The Old Banyan Tree*, OUP, 2000

Fahmida Riaz, *Godavari*, OUP, 2008

Shaukat Siddiqui, *God's Own Land*, Paul Norbury Publications/ Unesco 1991.

Partition and After

Before the creation of Pakistan, Urdu literature flourished in many centres, including Lucknow and Hyderabad. Delhi and Lahore were, however, always the hub of publishing and Lahore, in the new country, continued to be so. The contribution of Punjab to Urdu literature had always been notable: legendary pre-Independence poet-philosopher Allama Muhammed Iqbal, associated with the concept of Pakistan, and Faiz Ahmed Faiz, arguably Pakistan's most famous and beloved poet, both came from Sialkot. Maulana Mumtaz Ali set up a press in Lahore particularly for women writers in the early years of the twentieth century. (His publishing concerns were later taken over by his son, dramatist Imtiaz Ali Taj, and daughter-in-law, acclaimed novelist Hijab Imtiaz Ali). Ghulam Abbas, Manto and Ahmed Nadeem Qasmi all chose to write in Urdu rather than in their native Punjabi, as did the Sikh writers Rajinder Singh Bedi and Balwant Singh. Some of the early women writers, such as Mrs Abdul Qadir, Jahanara Shahnawaz and Fatima Begum, were Punjabis; the latter two abandoned fiction to play an active part in the Freedom Movement that led to the creation of Pakistan.

With Partition, most non-Muslim Punjabi writers left for Bombay and Delhi and many of the Muslims who were working in those cities moved to Pakistan. There was also, because of the attraction of the new nation, an influx of writers who had no prior connection with Punjab, Sindh or the regions of the Frontier, but nevertheless settled there and found new and fertile landscapes for their fictions, extending the topography of Urdu fiction. Karachi took its place in the post-Partition years as another centre of Urdu writing and publishing, and remains so to this day. A few of the best Urdu writers, such as Ismat Chughtai, stayed on in India, but they were read and published – and still are – with great alacrity across the border, as are younger writers such as the surrealist Nayyar Masud.

Urdu fiction continued to develop in Pakistan, and over the decades showed an especial predilection for the short story, which remains the most popular form with writers of literary prose. (You can be a great writer of fiction and never write a novel, but few novelists have managed to avoid the short story.) Many – even most – classic writers of long and short fiction remain in print, although today's commercial publishers favour genre fictions – romance, suspense, historical – that are often quickly adapted as television soaps and serials.

One writer who made a home in Karachi was among the finest mid-twentieth short story writers of the subcontinent, Ghulam Abbas, who published only three collections of short fiction in his lifetime. The late and able Khalid Hasan chose some of the best of these for *Hotel Moenjadaro*. In the title story, written in the late 60s, a Pakistani astronaut lands on the moon, to the pride of the progressives and the fury of the fundamentalists, leading to the bombing of the eponymous building. In other tales, harassed employees try to acquire property in post-Partition Karachi; a young man brings back his kind-hearted Welsh wife from London to Karachi to serve the new nation of Pakistan, but, disappointed with the jobs on offer, they end up running a school of western dance; a corpse is found dressed only in an elegant overcoat. Detached, concise and often satirical, Abbas's prose achieves its effects through understatement. Urdu, particularly in its fiction, has integrated influences from French and Russian writers into its home-grown aesthetic. (Since the nineteenth century, reformist critics had pre-scribed the rejection of old and decadent lyricism, and advocated socially relevant narratives in pragmatic, serviceable prose). Urdu is both precise and elliptical, which can make it seem too bare in translation. Perhaps Abbas's work has failed to reach an international audience for its lack of flourishes, rhetoric, and thick anthropological description.

Though his prose could also be chillingly precise, Abbas's more famous and prolific contemporary, Saadat Hasan Manto, was a far more dramatic and sensational writer. He had some success in Bombay before 1947, but the madhouse of Partition provided him with material for many of the stories, on which his international reputation rests, that he wrote in Lahore. Some of these, 'Toba Tek Singh', 'The Return', 'The Dog Of Titwal', and 'Mozelle', which often use sexual violence as political metaphor and por-tray both perpetrators and victims with equal dispassion, are included in Khalid Hassan's *Kingdom's End*. This selection of his stories brought Pakistani literature to international attention, gathering praise from Salman Rushdie and James Kelman, and reaching a section of Pakistani readers who had never before displayed any interest in Urdu literature. Even today, Manto is just about the only Urdu writer who is ever mentioned as an influence by Anglophone Pakistani novelists who know him through this translation.

Slightly younger than Manto and Abbas, the very prolific Ahmed Nadeem Qasmi also came from the Punjab. Like his contemporaries he brought the landscapes of his native region to Urdu literature. But whereas Manto and Abbas are equally at ease in urban and rural settings, Nadeem's best stories focus on village lives and conflicts, making him in many ways an archetypal regional writer. (More than one critic has made a comparison with the much later work of Daniyal Mueenuddin, favouring the older writer.) Qasmi's lyrical style (he is also a poet) is cadenced and inflected by Punjabi in a way that has influenced regional writers of his own and of latter genera-tions. His stories are tough and virile, but also tender, with an occasional undertow of sentimentality. *The Old Banyan Tree*, a judicious selection of stories from Qasmi's very long career, was exquisitely translated by Faruq Hassan.

Partition also brought young migrant writers to both Lahore and Karachi. Khadija Mastur was well-known as a left-wing short story writer before she came to Pakistan at the age of twenty, but it was in Lahore that she produced her first, prizewinning novel, *Aangan* (The Inner Courtyard). A bildungsroman, it chronicles, through the life journey of its protagonist, Aliya, the impact on India of World War II, the struggle for independence from British imperialism, and the search for a home in the new country. Neelam Husain's translation faithfully captures what the introduction refers to as Mastur's 'Spartan Urdu': the direct, unadorned language in which she told her dark, pessimistic tales of repressive feudal and bourgeois mores in colonial India, and of the self-seeking corruption that accompanied the making of a new society in Pakistan. (Mastur's last and, to me, best novel, *Zamin*, set largely in the first decade of post-independence Pakistan, is only available in English as a brief excerpt in *Cool, Sweet Water*, Tahira Naqvi's exquisitely representative selection of some of her most celebrated fictions.)

Dastak na Do a gentler, though equally unromantic, bildungsroman by Altaf Fatima, another migrant writer, covers some of the same ground though in a deliberately intimate manner and adds an unusual narrative twist. The perspective of Geti, its female protagonist, is juxtaposed with that of Liu, an immigrant Chinese shoemaker, through whom it touches, with his outsider's eye, on various aspects of nation, race, culture, history, migration and diaspora. It's also a novel that skilfully combines elements of literary modernism with the tropes of popular domestic fiction; its author discards the harsh realism and bare prose favoured by many of her contemporaries, including Mastur, for a richer and more textured style. This is ably captured in *The One Who Did Not Ask*, the translation by Rukhsana Ahmad, herself a dramatist and a writer of fiction.

Speaking of harsh realism, Shaukat Siddiqui, too, migrated from India, but is best known for his post-Partition fiction. His novel *Khuda ki Basti* is earthy, even crude; it is set among the poor and the proletarian in the underworld slums of Karachi from where it moves to nouveau riche residential districts and fancy hotels and back to the slums and provincial towns. It has been translated efficiently by David Matthew as *God's Own Land*. (The English title, obviously announcing an allegorical dimension, glosses the new nation in a way the original, which simply means 'God's settlement', does not set out to do.) The translation received no attention in England where it was first published, but has, in its Pakistani edition, become a cult book with a segment of English-educated Pakistani youth. Like *Dastak na Do*, *Khuda ki Basti* became a very successful television serial in the late 1960s.

Intizar Hussain is possibly Pakistan's most lauded living writer. He excels as a spinner of tales that combine myth and fable (Hindu, Buddhist and Muslim), history and memory. His novel *Basti*, translated by Frances Pritchett, combines these elements with an allegorical representation of the 1971 war that resulted in the creation of Bangladesh. Husain self-consciously retains and reworks the techniques of traditional Indo-Persian storytelling, using the *dastan* and *qissa* as templates. His poetic, allusive and at times recondite style often reflects the exoticism of manner and subject foreign readers seem to expect from 'Oriental' texts. Yet it sets him apart from many of his contemporaries who have been translated, as the complexities of experimental prose in Urdu (much of it influenced by existentialism, Latin American magic realism and Eastern European postmodernism) are hard to replicate in English, and translators have opted for realism in their choice of texts. Hussain, whose prose is deliberately fable-like, has emerged as the first among equals as a suitable candidate for translation.

Another experimental writer, Qurratulain Hyder, deals with the linguistic dilemma by translating many of her own magnificent novels into English. Since Hyder left Pakistan in the 1950s after living there for about a decade, there's an argument today about where her earlier works belong. She continued, however, for many years to write about the country she left behind; she's equally lauded in India and in Pakistan. The orginal Urdu edition of *Aag ka Darya*, one of the most famous novels of the subcontinent, was published in Pakistan before she left, and nominated for a major prize. This masterpiece of mid-twentieth century literature is impossible to summarise: it moves from Buddhist times to medieval, from the Mughal era to the glory days of the East India Company; and then to modern times and the creation of Pakistan, where it concludes. (It was criticised at the time by nationalist critics as being, at worst, anti-nationalist and at best unsympathetic to the creation of the new nation). The narrative is linked by a group of protagonists who seem to be reincarnated in every age. Hyder's own slightly reworked English version finally appeared in the late 1990s, fifty years after the division of the country and two decades after she wrote the novel.

In the wake of the success and controversy generated by Hyder's book, her younger contemporary Abdullah Hussein echoed many of her concerns in the prizewinning *Udas Naslein*, a multi-generational family saga about the Punjab in the first half of the twentieth century. Hussein, too, rewrote his own novel in English in the late 1990s; *The Weary Generations* is one of the very few translated Urdu novels to be published in Britain and remain in print. (Both Hyder and Hussein seem to owe some of their visibility in the west to their bilingualism.) The redoubtable Umar Memon, the doyen of Urdu literary translation, had already introduced Hussein to a western audience in Canada, in the representative collection of stories and novellas he translated. 'Downfall by Degrees', the collection's title story, is an intricate though understated experiment in postmodern multiple narration, which employs the strategy of using the primary narrator as psychological investigator and detective. 'Exiles' is one of the earliest representations of working-class Pakistani migrants in Britain.

Urduphone, Anglophone

So far, I have focused on outstanding, or at least good, fiction produced during the first forty-five years or so years of Pakistan. My brevity, however, reflects what has been made available in translation to date (largely in Pakistan and India) and also the paucity of good translations. While we might celebrate the fact that some of the best Urdu writers on both sides of the border can be read in English, there are hugely successful Pakistani novels such as those of Bano Qudsia – for example *Raj Gidh*, one of the most popular novels ever to be published in Pakistan – and Jamila Hashmi, which are not available and are unlikely ever to be. With the upsurge of English writing by Pakistani writers at home and abroad, and the demand for writing that somehow represents Pakistan – 'that Terrorist State' – to foreign readers, translations are no longer a priority for diasporic academics. There has also been a simultaneous dwindling of interest in full-scale literary translation in the western academy. Most translations are published in India, where a genuine interest in vernacular fictions often matches – and at times outdoes – the desire to read about life across the border. Another - more unusual, but growing – constituency is the English-educated youth of Pakistan, who are curious to know something about the history and development of literature in Pakistan. They feel their language skills aren't sufficiently adequate to read the originals, and need the aid of a translation.

Most Urdu fiction that is discussed online and sold (or even circulated free) in e-format is popular, accessible stuff — it is often turned into polished, and on occasion socially relevant, television drama. Young women writers such as Farhat Ishtiaq and Maha Malik excel at novels that deal with the problems and relationships of semi-westernised, educated middle class women. Other popular novels are tinged with Sufi religiosity, such as the work of Umera Ahmad and Hashim Nadeem Khan. All are familiar names, even for those who don't read them, via the (often very opulent) television adaptations of their novels, which run for weeks and are probably available in subtitled versions for Pakistanis abroad. These novels are unlikely ever to reach an Anglophone audience in book form, and certainly not in English translation; yet viewers might enjoy the television versions in their sitting rooms or on a Gulf-bound aeroplane. They are sometimes directed by western-trained film makers.

Another interesting phenomenon is how writers who are known in one genre in another language migrate to write teleplays in Urdu. Nurul Huda Shah, a bilingual Sindhi short story writer, is well known as a writer of Urdu teleplays, as is the celebrated Sindhi feminist poet Atiya Dawood, who has crossed the bridge of language to write both screenplays and an autobiography in Urdu.

Among these contemporary dramas and soaps, a massive historical drama came to the television screen in late 2010. Titled 'Dastaan', it is the life story of a woman who became a victim of Partition: abducted by a Sikh, she finally escapes captivity after his death and reaches Pakistan with her illegitimate son only to be received with confusion by her erstwhile fiancee and discreetly spurned by the rest of her family as a fallen woman. It is, I realised when I watched it on YouTube, utterly compulsive viewing. In spite of anachronistic costumes, and other minor flaws, it was both visually seductive and dramatically compelling. To my pleasure, I was given an entire set of DVDs of the serial on a trip home in January 2011, and also discovered that it was based on *Bano*, a novel by Razia Butt herself. What's more, I'd read the novel during the course of a research project on fictions of Partition, when it was reprinted in 1997, quite appositely, to mark the fiftieth anniversary of independence, with a note by the author expressing her disenchantment with the present state of Pakistan. In fact her subject matter was similar to literary works written on both sides of the border and in many languages, but it is perhaps presented in the novel with a louder ideological or nationalist message that is not entirely positive about the current state of Pakistan. The success of the televised version proves that the hold of the past is still strong; but when TV producers turn to novels that chronicle collective memory in epic style, they turn to the Butts and Hijazis rather than to the Hyders and the Husseins.

Butt and Hijazi continue to be bestsellers; new editions of their work stand alongside the country's masterpieces. Hijazi has a posthumous reputation as a supporter of the unpopular (with literary intellectuals) Islamic party, Jamaat-i-Islami, and no longer has a mainstream publisher. Butt, however, shares a publisher, the hugely enterprising Lahore-based Sang-e-meel, with Mastur, Hussain and other celebrated literary names. Yet the only way many of us Anglophones will ever be made aware of this popular fiction that forms the staple fare of the ordinary Pakistani reader, past and present, is via television when we see a familiar actor's face flash on the screen in an idle moment and stop to see what s/he's doing. The wonderful comic writer and essayist Shafiq-ur-Rahman remains un-translated. I hear there's an Indian translation of Khatoon's perennial classic *Shama*, but we are still waiting to see it in print. Three of the author's remarkable fairy tales, translated by Shahnaz Aijazuddin, are awaiting publication in Pakistan: we are lucky to include one in this issue of *Critical Muslim*.

One popular author has made it into English: no less than five titles by Ibn-e-Safi, the prolific writer of detective pulp, were recently published in India, one translated by the up-and-coming writer Bilal Tanweer, the other by Indian scholar-novelist Shamsurrahman Farooqi. (One of these is probably the worst books it has ever been my privilege to read; the others made for great entertainment on Kindle on an early morning trip to Rome.) With apologies, I won't include them in my list, as they read like vintage detective stories from anywhere in the world. Taken away from their Urdu idiom, they offer little that's distinctive apart from a kind of amusing kitsch. The impact of Ibn-e-Safi in the original is discussed elsewhere in this issue by Ziauddin Sardar.

Literary fiction, which is occasionally made into (brief) TV films, also flourishes on the pages of literary journals such as the Karachi-based *Dunyazad*, which publishes fine fiction from all over the world. However, though I have touched on books we are unlikely to see in English versions, my focus is on translated modern classics, and here is a final nomination for that status. One of the most interesting novels to be made available in translation is the complex, polyphonic and fascinating *Godavari* by feminist poet Fahmida Riaz, who has since continued to write fiction of the highest order. First published as part of a trilogy in the Karachi journal *Aaj* in 1993 and then in book form, the novella is told from the perspective of a Pakistani leftist intellectual in voluntary exile with her family in India. *Godavari* conflates the slow disintegration of the protagonist's marriage with an account of ethnic warfare and sectarian, anti-Muslim rioting in Maharashtra and the rise of Hindu extremism in the port city of Bombay. The eponymous character, a historical personage, only appears in narrations of the past. Godavari Parulekar, a communist, attempted to make the Worli aboriginals of the region aware of their oppression. The novel's contemplative heroine, 'Ma', muses on Godavari's journey as a metaphor for those ideals lost during the construction and consolidation of warring South Asian nation-states. 'Our history', Riaz says in the preface to the English edition, in words that can apply to many Pakistani fictions in any language, 'is indeed stained with blood, as the communal bloodshed mentioned in the story indicates....(yet) one can hardly fail to notice the struggle for justice and human compassion throughout history'.

IBN-E-SAFI, BA

Ziauddin Sardar

When I visited Bahwalnagar in May 1975, I found little had changed. A new generation of *goll guppa-wallas*, *chaat-wallas* and *paan-wallas* had taken over the stalls in Railway Bazaar. It was still the direct route from the Railway Station to our house in the centre of the town, where we lived and I grew up. I had left the city at the age of nine, when my parents migrated to London. And I expected no one would know me. Indeed, they did not know me. But they recognised me: I was the returning grandson of Hakim Sahib.

Abdur Razziq Khan, known locally and affectionately simply as 'Hakim Sahib', was one of the most distinguished citizens of the town. I called him Nana. He hated the Raj and the British with equal measure. Not least because the British had outlawed his profession: hikmat, the traditional Islamic medicine. He looked after his mostly rural patients from his surgery, 'Haziq Dawa Khana', which was situated in the middle of Railway Bazaar. Everyone in Bahwalnagar knew him; and everyone knew that his grandson had come from England to visit him.

I had arrived the previous night; and it was my first day in Bahwalnagar. Nana had asked me to meet him at his surgery after lunch. 'And bring a copy of the latest ibn-e-Safi with you', he had instructed.

I knew ibn Safi well. During my childhood in Bahwalnagar, the entire extended family, consisting of scores of uncles and aunties, were addicted to ibn-e-Safi. We read ibn Safi; and had ibn Safi read to us. He published two best-selling series of Urdu spy novels. The first, *Jasoosi Dunya* (Spy World), featured two detectives, Colonel Ahmad Kamal Faridi, the exceptionally clever and highly ethical Chief of Police, and his partner and assistant Sajid Hameed, a humorous and playful young man who appears to be careless but in fact has great presence of mind. The second, the *Imran* series, featured Ali Imran: a playful, highly intelligent detective who is also a master of disguise.

133

Two novels came out every month; and there was always a new ibn Safi to read every fortnight. Nana had assigned a cupboard in the house where all our ibn Safis were stored; and I was proudly put in charge of this treasure. It was also my responsibility to secure the new novels as soon as they hit the street. I remember that at a the tender age of seven or eight, I had to fight my way through the crowds that always gathered in front of newspaper vendors and street sellers to buy the latest adventures of 'Hameedi-Faridi' and Imran.

I set off for Nana's surgery at about three o'clock. As I walked on Railway Bazaar, I was beckoned by the *paan-walla*. 'Young Sahib, young Sahib', he shouted, 'you are the grandson of Hakim Sahib. Right? I will make a special *paan* for you — in your honour.'

It is practically impossible to escape a *paan-walla* anywhere in Pakistan. *Paan* is the heart-shaped leaf of the betel plant, a type of creeper, on to which a number of spices are smothered, seeds and nut are added, and the complete concoction is then folded into a triangular shape. It has three basic ingredients: *katha*, a reddish solution of the heart-wood of the tree Acacia Catechu Wild; *choona*, lime paste; and *chalia*, areca nut (which in botanical terms is not a nut, but a seed), which is also known as *supari*. Beyond these, a whole range of different spices, seeds, nuts and dried fruit can be added to give the *paan* specific taste and flavour. The most visible ingredient of *paan* is the *katha* which produces natural red colour. Folklore has it that *paan* was popularised by Queen Noorjehan, the mother of Mughal Emperor Shahjehan who built the Taj Mahal as a symbol of his love for his wife, Mumtaz Mahal. Noorjehan used *paan*, presumably with a lot of *katha* in it, as a lipstick! In Bahwalnagar, lipstick-coloured spit graces most of the city's walls, particularly if they have been recently white-washed.

The *paan-walla* picked a betel leaf from a tray, carefully dried it, covered it with *katha* with a round spoon, dropped a few drops of *choona* on one side, and placed a small pinch of *chalia* in the middle. 'Not too much *chalia*', I said. 'And make it small pieces. I find them too difficult to chew; I don't want to break my teeth.' 'Do not worry Sahib', the *paan-walla* replied as he continued to add other ingredients: cardamom, aniseed, grated coconut, cloves, rose essence, chutney… Eventually he handed me the paan.

'My best! I call it *Asmani paan*. Direct from the heavens through me to you.' I took the *paan* and placed it in my mouth: it simply melted away.

Ibn-e-Safi BA is as indigenous to Pakistan, and as ubiquitous, as the *paan*.
His real name was Asrar Ahmad; the 'BA' in his *nom de plume* was integral.
When Asrar Ahmad obtained his Bachelor of Arts from Agra University, in
the late 1940s, it was still rare for a Muslim to be so highly educated. He
was born in the small village of Nara in Allahabad, India, on 26 July 1928.
He published his first detective story in 1948 in a magazine called *Nikhat*,
which was printed in Allahabad. And then went on to write under various
pseudonyms, eventually settling for ibn-e-Safi BA after the success of his
Shola (spark) series. He was a progressive writer, and branded as such both
by the British and then the Indian authorities after them. Warrants were
issued for his arrest and he ended up escaping to Pakistan. *Jasoosi Duniya*
began in India in 1952; *Imran* series started in Pakistan in 1958. Ibn Safi
published his novels simultaneously in India and Pakistan, and kept the Subcontinent enthralled till his death by cancer, aged fifty-two, on 26 July 1980
(coincidently the same date as his birthday). He left some 232 novels behind
him. A whole generation of Pakistanis grew up on his novels, idolising
Hameed, Farid and Imran. This vast output took its toll and in the middle
of his career, between 1961 and 1963, ibn-e-Safi developed schizophrenia.
But he recovered to make a sensational comeback, with the bestselling
Imran novel, *Dairrh Matwaalay*.

Like the *paan*, ibn-Safi novels have three basic ingredients. First, there is
the language — the *katha*. Ibn-e-Safi writes with wit and panache, taking
great pleasure in word play. Imran frequently quotes and misquotes the
great Urdu poets Ghalib and Mir, as well as Confucius, to poke fun at himself. The dialogue is always crisp, scintillating, and punctuated with layer
upon layer of innuendos and puns. Yet, nothing is over written; everything
is precise and measured. Even the titles of the novels play with words:
Larazti Lakeeran (Shivering Lines), *Adhura Admi* (Unfinished Man), *Tabut Main
Chikh* (Scream of Iron) and *Lash Gati Raay* (The Singing Corpse). And the
villains are just delicious: Qalandar Bayabani, the spy story teller; Theresia
Bumble-Bee of Bohemia, who behaves like a chameleon; Gerald Shashtri,
the western expert in Sanskrit; and the most ingenious and treacherous of
all, Sing Hee. Second, the emphasis on virtue — the *choona*. Ibn Safi was a
highly moral man who took religious virtue seriously. Although religion
itself is never mentioned in the novels, his protagonists are highly ethical,
indeed critical Muslims: they follow the law impeccably, do not believe in

unnecessary violence, do not drink or gamble, and they never, never have sex. Even when the playful Hameed and naughty Imran are surrounded by irresistible glamour – in five star hotels, for example – they are not allowed even a side-ways glance at desirable pulchritude however enticingly displayed. Moreover, they are thoroughly professional, exceptionally rational and precise in their actions. The virtues are not overplayed, or thickly layered; they are just there, a natural and integral part of his characters. They should be, ibn Safi seems to suggest, the norms of Muslim society. Third, the plot — the *supari*. While the plots are crafted deftly, the pleasure in reading ibn Safi is not so much in discovering the mystery that will eventually resolve itself at the end, but how the drama is unfolded, how the story is weaved, and how the familiar set pieces are manipulated and twisted not just to surprise but to delight. Ibn-e-Safi wants his readers to be involved with his creation, to appreciate how the narrative is put together, to enjoy how his familiar tropes perform in unfamiliar situations, to savour the texture and every morsel of the story.

Then there is the *paan* leaf itself: the landscape of the story. The novels are set in an unnamed country. But we know that Hameedi-Fradi are defending India. But it is an India that stretches from North West Frontier to the Far East, and it is seen as a civilisation rather than a nation state. The Imran series is clearly set in Pakistan, but it is not a Pakistan that we would recognise. Ibn-e-Safi's Pakistan is a confident nation with unimpeachable integrity. And his characters are at ease everywhere. The entire globe is 'home'. The protagonists travel all over the world in pursuit of the villains (who invariably tend to be white men): plague-infected ghettos in the US, colonial settlements in South Africa, the congested streets of cities in England, and a fictional country known as Zero Land (where, naturally, everyone is a non-entity). There is also an awareness of progress and of the future. In the 1957 novel *Toofan Ka Aghwa* (Hurricane Kidnap), we find a loveable robot, 'Fauladmi', who performs household chores, controls traffic, and even settles minor disputes between citizens. But ibn-e-Safi is also aware of the downside of technology. In *Jungle Ki Aag* (Jungle Fire), written in the 1960, the villain invents a machine that turns three crippled beggars into a gorilla.

Before I could thank the *paan-walla*, I was assaulted by two young boys. One pulled my arms; the other was firmly attached to my right leg. They were intent on moving me in two different directions. It took some effort to disentangle myself and control the enthusiasm of the boys. 'Sahib! Sahib!' the boy attached to my arm was urging me to the *goll guppa* stall. And for old time's sake, why not?

'Only one *goll guppa*, please!' I pleaded with the *goll guppa-walla*. '*Teek hai, Teek hai* (OK), just for today. One is enough to get you hooked.' I opened my mouth as widely as possible, prepared to receive his bounty. But he recoiled in horror. 'No sir!', he said. 'Never! Never will I be putting my divine *goll guppa* in a mouth full of *paan*'. I quickly spat the remaining *paan* from my mouth; drank a few sips of tamarind water from the small glass he placed in my hands. 'Now you are ready for the *goll guppa* experience' he said exultantly and carefully placed a large *goll guppa*, full of chickpeas and tamarind water, in my mouth. As the *goll guppa* exuded its divinity in my mouth I found my body encrusted with a new effusion of boys all anxious to drag bits of my being in sundry directions. I managed to wriggle out and ran towards a bookseller. His wares were displayed on the street next to a pharmacy. He sat on a stool, a fan in his hand, surrounding by books and magazines. There were several ibn-e-Safi novels neatly displayed.

As far as I know, *goll guppa* is a totally *desi*, that is local, concoction. Not unlike ibn-e-Safi novels. Arrogant and ill-informed Pakistani literati have dismissed his work as derivative, not worthy of serious attention. He is said to have borrowed from Arthur Conan Doyle, Leslie Charteris, Ian Fleming and a host of others. Such dismissal says a great deal about the deep inferiority complex one detects in the Pakistani literati. Imagination is not something that Pakistanis, the *desis*, are allowed to have. The *desi* is always seen as inferior to the 'western'. Of course, there are shades of Bond in ibn-e-Safi just as there are shades of Bond in Robert Ludlum's Bourne novels. It's a genre for God's sake. In any case, by the time Ian Fleming published the first James Bond novel, *Casino Royale* (under the title *You Asked For It*) in 1953, Ibn-e-Safi had already published well over a dozen novels in the *Jasoosi Dunya* series and the characters and adventures of 'Hamidi-Faridi' had been well established. While Bond certainly knows his drinks, his gadgets and his weapons, Ibn-e-Safi's characters are more at home with Freudian psychology, Nietzsche, Confucius and Omar Khayyam. *The Saint* may be as suave as Imran, but his adventures are mundane and he cannot match Imran's ability to disguise himself or dodge bullets.

Ibn-e-Safi's literary output is about as Pakistani or Indian as one can get. No doubt, like most of us, he was influenced by what he read. He was honest enough to acknowledge those who influenced him. But *Jasoosi Dunya* and the *Imran series* are part of a very specific genre of Urdu literature that played with magical realism centuries before magical realism was invented. The genre can be traced back to the sixteenth century and to such classical novels as *Dastan-e Ameer Hamza* ('The Narrative of Ameer Hamza') and *Talism-e Hoshruba* ('The Magic That Robs the Wits'; translated by Shahnaz Aijazuddin as *The Enchantment of the Senses*). These are sprawling narratives of kings and Jinn, battles and romances, moral imperatives and ethical choices, deeply rooted in the imagination and the soil of the Subcontinent - just like the *goll guppas*. Ibn-e-Safi's plots are as multi-layered, complex, and convoluted as the stories in *Talism-e Hoshruba*.

'Do you have the latest ibn-e-Safi?' I asked the bookseller.

'Yes, Sahib', he shot back. 'The latest and the original'.

'Original?' I was intrigued.

'Yes, Sahib. You can't be too careful nowadays. There are vandals out there who produce fake copies of his work. Ibn-e-Safi has himself complained. But they don't listen.'

'Here', he said, handing me a novel, '*Khooni Panja* (Blood Claw). Hot off the press'.

I bought the novel and ran all the way to Haziq Dawakhana.

Hakim Sahib was sitting crossed-legged on a cushion listening attentively to a patient. I composed myself. I took a seat near him, keeping a respectable distance from the private space between a hakim and his *mareez*, the patient. When he finished, Nana looked up.

'I see you have got the latest ibn-e-Safi'.

He paused for a thought. 'Can you still read Urdu?'

'I think I can', I replied.

'Then begin at the beginning.'

Khooni Punja was from the *Imran* series. The comical and apparently incompetent Ali Imran, 27, Oxford PhD, also known as X-2, lives in a modest flat with his three faithful employees: his cook, the cook's wife, and his personal body guard, Joseph, an African. Handsome and a flamboyant dresser, he speaks several languages, and is an expert in a number of fighting arts. When he has to fight he fights like Jackie Chan: aiming to humiliate the opponents into submission rather than physically beating them up. He is a master of the Chinese 'Sung Art', which he learned from one of his arch enemies, Sung Hee, a Chinese criminal and spy. Imran has a string of agents working for him, but they do not know his identity; whenever any of his subordinates are in trouble X-2 appears mysteriously, as if he were a 'spirit', to save them. The most fearsome of his criminal opponents, Theresa Bumble Bee of Bohemia (T3B), is deeply in love with him. At the beginning of each novel, Imran appears in disguise as some insignificant character in the back-ground, ever present, but almost invisible. The readers themselves do not know it is Imran until well into the novel. What we do know is that an elaborate trap is being set. And we may suspect there is more to that beggar with the twisted body who insists on praising Allah incessantly, or the *paan-walla* who is trying to attract customers by juggling his '*Asmani paan*', or the incompetent motor mechanic who is taking forever to change a wheel.

'Well, get on with it then!' Hakim Sahib jogged me from my reverie.

I had forgotten to read; and I was struggling a bit with my Urdu.

'*It is possible that this event would not have happened. Or it would have. We cannot be sure that the riot was not used as a front for something else. It started innocently enough and then developed into wide scale looting. Shops were vandalised.* Paan-wallas *and* goll guppa-wallas *were robbed.*'

'What?' Hakim Sahib asked sharply. 'Read that again.'

'*Shops were vandalised.* Paan-wallas *and* goll guppa-wallas *were robbed.*'

'Carry on.'

'*Maybe we can say that another event was unfolding behind the riot. The initial impulse for the troubles was provided by the bulky man, with an ill-fitting suit, eating ravenously in the restaurant. A young couple arrived and sat in front of him. He looked at them while placing a handful of rice in his mouth. The girl was exception-ally beautiful. Did she look at him? Qasim did not know her. But he knew the man accompanying her. He was the son of a well-to-do businessman. He really liked the girl. Did she look towards him again? Qasim tried to ignore the couple and concen-trate on his food. His eye was caught by a Pathan, sitting at one end of the restaurant. Wearing an ostentatious shalwar kameez, in bright blue shades, the Pathan had fin-ished his meal. The waiter brought him some coffee and biscuits. The Pathan dunked a biscuit in the coffee and ate it as though he was performing an act of high ritual significance.*'

'What? What?' Hakim Sahib leaned forward as if he hadn't quite heard what I read. 'Read that again.'

'The waiter brought him some coffee and biscuits. The Pathan dunked a biscuit in the coffee and ate it as though he was performing an act of high ritual significance.'

'Carry on.'

'Qasim became aware that the couple were laughing at him. He tried to ignore them. But then they started pointing at him. They were openly mocking and humiliating him. Qasim just could not take it anymore. He picked up the chair next to him and threw it at the young man. Within minutes the restaurant was engulfed in an all-out brawl. Chairs, tables, plates, shoes — everything was flying. The brawl spilled out into the street. And the fight in the restaurant turned into a riot in the bazaar'.

I paused a minute to make sure Hakim Sahib was still attentive. He was. But there was a slightly troubled look on his face. 'Why have you stopped?' he said. 'Carry on.'

'Inside the restaurant, the lights went off. Everything fell into darkness. There was a scream. "Let me go, let me go", yelled a woman. It looked as though someone was trying to suffocate her. When the light came back a few minutes later, the young girl had disappeared. Her companion was lying on the floor, bleeding profusely. He had been stabbed. Qasim had been knocked unconscious. The restaurant was in total disarray. But the Pathan still sat on his table at the corner. He surveyed the scene. "Array baap ray", he said. "What a mess!"'

'That's enough, that's enough', Hakim Sahib shouted. He was agitated. 'I have heard enough. Where is my walking stick?'

I got up and handed the walking stick to him. 'Come with me,' he said. 'And bring that wretched novel with you'.

Hakim Sahib closed the door of his surgery. Walking stick in his left hand, he set off at a determined pace, with me walking as fast as I could to keep up. As we passed other shops in the Bazaar people turned to watch the parade and quickly ascertained Hakim Sahib was not in a very good mood. 'Something agitating you Hakim Sahib?' asked one. Hakim Sahib gave no acknowledgement but carried on walking, brandishing his stick with a no-nonsense swagger. Soon people started to follow us. After twenty minutes or so, we arrived at a large, dilapidated house. Hakim Sahib knocked at the huge wooden door with his walking stick. There was no reply. Hakim Sahib knocked again. 'Master Chaudhry, Master Chaudhry, come out', he declaimed. 'There is no point hiding from me!'

A window, adjacent to the large door, opened. A man, in a *dhoti* but naked from the waist upwards, leaned forward. 'Oh Merciful God', he said, 'is everything all right? Hakim Sahib you look too agitated. You should think of your heart at your age.'

'My heart is stronger than your brain', Hakim Sahib shot back. 'If I have told you once, I have told you a thousand times. Have I not?'

'What Hakim Sahib, what?'

'Not to peddle your fake novels Master Chaudhry!'

Hakim Sahib grabbed the novel from my hand. 'This, this trash. *Khooni Punja*. This is one of yours, isn't it? Why do you have to disgrace the good name of Ibn-e-Safi BA.'

'But, but... Hakim Sahib'.

'No buts'.

"But, but... Hakim Sahib how did you know?"

The question transformed Hakim Sahib. He became calm. 'Oh, Master Chaudhry', he said. 'It is so obvious. Ibn-e-Safi would never cause a riot in a street for a kidnapping to be staged in a restaurant. That's just grotesque violence. You have tried – unsuccessfully – to combine the opening sequences of two Imran novels: *Lash ka Qahqaha* ('Laughter of the Corpse') and *Mahaktay Muhafiz* ('Cheeky Protectors'). Anyway, who would want to rob the poor *goll guppa-walla*?'

'Those who want to eat the *goll guppas*!'

'Just shut up, Master Chaudhry and listen. This was not your cardinal mistake. Your unforgivable sin was to give Imran's identity away right at the beginning of the novel. Don't you know that only Imran says "*Array baap ray*", (Holy Father) that is his *takya kalam* (pet phrase). The moment someone says "*Array baap ray*", the reader knows it is Imran in disguise. And Imran never, never dunks his biscuit in his coffee. With or without high ritual significance. He is a tea drinker.'

'I am really sorry, Hakim Sahib.' Master Chaudhry slipped a *kurta* over his head and came out. 'I cannot apologise enough for causing you so much distress. Please accept my sincere apologies for the same. Next time I will try and do much better.'

'What do you mean next time? There will be no next time. Next time you will put your own name on your own trash.'

'But Hakim Sahib no one buys novels with my name on them. Ibn-e-Safi sells. I have to try and make a living somehow!'

Hakim Sahib became reflective. 'That's true', he replied. 'People do not appreciate *desi* literature. Particularly when it is so bad.' He paused for thought. 'Ok then, if you are determined to have a career writing fake novels, make sure you don't give the game away on the first two pages. But try and keep your hands off our national writers. This *farangi* fellow, what's his name, Sheik Spear, fake his books. Who knows? You may capture an international market!'

PAPERBACK WRITERS

Bina Shah

In the last three years, Pakistani literature has been undergoing a 'boom', an odd appellation that makes me think of both Pakistan's nuclear ambitions and the exploits of its cricket star Shahid 'Boom Boom' Afridi: all fire and drama that creates a blinding flash, performs inconsistently, then burns out quickly. Certainly Pakistani writing seems to have exploded in the world's eye, with today's contemporary English writers climbing to the top of best-seller lists, winning major literary awards, and novels being adapted into major Hollywood screenplays. But are we simply the flavour of the month, or is there a deeper evolution of our nascent literary tradition that will continue to expand and flourish in the next decade and beyond?

How many books does a boom make? Well, Mohsin Hamid's second novel *The Reluctant Fundamentalist* was shortlisted for the Booker Prize in 2007, Mohammed Hanif's *A Case of Exploding Mangoes* won the overall Common-wealth Best First Book Prize in 2008, Daniyal Mueenuddin won the 2010 regional Commonwealth Best First Book Prize for short story collection *In Other Rooms, Other Wonders*, and was nominated for a Pulitzer Prize. Aamer Hussein's novella *Another Gulmohar Tree* was nominated for the regional Commonwealth Best Book in 2010, while Kamila Shamsie's *Burnt Shadows* was shortlisted for the Orange Prize in 2009. HM Naqvi's debut novel Home Boy won the $50,000 DSC Prize for South Asian Literature at last year's Jaipur Literary Festival.

Publishers, editors, literary agents and critics all over the world suddenly sat up and paid attention to Pakistan, a nation that since the events of 9/11 had been regarded as a hotbed of Islamist extremism, an incubator of global terrorism, and a political and societal basket case, especially when com-pared to its larger and more stable neighbour, India. But the books pro-duced by Pakistanis in the decade of the 'War on Terror' were filled with narrative tension, and infused with the themes of love, war, death and politics that colour so many great works of literature across the centuries and around the globe. A small group of talented Pakistani writers have made their way to the top, and it seems they will be leading the way into the future, holding court for years to come, which is a triumph for both Pakistan and for its writers. But there are caveats to consider when examining the 'boom' from a critical angle.

My own journey of discovering the English-language Pakistani writers and then joining their ranks has been not so much an academic process but one of personal and joyful navigation of uncharted waters, new territory that seemed strangely familiar in indirect ways. I'd spent the first part of my childhood in America, and had then come back to Pakistan to attend an American school while trying to adjust to a life back in a country that made no sense to me. As a result, I was always a young woman with an identity crisis so heavy that you could see me leaning to one side as I walked the halls of my school. Being unable to speak or read Urdu at anything beyond the most basic level, I thought the traditions of Pakistani literature were inaccessible to me. Then I discovered Pakistani writing in English born of both Urdu post-colonial writing and the post-colonial literature coming from India in the late 1970s and early 1980s.

For me, the first Pakistani writing with an ear to the sensibilities of both Urdu and other languages was Saadat Hassan Manto, who found his own identity as a leftist and socialist in the new Pakistan first by translating the works of masters such as Anton Chekhov, Victor Hugo, and Oscar Wilde, and later by turning to writing about the subcontinent. I devoured Khalid Hasan's English translations of his short stories and essays which dealt with the darkness of the human psyche, as humanist values progressively declined with the violence and turbulence of Partition. The influence of his work, thematically if not linguistically, can be seen in much of today's contemporary Pakistani English literature, which is by turns dark, richly comic, potently tragic, and always overlaid with tones of despair at the mess our country has managed to find itself in after sixty-five years of lurching from one crisis to the next.

Along with Manto, Indian writer Ismat Chughtai was one of the four pillars of Urdu writing in South Asia; her work dealt with gender identity and sparkled with honesty. She paid little heed to the social conventions of the time. Great friends with Manto, she was a feminist, and advocated freedom for women both in her own life and in her writing. She was rebellious, writing progressive fiction and wanting change and independence for women in post-Partition South Asia. Her work has also influenced later generations of Pakistani writers, especially women, and much of Pakistani women's writing in English today owes its origins to the space that Chughtai opened for them in the 1950s.

I've certainly drawn my own inspiration from her work, by espousing in my own novels and short stories a type of feminism that is angry, militant, and unwilling to accept the unjust patriarchal traditions of South Asian culture. And yet we Pakistani women who must be so tough in everyday life always manage to find a tender, warm core in ourselves and in dealings with our allies – be they family, friends, children, or colleagues. Pakistani women's writing walks that fine line between anger and tenderness, between humiliation and pride, between annihilation and survival. It is coloured with defiance and love, which is what makes it so powerful to me as both a reader and a writer.

As a child I saw my father carrying an illegal copy of Salman Rushdie's *Shame* in his briefcase; I worked out the combination by peeking over his shoulder while he was opening the lock. Once I'd spirited away his copy I sat down to read it, and was in turn horrified and fascinated by Rushdie's cynical portrayal of Pakistan and its political leadership, and its controversial imagining of the relationship between Zulfikar Ali Bhutto and General Zia, with Bhutto's daughter named 'the Virgin Ironpants'. These provocations, and the book's theme – that violence is born out of shame – caused the book to be banned in Pakistan. It paved the way for Mohammed Hanif's later novel, *A Case of Exploding Mangoes* (2009), which treats General Zia and other players of the day with similar satire and scathing cynicism. Both books produced in me an odd sense of revulsion, because my father had served as a cabinet minister (under Mohammed Ali Khan Junejo) during General Zia's regime, and my parents told us of all their interactions with the General, and their description of him as a benign, kindly figure clashed hard in my mind with the portraits of lurid violence and sexual repression that Rushdie and Hanif painted in their novels.

Soon I discovered the godmother of Pakistani writing in English, Bapsi Sidhwa, who astonished the world with a lively portrayal of the Parsi community in her debut novel *The Crow Eaters*, and followed it with her tale of a young Punjabi woman given away as a bride to a tribal Pathan in the harsh mountains of Northern Pakistan in *The Pakistani Bride* (1982), earning worldwide acclaim. Her frank account of the sexual relationship between the adopted Punjabi girl Zaitoon and her harsh Pathan husband found its way into my own sexual awakening: I simply didn't know, living in conservative Pakistan, that Pakistani men and women had sex and enjoyed it. Sidhwa taught me that they did. Her insistence on portraying South Asian women as sexual beings and her success in bringing the world's attention to women's issues in the Indian subcontinent set her apart as the writer to whom I first turned when I wanted to understand the inner layers of sexuality and relationships in Pakistani society.

Pakistanis who wrote in English through the 1980s and 90s were not widely published or widely read, but Muneeza Shamsie created space with the publication of her 1997 anthology *A Dragonfly in the Sun: An Anthology of Pakistani Writing in English*. Included in the anthology were works by writers such as Zulfikar Ghose, Sara Suleri (whose 1991 non-fiction memoir *Meatless Days* won accolades for its lucid prose and its clear-eyed yet poetic remembrance of her family life in 1960s and 70s Pakistan), Adam Zameenzad, Tariq Ali, Hanif Kureishi, the short story writer Aamer Hussein (author of several lyrical short story collections, including *Mirror to the Sun* and *Cactus Town*), Moniza Alvi and Sorayya Khan.

I was overjoyed to discover, at the age of eighteen, the writings of Hanif Kureishi; undergoing my own identity crisis as a Pakistani with an American upbringing, I had no idea that there were other young Pakistanis who felt the same sense of isolation and alienation, until I read Kureishi's books. Then I fell in love with their defiance and fashioned myself as a punk in black clothes during my undergraduate years at Wellesley College, where the young ladies in pearls and heels looked at me askance as I strode through the campus in my spiked, gelled hair, violent red lipstick, black leather jacket and motorcycle boots.

The movement continued, expanding slowly but gradually, with Kamila Shamsie producing a steady series of novels in and about the city of Karachi: *In the City By The Sea* (1998), *Salt and Saffron* (2000), *Kartography* (2002) and *Broken Verses* (2005). Uzma Aslam Khan added her voice to the mix with *The Story of Noble Rot* (2001) and *Trespassing* (2004), which was shortlisted for the Commonwealth Eurasia Region Prize. Mohsin Hamid's debut novel

Moth Smoke (2000) stirred excitement and won critical acclaim for its bad-boy rendition of societal tension and class differences in modern-day Lahore. Sehba Sarwar wrote 2006's *BlackWings*, Maniza Naqvi followed her debut novel *Mass Transit* (1998) with *On Air* (2000) and *Stay with Me* (2004). Short story writer Aamer Hussein published the celebrated collection *Insomnia* in 2007, then switched to longer fiction with the novella *Another Gulmohar Tree* in 2009 and the novel *The Cloud Messenger* in 2011.

With the reputable Oxford University Press in Karachi, and two new publishing houses, Alhamra in Islamabad and Sama in Karachi, seemingly committed to fostering Pakistani writing, and with friendly help from publishers in next-door India, Pakistani writing in English began to achieve critical mass. By this time, I was able to place myself in the tradition as well, as my short story anthology *Animal Medicine* was published by Oxford University Press in 1999, and my debut novel, *Where They Dream in Blue*, was published by Alhamra in 2000. At the time my father was serving his second stint as a cabinet minister in the regime of another army dictator, General Pervez Musharraf. My second novel, *The 786 Cybercafe* (2004), and another collection of short stories, *Blessings* (2007), were both written in the shadow of dictatorship.

As a writer, there are certain questions and concerns that I hold about my work and the larger movement of English writing that comes out of Pakistan. The first is a common question that every Pakistani writer working in English has heard at some point or other in their lives: 'Why do you write in English?' This is a question that annoys and amuses me in turns whenever I hear it. The people who ask always do so with a pained look on their faces, as if you're committing a sin that hurts them more than it does you. 'Why aren't you writing in Urdu?' they ask. I always reply by asking them, flippantly, if they've heard me speak any Urdu, and if so, why they think I'd possibly be able to write more than my own name in that language.

But the question of whether or not English is a suitable or politically correct language for Pakistani writers is a post-colonial hang-up that we have to get beyond if we're to thrive as writers on the international literary scene. English is our heritage as much as our own regional and national languages. Let's go back to the origins of Urdu, and remember that it originated as a 'lashkari' language, a vernacular created so that soldiers speaking Turkish, Persian or Hindi could communicate with one another during battles and troop manoeuvres. It continued to hold the status of a working, and working class, language until it was adopted by the princely courts of Lucknow and Hyderabad Deccan, where it developed into the courtly, elegant language of Mirza Ghalib, Momin Khan Momin, and other poets who flourished under the rule of Bahadur Shah Zafar (himself a prolific poet) in the eighteenth and nineteenth centuries. Later, the work of Allama Iqbal, Pakistan's national poet, who wrote in Urdu and Farsi, cemented Urdu into the minds of Pakistanis as the language of literature.

As the daughter of a Sindhi family, I was raised to view Urdu and Urdu speakers with a certain amount of suspicion: I was born during the days of the language riots in Karachi, when in 1972 the Sindh Assembly passed a bill declaring Sindhi to be the official language of Sindh along with Urdu. The Muhajir communities, envisioning losing their hegemony over the province, rioted in Karachi, forcing my father's relatives who'd come from Matiari to visit my mother and me to remain trapped in my mother's household in Karachi for several weeks until it was safe for them to go back to the village. It was an unpleasant time for my stranded relatives as well as for my maternal grandmother, forced to feed, house, amuse and entertain a dozen unexpected ladies who lived in strict purdah. With such a fiery association, Urdu would never have been the language in which I'd have chosen to express myself. Such is the pride and stubbornness we non-Urdu speakers feel about the issue of language.

Never mind the fact that English is the language of our former colonial masters, or that our parents were educated in convents by English-speaking nuns and priests, where they learned to sing hymns to Jesus and read from the canon of English literature. English is a practical choice for the writers of my generation: it's a global language, one that makes us immediately accessible to international readers without having to go through the pain and inconvenience of translation. Our generation, educated in English and lacking the sentimental ties to Urdu held by the previous generation, simply doesn't see the logic of writing in Urdu or limiting our audience to a local readership anymore. Many of us don't read Urdu with ease, let alone write in it. English is a language of directness and precision, a growing, changing force, able to accommodate great diversity in style, syntax, rhythm and tone. This works well when attempting to house the hugely divergent works of our Pakistani writers: Mohammed Hanif's tragi-comic and satirical sensibility, Mohsin Hamid's architecturally simple yet ideologically vast novels, Danyal Muennuddin's more textured, layering-characters-in-context approach, or Kamila Shamsie's intricate woven layers of history, tradition, and human relationships.

Is Pakistani women's writing being ignored or overlooked in the Pakistani literary 'boom'? I'd posed this question in an article for the *Guardian* called 'The Pakistani Literary Boys' Club'. But William Dalrymple and Kamila Shamsie both believe that the prevalence of male writers was not due to any gender bias. Dalrymple called it a 'reflection of relative sales by a crop of boys in a particular year'. Shamsie echoed this opinion: 'It's mostly the male writers who have had books... in the last two years when there's been all this hoopla over Pakistani writing.' Faiza S Khan, literary critic and editor of the *Life's Too Short* literary review, adds: 'I think it's a complete coincidence. Maybe even the opposite: women being overrepresented for being women. Most of the women's writing I have read has been subpar. There have been more women writers to male than in the UK, and I think the people being overlooked are not women but the quiet domestic writers.' I disagree with Khan that women's writing is 'subpar', but I understand and share her impatience with a particular sort of sensual, overly sentimental novel that has been the starting point for many Pakistani women writing in English. You know the kind: 'Sara must go back to her family history to uncover the dark secret about her maternal great-grandmother before she can free herself from the past and go on to live a life of freedom and love.' Sara also probably puts on or takes off the hijab and discovers her identity as a Pakistani-American woman along the way; Pakistan is her past but America/England/Australia is her future...

I participated in a panel discussion, 'Women Writing Women', at the 2012 Karachi Literature Festival which explored the question how women's writing is perceived in Pakistan. Two of the panellists, Nafisa Haji and Maniza Naqvi, declared their aversion to being labelled as 'women writers'. They felt the term casts unfair aspersions on their subject matter and who they perceive their readership to be. I stated unequivocally that I wrote as a woman, for women, about women – and was promptly misquoted in *Dawn* the next day as saying that I wrote 'only for women'. It's a great pity that Pakistani women writers feel so afraid of being marginalised that we hem and haw and hesitate to be identified as women writers - a telling indication of our fear of gender bias in the field.

A Pakistani writer who bridges the gender divide with panache is Moni Mohsin, whose 'Diary of a Social Butterfly' column, which skewers Pakistani high society, has been immensely popular in the independent newspaper *The Friday Times*, a well-received publication which serves up a heady mix of political analysis, cultural articles, and society and political gossip. Mohsin is sometimes compared to Jane Austen because of her astute observations and wry humour cleverly disguised in the faux-stupid voice of a Lahori 'begum' whose obsessions in life are purely material, to the dismay of her more politically aware husband (echoing Mr and Mrs Bennett in *Pride and Prejudice*). It's this kind of confidence and attitude that Pakistan's women writers need, as well as technical virtuosity and skill, combined with plots and themes that address weighty issues but avoid autobiographical or clichéd tropes, in order to make their voices heard and achieve critical success on the same scale as the male writers on the top of the list.

The men don't deserve to be let off the hook either: one of the particular failings in novels by Pakistani men is the inability to produce a complex, well-developed female character. Some novels, like Hanif's *A Case of Exploding Mangoes* and H M Naqvi's *Home Boy* avoid the issue by simply not including major women characters in the first place. In other novels, like Nadeem Aslam's *Maps for Lost Lovers*, or in Muennuddin's short stories, the women are portrayed as evil and scheming, manipulative and cruel, the perpetrators and perpetuators of patriarchy even more than men. Mohsin Hamid's *The Reluctant Fundamentalist* presents us with Erica, a depressed blonde white woman who isn't even capable of functioning in real life, let alone to hold up her end of a challenging relationship with a Pakistani man. Male writers either create women as caricatures or foils, not human beings with autonomy and sovereignty equal to that of the men in their work.

There are two exceptions to this sad rule. The first is Aamer Hussein who writes about Pakistani women with, as I noted in my review of his short story collection *Insomnia*, 'unflinching honesty'. His empathy and admiration for woman is one of his hallmarks, becoming even more pronounced in his novella *Another Gulmohar Tree*, with its hugely sympathetic female protagonist Lydia offering her own journey and perceptions as an equal narrative to that of her husband Usman's. Hussein never takes a false step in describing the thoughts, dreams, and motivations of the women that people his stories. They serve as friends, collaborators, lovers and muses, but from a position of strength and equality, not weakness or sexual objectification. The second exception is Mohammed Hanif's latest novel, *Our Lady of Alice Bhatti*. This book is unusual in that it has a female protagonist and that half the book is written from Alice's perspective. Not only this, but Alice is a strong woman, a Christian nurse in a Muslim society, who falls in love with a Muslim police tout and defies societal conventions to marry him. But the book isn't just about her marriage; it's about her will to survive in a hostile environment and her ability to work miracles in the lives of people around her. Alice is no victim: she's a fighter. Hanif elevates Alice Bhatti from the second-class gender and religious status she was born into, and transforms her into a holy icon, a saint: no small feat in a country whose patriarchy threatens to colour even the nascent English-language literature movement with its muddy waters.

Another question worth asking: are Pakistani writers garnering the acclaim they deserve for their literary talent, or for their ability to tailor their output to the demands of international publishers, with their need to portray Pakistan as a 'war-torn country', ripped apart by decades of political and social turmoil and upheaval? Have they been spurred on by terrorism and other lurid political developments in the region over the last decade, including the assassination of Benazir Bhutto and the capture and killing of Osama bin Laden? Simply put, is violence and terrorism sexy to Western readers, and are Pakistani writers pandering to that trend?

Several Pakistani novels deal directly with the events of 9/11 and the 'War on Terror': Hamid's *The Reluctant Fundamentalist*, Shamsie's *Burnt Shadows*, Aslam's *The Wasted Vigil*, and Feryal Ali Gauhar's *No Space for Further Burials*, to name a few. It's tempting to say that these novels capitalise on the Western world's desire to see Pakistan as a disaster zone, and Pakistanis as rogue Muslims who can easily betray or harm their Western allies. But these novels examine themes and events that have had tremendous influence on these writers by way of their identity as Pakistanis, Muslims, and artists charged with the responsibility of observing and interpreting what's happening around them to their readers and themselves. The events of 9/11 and the War on Terror have been so overwhelming, so all-surrounding, that it's inevitable they would eventually filter down into the writing of Pakistanis, not as a cold-blooded consideration of market trends, but as a product of psychology, society, and the creative process.

My own novel in progress, *Peter Pochmann Goes to Pakistan*, tells the tale of an American businessman who comes to Pakistan for a three-day business visit, but due to a string of increasingly poor decisions, he finds himself stranded in Pakistan, his bag stolen, in trouble with the police, and almost sparking off deadly riots and a coup. Pochmann spends much of the novel in fear of being killed by terrorists in a post 9/11 Pakistan hostile to America and the War on Terror. I wrote the short story the novel is based on back in 2008; weirdly, it seemed to be prescient of events surrounding the case of Raymond Davis, the CIA contractor who in 2011 shot and killed two men at a Lahore intersection. I couldn't honestly say that I had written a story meant to capitalise on those events and the greater atmosphere of 'Emergency Pakistan', but they have certainly coloured my work and given it a creative impetus that would not have emerged had I been living in, say, Geneva or Seoul.

Some Pakistanis argue that Pakistani writers today are only showing the bad side of Pakistan in order to gain financial and critical success, and that they should take greater pains to present a balanced view. I'm hesitant to throw that kind of accusation around at anyone, no matter how truthful the observation may be. Social responsibility tends to strangle creative freedom, and it's a short distance from political correctness to propaganda. I think that readers are intelligent enough to discern a novel that portrays social and political problems with sensitivity and honesty from a novel that exaggerates and distorts Pakistan to serve the author's own aims.

Still, there's a reason that *Granta's* issue on 'Pakistan' devoted to 'Corona Burst of Talent' continues to sell well, while local anthologies such as the *Alhamra Literary Review* (which I edited for two years) are now defunct, and the *Life's Too Short* review, the print magazine of the 'Life's Too Short' short story competition edited by Aysha Raja and Faiza S Khan, has gone out of print barely a year since its publication. While *Granta* is naturally more well-established, has a formidable reputation and enjoys clout in the international literary world, the special issue on Pakistan has been seen as portraying only one aspect of Pakistan: the War on Terror years, the political upheaval, the instability, the danger and death of this country. The home grown anthologies, which portray quieter aspects of Pakistani life, urban and rural, across social classes, humorous and serious, simply aren't as 'sexy'. And un-sexiness equals death in a publishing world that demands taglines, headlines, and recognisable by-lines in order to sell copies.

Pakistan has been described as the most dangerous country on earth. That's a pretty exciting place in which to be a writer, and if international acclaim follows for our talent as much as for our circumstances, I can't think of many struggling artists who would refuse the attention. As long as tensions continue to simmer between Pakistan and India, between the Muslim world and the West, as long as Pakistan's own internal conflicts continue to bubble, international readers will keep hungering for narratives about the country. And let's be honest: there will always be writers willing to serve those up to them, and they fulfil a need for a kind of 'immediate fiction' that's long on sensationalism and short on literary worth or beauty.

But we're in a unique position as writers in Pakistan, and not just because we have bombs and the Taliban to contend with. Because of our history of colonialism and our current generation's ease and facility with English, Pakistan is the only Muslim country in the world with a large number of English speakers; due to Western (and in the case of these current writers, mostly American) education and exposure to Western literary traditions and creative writing programmes, Pakistani writers meet a demand for literature about Pakistan produced in English. Yet we have to be careful to prioritise artistic demands, not market demands; and to avoid writing to a formula dictated by market forces in order to strengthen the movement and contribute to its long-term success. Our responsibility as writers demands this much from us.

So, back to the original question. Pakistani literature: boom or bust, bang or whimper? Based on the length and breadth of Pakistani writing in English, as well as its scope for future success, I'd rather call it a long-standing movement with history and depth than compare it to the birth of a new star, with all the attendant flash and glory. Booms have a way of petering out after their initial brilliance; gold booms gave way to ghost towns, whereas there's nothing to suggest the rich vein of Pakistani literature has begun to run out just yet.

Nor does it make any sense to pit the Pakistani English literature movement against the Indian tradition, cultural competition with our neighbour being one of our favourite cross-border sports along with cricket matches and the nuclear arms race. One of Pakistan's extraordinary voices, Mohsin Hamid, does not see the celebration of Pakistani literature in competitive terms. In an interview with *Newsweek Pakistan* about the Karachi Literary Festival, he says, 'It's not a race, we're not contesting with anyone. It's about direction, and I think we're headed the right way.' Hamid adds that events like the KLF have become part of the 'writing ecosystem' of the country, which now offers more, if still not quite enough, writing-related job opportunities.

In the week following KLF 2012, Ameena Saiyid, in her introduction to a talk by Vikram Seth, spoke about how the three years of the Karachi Literature Festival's success heralds a 'Pakistani Spring' in literature. It is this image I'd like to hold on to as the one that Pakistani literature truly deserves, rather than one of a boom: a flowering, the growth of new things, the planting of seeds, and patient readers and writers waiting to reap the fruits of their germination for generations to come.

COKE STUDIO

Bilal Tanweer

There are no billboards on the streets. For the last four years, a week or so before the new season of Coke Studio is launched, most of the important billboards in major Pakistani cities are taken up by snazzy advertisements announcing the featured artists of the season. It's the biggest annual ad campaign for any TV program and this is Season 5. It's being touted by many to be the mother of all seasons, mainly on the basis of a wildly circulating promotional video of Episode 1 of the new season. The first artist on the promo video is a rapper: Bohemia. The video shows him in a hoodie and dark glasses, slamming out a rap number in Punjabi. 'This is an opportunity for me to tell you what rap is — it's poetry, it's a message,' he says in a close-up shot of his three-second interview. The video cuts back to the song. By his side are the Viccaji sisters – Zoe and Rachel – who do backing vocals and harmonies but they appear to be in a more prominent role for this number.

The clip is followed by Hadiqa Kiyani, among Pakistan's leading female vocalists, singing what sounds like the hard rock version of an AR Rahman's composition. She is singing the Sufi poetry of Bulleh Shah. She's followed by Atif Aslam, arguably Pakistan's biggest rock star, also a sensation in India for the last four years. He has teamed up with 'Qayaas', an underground band, to do a version of a Nusrat Fateh Ali Khan *qawwali*. The last singer on the promo is of Humayun Khan's who is singing *Larsha Pekhawar Ta*, a popular Pushto folk song.

The absence of billboards is unexpected. For the last three years or so, Coke Studio is the soft drink brand's main marketing strategy in the country. In fact, the entire marketing campaign of Coca Cola Pakistan is designed around Coke Studio: artists featured in the program are on Coke bottles, cans, television adverts, newspapers, television, radio and billboards. But there is no visual clue of it this year. Maybe it is a scaling back by the soft drink company. But the other interesting thing I notice is that on Coke Studio's Season 5 website there is no 'About' tab either – nothing to introduce a newcomer to Coke Studio. Taken together, these could mean a number of things, but they unmistakably do mean that no one needs to be told What Coke Studio Is and What It Does; and second, nobody needs reminding that Coke Studio will start airing on 13 May. It's common knowledge.

If there is a confirmation of Coke Studio's status as a cultural behemoth in Pakistan, this is it.

Coke Studio is a world apart from Music Channel Charts, the programme I grew up on, and where I first encountered rap. The song was called *Bhangra Rap*, a mix of Punjabi bhangra with rap. The lyrics were a smooth and unselfconscious mix of Urdu, Punjabi and English. The song was sung by a young man, Fakhr-e-Alam, who in the music video sported a huge locket with a Peace sign and danced some serious moves in his baggy, torn-knee jeans. My younger brother and I loved Fakhr-e Alam and his music and everything about him. We had memorised *Bhangra Rap* by heart and sung it in chorus with friends.

Growing up in the nineties, our entertainment options were limited to street cricket and two TV channels - a private one and a state-owned one. The transmission times for both channels were around eight to twelve hours a day and almost everyone we knew had memorised the entire week's TV schedule. MCC aired on the private TV channel, NTM (later renamed STN), and featured young men (all of them men, except for a handful of female vocalists in a few scattered exceptions) who looked like creatures from another planet compared to everything else on TV: they had unsuitably long hair, wore chains around their necks, jeans that were either tight or torn and their music was loud and brash. These boys made my middle-class parents deeply uncomfortable, for they projected an image which was perhaps my parents' very worst nightmare. For them, these boys were of an age where they should've been worrying about jobs and earning a livelihood. Instead they were running after girls on their bikes and making sounds in the name of music that positively punished my parents' sensibilities.

My brother and I, on the other hand, loved everything about this programme. It was decidedly different in its energy, sound and look from everything else we had seen on TV. It lacked polish but we hardly cared. Almost all the videos were cheaply recorded and produced at home by amateurs.

The videos were all shot around predictable locations like garages and apartment rooftops and the Karachi beach makes an obligatory appearance in most of them. Not surprisingly, most of them were shot during the day too (lighting/studio services being too expensive).

My mother would sit and monitor us as we watched the show. When we got too excited (which happened often when our favourite band/number was ascending the charts), she would disapprovingly start pointing out everything that was wild and uncivilised: 'Look at the way this boy is jumping. Baboon. Look what he's wearing. I bet he got that from the flea market.' The jibe that stung most: 'Look how this boy is aping the *firangis* (westerners); seems like he's smelled some white man's knickers.' We had little choice but to ignore her taunts and focus squarely on the music.

MCC was a ground breaker. Its competitive format drew legions of followers and encouraged hundreds of young men to make their own music videos. Despite its limited production values, MCC was an astounding success. During the four years it ran, MCC introduced many young musicians who went on to define Pakistani pop music: Ali Haider, Nadeem Jafri, Fakhr-e-Alam, Saleem Javed, Amir Zaki, Strings, Junoon, Amir Saleem, Bunny, Khalid Anum and many others. MCC also redefined the way the Pakistani urban youth imagined themselves. One of its major bands, 'Vital Signs', became a major force on the pop scene in Pakistan.

MCC disappeared almost as suddenly as it had appeared. As cable television penetrated Pakistani cities, local television lost viewership and the audience switched to MTV, Channel V and Bollywood music in a big way. MCC closed shop in 1994. By then, Pakistan already had a nascent but confident pop music scene, a maturing concert circuit and sponsors willing to foot the bill.

A lot has changed in Pakistan since. The country has become polarised by ethnicity, religion and class. The contradictions and ideological confusions of the nation are also reflected in the pop scene. One of the country's biggest pop stars, Junaid Jamshed of 'Vital Signs', abandoned music, embraced the life of a religious preacher of the evangelical Tableeghi Jamat, grew an absurdly long beard and established his own fashion label. Ali Azmat, ex-vocalist of the most successful Pakistani rock band, 'Junoon', became a conspiracy theorist who blames 'Western and Hindu Zionists' for all the ills of the country, holds the US responsible for funding terrorism in Pakistan, prophesises that Pakistan will transform in the near future into the military bastion of all the Islamic countries, and idolises the Pakistani military as God's gift to the Muslim world. Then there is Najam Shiraz who made his debut on MCC, and who now sings moving na'ats (religious devotion songs) alongside his standard pop output. There are a number of soft and hard, red and white revolutionary bands. One band, 'Laal' (literally, Red) espouses Marxist-Leninist-Stalinist ideology and sings revolutionary poets like Habib Jalib. There are others like Shehzad Roy and Strings, who sing of economic prosperity, law and security, and education for all and wish to see a culturally liberal and economically viable Pakistan, integrated in the world economy. In other words, Pakistan's cultural imagination is as fractured both vertically across classes and horizontally across ethnicity and ideology as the nation itself. There seem to be few instances where art could transcend these rigid boundaries.

Coke Studio emerged as a clear attempt to bridge the cultural fragmentation of Pakistan against this background. The first episode of the first season was aired on 8 June 2008. Broadcast on a number of television channels, with Video and MP3 files available for immediate download from its official channel on YouTube, it received instant critical and popular acclaim. The show's accent was firmly on bringing tradition and modernity together in a new synthesis. It made a conscious and sustained effort to work out a way to engage with the traditional folk music of the Subcontinent using the vocabulary of Western music, which is more accessible and familiar to the younger audience. Through Coke Studio many folk musicians and their work have been introduced to a new generation, allowing them to access a deep and rich cultural heritage that was withering on the margins.

The young filmmaker and blogger Ahmer Naqvi was swept off his feet when he first saw Coke Studio. 'We all grew up as Junoonis and Vital Signs fans. There was little else that was available culturally to us as young Pakistanis', he says. He, and countless young men and women of his generation, grew up with only a vague sense of the traditional music of their region. 'Coke Studio grabbed us because it was an amalgamation of things that were already present in our subconscious and all around us, but we never really paid attention to them,' says Safieh Shah, who wrote a detailed comment on every Coke Studio episode in the last season in The Friday Times. 'Coke Studio not only brought all those things together but did it in a way that was accessible to us.' Aamer Ahmad, who was the recording engineer on Season 2, the season in which Coke Studio found its feet and gained popularity as the cutting-edge of Pakistani music, concurs. 'Coke Studio provides people a platform where they can come to talk, chill, relax. It's like when you put a dhol wala, a drummer, and a guitar player in a room and they automatically make music. Because that's what they do.'

To understand Coke Studio we need to appreciate Rohail Hyatt, the producer and the driving force behind the show. Hyatt was a founding member, producer, song writer, guitarist and keyboardist of 'Vital Signs'. The band was formed in 1986 and exploded onto the Pakistani music scene with *Dil Dil Pakistan*, one of the most popular songs the music history of Pakistan. It became, and continues to be, the pop national anthem of the country. In a 2003 BBC poll of the ten most famous songs of all time, *Dil Dil Pakistan* ranked third. Vital Signs also scored two important firsts in Pakistani pop history: they were the first local band to land a major sponsorship deal (Pepsi) and the first to tour the United States. The band also did a number of cross-country tours, a rare achievement. Vital Signs broke up in 1998. Rohail joined the advertising industry until he returned to music with Coke Studio ten years later.

Hyatt is a naturally shy person whose dislike for interviews is well-known. Not surprisingly, he did not respond to my multiple requests for an interview. However, in an interview for *Dawn*, he stated that when he stumbled into classical music a year before Coke Studio, 'I was pretty blown away by the fact that here I was, a musician all my life, and I had no idea about a treasure of an art form that we had and it was so different from the western music that we had grown up with.' He felt that 'we as a people needed to experience our heritage, so this stems from one small experience into discovery.' Hyatt, says Haniya of the singing duo Zeb & Haniya, 'has very distinct likes and dislikes. His aesthetic met the traditional music of Pakistan—and something clicked.'

In Coke Studio, Hyatt focussed on two specifics: production quality and freedom for the artists to experiment without commercial pressures. 'Right from its inception', says Louis Jerry Pinto, who is better known as Gumby and is considered to be Pakistan's finest drummer, we wanted to 'have better production values and quality sound'. The high production values are there to be seen. Indeed, television advertisements and a few music videos aside, audiences have not seen a television production of such visual quality and sophistication on local TV channels.

Gumby, who has been a core member of the Coke Studio house band from the first season, says that the producers decided to be flexible in both approach and outcome. 'We said to each other let's keep it open-ended and let's not give it a label.' Pakistani artists have frequently complained about commercial pressures, which have stalled their creativity. Hyatt has spoken about this himself. He told *Dawn*, 'As an artist, I know during the times of Vital Signs, every time we wanted to do what we really wanted to do, there was somebody telling us that "no one is going to listen to this". It always used to be a really weird thing to give in to — my creative expression [to corporate sponsors or record labels]'.

The artists who have performed on Coke Studio wax lyrical about the creative freedom it provides. The 'beauty' of Coke Studio, says Tina Sani, a renowned *ghazal* singer who performed to great acclaim in Season 4, 'is Rohail's openness. Nobody was thinking of the commercial aspect or the audience. Rohail only suggests and you as the artist have the free-hand.' Quite a contrast with the commercial TV channels that dominate the air-waves, where ratings dictate everything, Sani says. Muazzam, one half of the Rizwan-Muazzam Qawwal Group, concurs, 'One thing we appreciated about Coke Studio is its environment,' he says. The duo belongs to the Nusrat Fateh Ali Khan's *qawwal gharana* (extended family), and their rendi-tion of the traditional *qawwali*, *Nayna de Aakhay*, was one of the big hits of Season 3. 'It works because people at Coke Studio understand music. No matter who you are, you are dealt with on your own terms. You are not bound in any way or forced to think in a certain way. This kind of respect boosts the artist's confidence. We have collaborated many times internation-ally and have also toured around the world. But this is the best collaborative experience we've ever had', says Muazzam.

'We had a lot of freedom in choosing our songs and even the arrange-ments,' says Haniya. 'It is a very collaborative process. You can be as involved or uninvolved as you like.' The degree of involvement depends on the artist. But it seems that those who are able to harness the qualities of the Coke Studio house band flourish the most. Big bands tend not to do too well in Coke Studio. The major hits have come when individual artists have paired up to exploit the genius and the quality of the Coke Studio house band which comprises some of the best musicians in Pakistan.

The process that Coke Studio follows in making its music was outlined in a video released at the end of Season 4. It describes the production process of a *qawwali* which was one of the highlights of the season. It starts with the invited artists doing a raw recording of the song they wish to perform. A number of other steps follow where the percussionists work out the rhythm structure and align it with the Western rhythm structure. Once the rhythms and beats are agreed, the house band gets involved and finds ways to retain the core improvisational aspect of Eastern music and works out a structure that could allow the two to function together. Finally, everyone rehearses together to produce the finished song.

While Coke Studio pays remuneration to artists, the immediate financial gains for appearing on the show are limited. But it does offer something that promises bigger financial rewards: exposure. Artists who do well on Coke Studio gain a global audience for their work. 'Coke Studio has put us on the map,' says Zeb of Zeb & Haniya. 'We went to France and were surprised to find people singing our songs.' Zeb & Haniya broke onto the Pakistani music scene in 2008 with their album, *Chup* – an instant hit. But their rise to international stardom came after they performed on Coke Studio in 2009. In India especially, where Coke Studio has a huge following, Zeb & Haniya performed extensively and went on to collaborate with Indian artists.

Global exposure is life blood for Pakistani artists. Making a viable living from local royalties has never been an option for musicians in the country. Indeed, many folk singers live in abject poverty. The celebrated Zarsanga, who, at sixty-five is considered the Queen of Pashto folk music, was forced to live in a tent on the roadside in Khyber Pakhtunkhwa province after her house was washed away in the 2010 floods. Even mainstream singers such as the celebrated Mahdi Hassan, known as 'King of Ghazals', faces hardship to pay for his medical care. Part of the problem is the rampant piracy that undermines the royalties of the artists. According to an artist interview, in the 1980s, an estimated thirty copies were pirated for every original cassette sold in the local market. Twenty-five years on, with the digitisation of music and the advent of the Internet, the entire business model of record labels has been comprehensively defeated in Pakistan. Even concert performances, which were the most significant source of income left for the artists, have suffered a serious setback in the deteriorating security situation. Now the few concerts that happen, happen indoors.

Coke Studio provides international exposure and serves as the flag-bearer of the enigmatic and creative side of Pakistan. 'I see Coke Studio as a platform. A big platform for the artists, especially for those who are not in the mainstream', says Muazzam. Coke Studio also helps with engagements in the local circuits. Salman Albert, a guitarist for the rock band Entity Paradigm, says 'exposure to the Western and Indian market is definitely there but even locally, after Coke Studio one gets many more concerts'.

But not everyone agrees that an appearance on Coke Studio would automatically lead to financial rewards. 'Coke Studio has not enabled any artist to make money off music, and it does little other than providing fame, which helps them get more concerts', says Fasi Zaka, broadcaster and respected long-time commentator on the Pakistani cultural scene. 'TV has always done that for the artists. But that doesn't mean it is bad. I think Coke Studio remains a great experiment in Pakistani music - mining folk influences and bringing a contemporary touch to it.'

Zaka and the noted cultural critic Nadeem Farooq Paracha have been staunch critics of corporate sponsorship in music. 'The problem with corporate money has been that it influences in directing the output of the artist', says Zaka, explaining his stance. 'So socially conscious artists would have to water down their artistic output because of corporate money involved and because corporations do not wish to be associated with anything political. For example, Shehzad Roy after his single *Laga Reh*, suffered because no sponsor wanted to touch him due to the overtly political nature of his song.' However, both Zaka and Paracha have now changed their views.

For Paracha the reason lies in the rise of militant Islam. 'I have revised my earlier position because frankly speaking I wonder if we have the luxury now. The radicalisation in our society has increased and nothing much is happening on the cultural front. It would be all right to criticise Coke Studio as a corporate brand game if we were an open society. To criticise Coke Studio in the present situation would be nihilistic.' Zaka has other reasons. 'For the music in Pakistan now, corporate money is an essential input. All the revenue streams for artists have dried up and the market isn't promoting these artists or their music. Also, with the digitisation of music, corporations affecting the output of socially conscious artists have become a minor issue. Artists who have something political to say can still say it'.

The artists themselves vigorously support corporate patronage. Gumby, who has been in the industry for over fifteen years, feels strongly.

To critics who say it is commercial, I ask: What's your point? Everyone is commercial. If corporate sponsorship did not exist in this country there would be no music. Coke is getting brand value for this money. And over the last few years, one has seen the conservative thinking in the corporate world also change and now one sees a certain level of sincerity in their efforts too: they are genuinely interested in promoting music.

But would Coke sponsor something that does not have the potential to be so popular, for the sake of music? 'If some people believe that Coke is doing it for the music, that just tells you how good a spin they have managed to put on it,' argues Zaka. 'But ultimately, we have to judge the net effect - it's good. If their aim is to sell their product, they could also do it by buying a lot of air time and running thirty-second advertisements. But if they are doing something that also benefits culture and music, then it is good.'

Coke Studio is indeed good: it is good for Pakistani music, good for our cultural heritage, good for musicians, and ultimately good for the audience – music lovers all over the world. It is something, says Aamer Ahmad, 'that we as a culture should have done sixty years ago. We should be doing it on a much larger scale, our government should be doing it.' When Coke Studio first appeared on the scene, the music industry was in the doldrums and all the music channels were losing money. 'It's not like they weren't spending: they were pouring enormous amounts of money into making jingles', says Ahmer Naqvi, who worked on Pakistan's first English TV Channel, Dawn TV.

There is a broad consensus amongst the Pakistani musicians that Coke Studio has indeed become a benchmark of quality. Music production in the country will now be judged in relation to Coke Studio. But there is also an unmistakable feeling that it has become repetitive and predictable. 'There was more creativity in the first two seasons', says Salman Albert. 'Now all songs have the same sound. Every song should have its own sound, music arrangement should be varied. New players should be introduced for each song. They have to do something radically new now to stay at the top.' Gumby agrees: 'it has become predictable and people have started taking it for granted. But Rohail has a certain sound and sensibility and I have no problems with it. For me, the first two seasons were more open-ended and by the fourth season we did not have much creative input.' Perhaps this is why Gumby does not take part in Season 5; he has left for other projects providing a space for new producers to bring a fresh perspective. Tina Sani echoes similar sentiments. 'Yes, it has become somewhat formulaic and a pattern seems to be followed. But there is no problem with it. We shouldn't be too pushy. What Coke Studio should avoid doing is chasing its own tail. Focus on making newer things. We should all encourage it.'

Such self-reflection and criticism is a good sign. Perhaps the most promising development is that Coke Studio has spurred other ideas on similar lines. Because of the unprecedented success of Coke Studio corporate sponsors now are keen to support more ventures that promote quality music. One example is Uth Records ('Uth' is pronounced 'Youth') which is sponsored by Ufone, a national mobile phone company. It is a reality show where aspiring musicians, irrespective of age and background, who have not yet released an album, are paired with industry professionals to produce a single. The show, produced by Gumby, just completed Season 2 and has received over 4,000 submissions by young musicians all over the country.

Even for artists not in music, Coke Studio serves as an inspiration. 'As a filmmaker, it has given me the belief that somebody like me can do something new and challenging,' says Ahmer Naqvi. 'It has also given me confidence in the audience too. If I do something that is sophisticated, the audience is going to come up to it.'

If we judge the cultural scene in Pakistan on its own terms, the distance it has travelled from twenty years ago is heartening — given that the political instability has persisted and the country has spent every year firefighting a different sort of wildfire. But the experiment called Coke Studio much like Pakistan itself continues to chart an unpredictable way forward—albeit with far greater aplomb.

DISCOVERING THE MATRIX

Muneeza Shamsie

Ever since I was a child growing up in Karachi I have been aware that the usage of words is a matter of paramount importance. My father, Isha'at Habibullah, an executive in a British multinational, had been educated in England from the age of eight. He read the *Illiad* in Greek, threw in Latin phrases to reinforce his arguments, and was immensely conscious of good English, the dominant language in our home and our social milieu. My mother, Jahanara Habibullah, however, spoke beautiful Urdu, her first language. She received a private education in Urdu, Arabic and Persian and also learnt English. After Partition, she exchanged copious letters with her two sisters in Rampur, which had become a part of India.

Her family included great poets and patrons of art and literature. One, Fakhra Masuduzzafar Khan, was a gifted artist. She illustrated the verses of the celebrated poet Ghalib with fluid pencil drawings of women with large slanting eyes, wavy tresses and swirling attire. My mother treasured these as she did a letter by their eldest sister, Rafat Zamani Begum of Rampur: it was entitled 'Pakistani Behen Key Naam' (in the name of my Pakistani sister) and presented by a Rampur scribe in formal black calligraphy. When I acquired my first copy of *The Arabian Nights* I was told that Rafat was a 'true-life Sheherezade'. Once upon a time, she created extraordinary tales – positive cliff-hangers – in the tradition of the Urdu dastaan to entertain her kinsman and husband, the ruler of Rampur. To the best of my knowledge these tales were never recorded; they now belong to that lost genre of sub-continental women: the oral tale. My mother also composed wedding poems (*sehras*) for her brothers and her children. After Partition she contributed autobiographical articles to Urdu-language Indian journals, describing the sumptuous, almost forgotten customs and rituals she had witnessed. She incorporated extracts from these artices in her memoir, *Remembrance of Days Past: Glimpses of a Princely State During The Raj (*2001).

My mother was a tall, spectacular beauty, with a sensitivity, gentleness and innocence that added to her charm. Her home was the pride and centre of her world. She didn't know where to turn when my father fell seriously ill: to her it seemed the end of everything. Her sisters urged her to write down her memories to help keep her together. Slowly, she started to jot down vignettes, which she returned to after my father died in 1991. She received a great deal of support and encouragement in this endeavour from a family friend, the distinguished Urdu writer and scholar Shanul Haq Haqqi. Finally she cyclostyled the completed manuscript for relatives and others, and gave a copy to Ameena Saiyid, the Managing Director of Oxford University Press (OUP) in Karachi. She thought the matter would end there. But Ameena wanted to publish it, albeit in English translation as she had not yet started OUP's Urdu programme.

Remembrance was illustrated extensively with old family photographs. My mother includes family history and anecdotes along with detailed descriptions of the musical, literary and culinary traditions of the Rampur court as well as its sumptuous celebrations permeated by music, poetry and song for almost every occasion: for the rainy season, marriages, births, religious festivals and even a coronation durbar. My daughter Kamila Shamsie drew on this account for her second novel *Salt and Saffron*.

The memoir describes her transition from life in the women's quarters (*zenana*) into the outside world, a change precipitated when Fakhra, her sister, developed tuberculosis. Her uncle, Saiduzzafar Khan, was an Edinburgh-trained doctor and founding Professor at King George's Medical College, Lucknow. He advised treatment in Switzerland. My grandfather, Sahibzada Sir Abdus Samad Khan, duly made arrangements. As was the norm, a journey to Europe meant Fakhra and my mother, aged seventeen and sixteen respectively, discarded *purdah*, as did their mother. In *Remembrance* my mother says, 'in those days it was unheard of for a young *purdah nashin* girl to leave India', and it caused a furore. Fakhra's fiancé broke off their engagement. Their grandmother 'could not endure the pain of seeing us leave for such a distant country and also without *purdah*. She passed away a few days later.'

My mother describes her excitement at the new world which unfolded before her. They sailed to Venice, spent a month at a sanatorium in Montana, and once Fakhra was well, they travelled to London. Life in India would never be the same again. On their return, they plunged into a glamorous whirl of parties, balls, *shikar*, and summers in Mussoorie: there she met my father, a childhood friend of Saiduzzafar's son, Mahmud, who is best remembered today as the Marxist Sahibzada Mahmuduzzafar Khan. My mother married of her own choice in 1942, and moved to Lahore where my father was posted. She mentions with pride his distinguished career in Pakistan's private sector.

She was eighty-four when *Remembrance*, her first book, was published in 2001. In the same year Kamila's novel *Salt and Saffron* appeared, as did my anthology *Leaving Home*. An Indian journal ran reviews of each – by mother, daughter and grand-daughter – on three consecutive pages. Suddenly people began referring to our 'literary line' and our 'literary genes'. My mother was particularly excited at OUP's publication of the Urdu version in 2003, 'because you see, these are my own words'. On another occasion, when she had been working until late on her manuscript, she said, 'I just couldn't stop. Now I know why you write.'

My mother lived long enough to see the advance copies of the Urdu edition. On the last night of her life she rang my father's sister, Tazeen Faridi. 'All these years', she told Tazeen, 'I was turned into a housewife and made useless! I should have been a writer!' She died peacefully in her sleep in the early hours of the morning. Her book lay on her bedside table, with pencil markings to indicate the passages she planned to read at her book launch (which became a wonderful memorial instead). On the lower shelf sat five other books: two anthologies by me, three novels by Kamila.

My aunt Tazeen was bowled over by my mother's last words. She knew, as I did, that such a self-revelation at eighty-six was momentous indeed. Tazeen and I were kindred spirits though we had very different personalities. She was a fiery social worker and feminist. She had participated in the Pakistan movement, done relief work in Pakistan's refugee camps, travelled in a donkey cart for development projects in Lyari, a Karachi slum, and was a founder member of the historic All Pakistan Women's Association (APWA): she later became its president. She lived near us in Karachi. Her husband and my father had both become heads of their respective multinational firms. She understood why I needed a life beyond the domestic sphere, as she did. I found my voice through journalism and the reclusive act of writing and criticism; Tazeen was an extroverted and dedicated activ-

ist. For her, words had to be translated into deeds. As a child, I assumed she
was a writer; she used to contribute articles to the Pakistani press on issues
related to welfare and women's empowerment. In 1960 she wrote a book,
The Changing Role of Women in Pakistan.

Inam Fatima Habibullah

From Tazeen I learnt that her activism was influenced by her pioneering
mother, Inam Fatima Habibullah, the Muslim League activist, reformer,
welfare worker and writer. When I was growing up, I perceived Inam Fatima
as a tiny, soft-spoken, gentle and widowed lady, who continued to live in a
greatly changed, decaying post-Partition Lucknow. There would be these
Chekhovian family gatherings (subject to visas and Indo-Pakistan hostilities)
where her children and their spouses would chat, reminisce, quarrel and
then go their own way. She always spoke Urdu and was very keen that I
should not forget my faith and culture. At nine, I had been sent away to
boarding school in England. My trips to Pakistan every second year often
included a tour to Lucknow and Rampur. I also wrote Inam Fatima letters
from Sussex, in childlike, increasingly deteriorating Urdu. She was very
appreciative of the effort.

During my early years in England, she published a slim book of prayers,
translated by her from Arabic into Urdu, which she gave me. She also
brought out *Nazar-e-Aqeedat* (c.1955), a collection of Urdu stories about the
Prophet which she wrote for her grandchildren. The book begins:

'Waris, Wajahat, Nazli, Shama, Muneeza, I said to my children, until now
you have listened to many stories, but I want to tell you some true stories,
about true events. Will you listen with all your heart?

All of them answered "Yes!"

Then listen. My beloved children.'

I was thrilled to see my name published in a book – and in the opening
sentence too!

The photographs I have of the young Inam Fatima bear no resemblance to
the grandmother I knew: they reveal a woman with dark, determined eyes,
a strong square jaw and carefully arranged waves of hair peeping out from
the gauzy sari over her head. Tazeen gradually filled me in on her early life.
Inam Fatima had grown up in purdah in a scholarly family and was educated
at home. Her humanitarian work was influenced by her *purdah*-observing

mother, who stayed in her village during a cholera epidemic to tend to the sick. Inam Fatima and her elder sister, Nisar Fatima, both married 'progressive', university-educated, feudal landlords. Both men were good friends, active in public life, and belonged to that order, the Taluqdars of Oudh, which Nisar Fatima's celebrated daughter, Attia Hosain, would capture so vividly in *Phoenix Fled* (1953), a collection of stories, and her novel, *Sunlight on a Broken Column* (1961).

Inam Fatima's husband, my grandfather, Shaikh Mohammed Habibullah, a strong-willed autocrat, was among the earliest Indians to serve in the colonial civil service. He admired the English greatly. Rather more unusual was his criticism of feudalism. He would not allow his young sons to visit their hereditary estate for fear that they would develop grandiose notions and grow up idle. He wanted them to have a profession and resolved to educate them in England. In 1920, his three boys left India for England; the youngest, my father Ishaat, did not return to India for sixteen years except for a brief visit after leaving school and joining Oxford.

In 1924, Inam Fatima travelled to England. She was accompanied by her husband (she refers to him as Sahib) and their bright, much-indulged, English-speaking daughter, Tazeen, aged five. She has recorded that momentous journey in a travelogue *Tasiraat-e-Safar-Europe* (Impression of a Journey to Europe). Re-reading *Tasiraat* today, I am riveted.

Inam Fatima had never seen a city as large as Bombay, nor indeed the sea; she is enchanted by the play of light upon the water and the sight of flying fish. But she is worried about the food on board the ship. Is it *halal*, permissible, or not? She dares not eat anything except boiled vegetables. She asks Sahib to consult a Turkish gentleman identified as a learned *alim*. He is an official in Ataturk's new government. He answers with disdain: why should she doubt the contents of any dish unless she has witnessed the fact that it is forbidden? He proceeds to make disparaging remarks about India and Indian Muslims, which includes an obnoxious attack on *purdah*. Sahib loses patience and puts him in his place. But Inam Fatima wants to learn more about women in Turkey. She questions him on women's empowerment, and education: she wants Muslim girls to learn Arabic and train Indian Muslim teachers. Soon the Turkish gentleman is quite won over: he sends her translations of works by Turkish women writers. She had been in *purdah* until she left for England. I have no idea if she was already involved in welfare work, or if she had been active in the women's conferences and clubs in India. These were part of a larger reform movement which included the establishment of schools for Indian girls and the birth of Urdu magazines for women. Inam Fatima's *Tasiraat* reveals that she is quite conversant with the reformist discourse of Indian Muslims of her day. She believes that the key to the betterment of Indian Muslims lies in a proper understanding of the scripture, which to her is perfectly compatible with modernity and change. This theme re-occurs, somewhat exhaustingly, throughout, including references to lectures by Islamic scholars in London and conversations with Muslims, both Indian and British.

In *Tasiraat*, Inam Fatima's detailed descriptions of London and its tourist attractions, including Crystal Palace, provide a vivid glimpse of an intact pre-World War II city and the hub of Empire. She reads newspapers assiduously and is fascinated by court cases. She takes a dim view of English food however, including that choice English meal – roast meat (*bhuna gosht*) and boiled vegetables (*ubli hui sabzi*). She is traumatised by her first visit to the 'theatre': a variety performance with a scantily dressed dancer displaying bare skin who keeps throwing herself against men. Later she goes to a popular play at the Haymarket. The plot revolves around an Indian Raja who, despite a splendid English education, has failed to imbibe true Englishness – in other words, humanity (*insaniaat*). Surrounded by prostrating yogis and *dhoti*-clad men, the bejewelled Raja aids and abets a crime, and compounds it by planning to kidnap and marry an Englishwoman and murder her husband. Inam Fatima records that the play depicts Indians as savages. She was deeply pained by it.

The whole is overlaid by her emotional journey, as a mother, beginning with her yearning to see her boys again, her undiluted joy in their company and the days of deep depression when she has to leave them. Her close bond with her homesick sons, Ali Bahadur "Sonny", Enaith "Bubbles" and Isha'at, highlights the magnitude of Inam Fatima's sacrifice, though she never complains. She is only grateful that she has the opportunity to see them again. She never doubts that they are receiving the best education possible.

At the end of the journey, a conversation of great import takes place. Sahib suggests that now she has travelled so much she can discard her purdah in Lucknow. She agrees, but adds that 'if I am to lead a life outside purdah then it will be spent in the service of nation and community.' She was ostracised and shunned by many when she finally discarded purdah. This did not deter her. She became Lucknow's Municipal Commissioner, and set up the Muslim League's women's wing in 1938, having been elected to the 1937 Legislative Assembly. She set up schools for girls and fought for Tazeen's right to attend university, whereas Tazeen's father wanted her to be educated at home, followed by finishing school in Switzerland.

Attia Hosain

In the 1920's, an increasing number of privileged girls began to attend English medium schools. Inam Fatima's widowed sister, Nisar Fatima, sent her daughter Attia to the La Martiniere School and later, the Isobella Thoburn College. Attia became the first woman from a feudal family to graduate from Lucknow University. She married Inam Fatima's eldest son, 'Sonny', on his return from England. I grew up hearing that they had eloped. But it transpired that they were the first in the family to defy the age-old custom of arranged marriages. They declared, against all prevalent norms of propriety, that they were in love and wanted to marry. It was a scandal.

Sonny, a civil servant, was awarded an MBE for his work during World War II and posted to the High Commission in London in 1946. After Partition, the family retained their British citizenship. When I arrived in England to study, Attia was working for the BBC Urdu Service and had published *Phoenix Fled*, which remains a particular favourite of mine. Its tight, evocative tales present a finely-tuned distillation of a world that had been passed on to me by my elders through conversations. My favourite is the much anthologised title story, about an old woman abandoned in her home, confusing the violence of Partition with that of the 1857 uprising against the British. In 'White Leopard' a young aristocrat recognises the innate human qualities of a man branded a dacoit, while 'Time is Irredeemable' and the 'First Party' describe the huge differences between traditional young women and the westernised men they are married to. In all of Attia's fiction there are images of the Lucknow I had glimpsed. Those beautiful houses with dark woodwork, arched doorways and coloured window panes filtering bands of red, blue and green light, which so fascinated me as a small child: an ambience very different to my two other worlds, urban Karachi and lush rural England.

The publication of Attia's novel *Sunlight on a Broken Column* caused tremendous excitement in the family and our Karachi social circle. But when I returned to my boarding school in Sussex and tried to talk about it, no one was interested. 'What is this novel you and your sister keep talking about?', a teacher asked me, 'I've never heard of it.' So *Sunlight* was consigned to a private space; a subject I could not discuss, any more than I could mention Inam Fatima's books.

In *Sunlight*, the characters seemed to echo aspects of so much that I had witnessed or heard, because in 1947 our family was divided between India and Pakistan. This led to stark political differences between siblings, including violent, often vicious, arguments over Partition at the dining table. The narrator, Laila, an orphaned literary heiress, sees her secure traditional world transformed when her grandfather dies and she is sent to live with her anglicised uncle and his wife. The novel describes her friendships, college life and the return of her two cousins from England; they bring with them new influences, new ideas, new lifestyles. Laila's struggle for empowerment coincides with India's struggle for independence. Attia describes the polarisation between the Congress and the Muslim League. A host of characters provide a panoramic glimpse of a gracious, elegant and glittering culture. There is also biting criticism of the feudal system and its iniquities.

In Inam Fatima's *Tasiraat*, there are frequent references to Dr. Saiduzzafar Khan. In 1920, he too sent his twelve-year-old son Mahmud to school in England. When Inam Fatima met Mahmoud, she was impressed by his passionate concern for reform, progress and education in India. At Oxford Mahmud became my father's mentor and introduced him to Marxism. In India his left-wing views influenced Attia. He married a fellow Marxist, the gynaecologist Rashid Jahan, author of *Wo*, a highly regarded collection of feminist stories and plays. In 1932, Rashid Jahan and Mahmud co-authored with Ahmed Ali and Sajjad Zaheer the radical story collection *Angarey* (Sparks), which outraged the orthodox and was banned by the government of India. This began the Progressive Writers Movement, generating a modern and dynamic literary discourse that transformed sub-continental literature.

Zohra Segal and Hamida Saiduzzafar

One person who remembers this era is the Indian actress Zohra Segal, who celebrates her hundredth birthday as I write this. Zohra's film and television credits include *Jewel in the Crown*, *The Courtesans of Bombay* and *Tandoori Nights*. Occasionally she would come to Pakistan to visit her sister Uzra Butt, a television and stage actress, in Lahore. They would travel to Karachi, where I would meet them at my mother's gatherings. I realised that both sisters must have battled against many taboos and prejudices in the old days, because in traditional society the performing arts were not considered professions fit for respectable women.

Zohra Segal's memoir *Stages: The Art and Life of Zohra Segal* (1996) describes her discovery of dance. She was educated in purdah at Queen Mary College, Lahore. After her mother's death, her uncle, Dr Saiduzzafar, took her under his wing. When she left school, Zohra wanted to attend drama school in England. Her uncle agreed to this; and she travelled with him by car across India, Persia, and Turkey to Europe. Her wardrobe included 'a lovely beige silk burqa with a transparent georgette veil to cover my face and breeches made specially for me like jodhpurs, which I wore with shirts and a jacket'. The burqa was discarded as she travelled westwards. They met up with Mahmud en route. A chance remark by him led to her resolving to become a dancer: her uncle took her to Germany and placed her in the Mary Wigman School of Dance. She toured Europe and America with the actor Uday Shankar and his troupe and worked with the pioneering Prithviraj Theatre in Bombay.

Mahmud lives on as a much-loved family legend. I have no memory of him, but I did meet Mahmud's sister, Hamida Saiduzzafar, a highly regarded eye surgeon, in Rampur. She was a warm, affectionate, unassuming woman. She died suddenly, leaving behind fragments of a slim, but immensely valuable memoir, published posthumously: *Autobiography: Hamida Saiduzzafar Khan 1921-1988* edited by Lola Chatterjee (1996).

I was fascinated by Hamida's narrative. She creates vivid images of her family, including her father's remarkable career. She also tells of his love for mountaineering and hunting. When she was very small, he seemed a rather absent, forbidding figure who frightened her and never consulted her mother on any decision. At that age, her mother was her great refuge. She was a shy and retiring woman, although she had discarded purdah at her husband's behest, entertained his Indian and British guests in style, and learnt English from Mahmud's governess.

Hamida tells of her first meeting with Mahmud when she was seven and he was eighteen. He had come to India for a brief trip and soon they were firm friends. She comments on his great gifts for drawing, painting and sculpture, which he neglected because he 'devoted his time and energy to politics'. He introduced her to western classical music and jazz. He returned from Oxford, a Marxist and nationalist, wearing a Gandhi cap and determined to speak only Urdu. His radical views upset his father; his marriage to Rashid Jahan, without the normal celebrations, upset his mother. But Hamida found in Rashid Jahan a kindred spirit, a sister-in-law who was 'great fun and a wonderful conversationalist' and who 'had been a tomboy too'. Rashid Jahan would often tell Hamida about the lives of 'women, their problems and their suffering in a male-dominated world', and read out the stories she had written. Hamida's account of her medical education in Lucknow describes the prejudice displayed by male professors, who believed that women doctors should not be taken seriously. They would get married and leave the profession anyway. Until 1945, Hamida tells us, it was the norm for women doctors in North India to specialise only in gynaecology. But she wanted to be an ophthalmologist. Despite her father's support, she had to fight a considerable battle before she was accepted in the Eye Department.

I was amazed at how little I had known about her. I wondered what course our conversations could have taken as I too was interested in science. I was the only girl in my class to take chemistry at A Level. My headmistress in England wanted me to study science at university but there were no careers for women scientists in Pakistan. In fact, there were hardly any careers for women at all. My parents wanted to send me to finishing school, an enthusiasm he shared with his father. I was appalled. Finally a compromise was reached. My headmistress insisted that I would benefit greatly from London's cultural life; and I was sent to Queen's, an exclusive secretarial college in South Kensington.

I returned to Pakistan at nineteen, married at twenty-four, and soon made another discovery. My mother's close relative in Delhi, Hamida Sultan Ahmed, was an Urdu writer. She was active in Delhi's Urdu scene and came to Pakistan occasionally. She lived in a traditional Old Delhi home with a large courtyard, flanked by long verandas with stone pillars and fluted arches. This was the world into which my maternal grandmother, Hamida Sultan's first cousin, was born. Hamida Sultan had published critical works and novels of which *Rang Mahal* (1960) was the most noted. Set in old Delhi, *Rang Mahal* is fascinating: it seems to me to be the women's answer to Ahmed Ali's evocative and nostalgic English novel *Twilight in Delhi*.

Hamida Sultan recreates, without sentimentality, traditional purdah life in an aristocratic Old Delhi household in the 1920's and 1930's. With wonderful and unflinching eye for detail and dialogue, she captures the segregated household of a wise, widowed matriarch and the intricate relationships and hierarchies of daughters-in-law, children and grandchildren. Young girls are married off in their early teens; childbirth is often life-threatening; there are tales of suppressed sexuality, undying love, mismatched couples, miserable marriages – and happy ones. At the heart of the drama, there is the lively, mischievous and literary Chammo. The decline of the Raj and the emergence of the independence movements and modernity are explored amid descriptions of changing seasons and their rhythms, the clothes, ornaments and rituals.

Kamila Shamsie

Hamida Sultan derived genuine delight from my love of literature. By the time I discovered her work, I was a part of a lively English language literary circle in Karachi and had given much thought to colonialism, nationalism, literature and gender. I also taught music and mime to mentally challenged children. All this fed into my journalism, although for years, I wrote in secret because I had no confidence. Eventually my articles began to be accepted in the English language press. In 1982, *Dawn*, a major English language paper, asked me to contribute to a new magazine supplement. Among other assignments, I was asked to interview authors and write book reviews.

My younger daughter Kamila was around eleven when she announced that she wanted to be a writer. I am often asked what I did to encourage her. I don't think I did anything. But the fact that she grew up, as she says, in a house full of contemporary novels must have helped. As a young girl, she was often busy writing stories. I have 'always responded', she says, 'as a proud mother rather than a critic'.

It is indeed difficult for a mother to be critical of her daughter's work. I simply derive great pride and pleasure from reading her work. While she was growing up, I was anxious not to burden her with gratuitous advice and expectations. Later, when she was at college and working on her first novel which became *In The City by The Sea*, I was really struck by the difference between her first and second draft: in the latter, she jettisoned huge chunks of rather nice writing because it did not impel, or add, to the plot or narrative. I thought, well, if she can do that now, she should be all right.

In an article in the *Guardian*, 'A Long Loving Literary Line', she says she 'grew up with a curious mix of awareness and ignorance' about her matrilineal literary heritage. Since she wanted to write English fiction from childhood, at first she did not think relatives writing in Urdu or producing English memoirs had much to do with her. But she was very aware of Attia, her great aunt, who had attained Kamila's 'great dream – publication by a house at the center of English literature'.

Attia was very ill when she heard that Kamila's first novel had been accepted for publication. I am told that she smiled, shut her eyes and slipped into a coma. I often wondered what she would have thought of Kamila's subsequent work, particularly her second novel *Salt and Saffron* about Partition, which belongs to the same matrix as *Sunlight*. Often I find random family resonances in Kamila's novels, which explore the troubled times in which we live. But the one trope runs through all: the women she portrays across the generations refuse to succumb to stereotypes. Over the years Kamila has come to understand the importance of growing up in an environment where 'the written word mattered so deeply'.

Looking at all these books produced in a single family, it seems to me that they represent the long and continuous struggle of Subcontinental women to assert their voice and claim their right to speak. But more than that, for me and my family, they embody a tradition that nurtured us. It will remain with us – always.

NOT TALKING ABOUT PAKISTAN

Taymiya R Zaman

I drew a secret line around the borders of Pakistan and rarely stepped over it. In the fall of 2007, I began teaching Islamic history at a small liberal arts college in San Francisco; even though my classes on South Asia and the Middle East could easily have included Pakistan, I made sure to exclude Pakistan from all my syllabi. To avoid ever having to talk about Pakistan, I changed the name of a course a predecessor had titled 'History of South and Southeast Asia', to 'Indian Civilisations'. This now meant that the course took a leisurely route through the Indus Valley Civilisation, the coming of the Aryans, the spread of Jainism and Buddhism in North India, the rise of the Mughal Empire and concluded with British colonial rule and the formation of India and Pakistan in 1947. But, after an emotionally charged lecture on Partition, I would begin a section on modern India and say nothing of Pakistan after the moment of its creation. My class, 'The Modern Middle East', covered American wars in Afghanistan but my syllabus screeched to a halt at the Pakistan border. Although the country inevitably featured in class discussions about US foreign policy, I assigned no readings on Pakistan. In my other classes, I stayed away from the twentieth century, which meant that the question of Pakistan never arose.

Outside the classroom too, I was something of an expert at not talking about Pakistan. This was a feat, given the interest that Pakistan generated. Being Pakistani meant that well-meaning students would frequently tackle me in corridors and ask me what I thought about 'the current situation' in Pakistan. Most of the time, this was an excuse to tell me what they thought, namely that America needed to bomb the hell out of Pakistan because the country was a den for terrorists. In some instances, the student would add, as a considerate afterthought, that he hoped my family was safe. I would respond to student comments such as these with non-committal statements about the banality of the nation-state. My retreat into vagueness would diffuse the conversation, and

I would hurry away. This constant bombardment and the defensive manoeuvres it called for left me with little energy for words, and no space at all to know what I thought about the Pakistan in which people around me were interested. What I did know was that there was a Pakistan somewhere that belonged to me and it was under attack; this meant that I needed to protect it because doing so was the same as protecting myself.

When asked to give guest lectures on Pakistan, I would analyze the politics of talking about Pakistan instead, and refuse to discuss the place directly. Once, I was asked to make a presentation on the Pakistan Earthquake of 2005, and I agreed only because I trusted the professor who had invited me to speak to her class. I was tired of images of suffering, helpless brown people waiting for Angelina Jolie's benevolence, and I wanted the class to know about the heroic efforts on the part of Pakistanis for their own people. I saw my talk as an offensive on behalf of Pakistan rather than the solitary, defensive war I was fighting. In another instance, at a student event focused on injustices around the world (which included the usual images of the suffering and the brown and the female and the poor), I spoke about the injustice of intervening in other countries in the name of justice, a point I would make in my own classes without directly referencing Pakistan. Both talks were well-received, and I appreciated the sensitivity and intelligence of the students with whom I spoke afterwards. Students such as these helped me remember that there were possibilities that lay outside the daily blur of pain through which I experienced my surroundings.

In those years, even among members of the South Asian and Arab diaspora, I found myself repeatedly defending Pakistan against constant attacks. I don't remember each encounter, only a vague combination of disappointment and irritation at the end of evenings meant to be a reprieve from work, and shock that suddenly it was perfectly appropriate for people to talk about the failures of Pakistan even in the presence of Pakistanis. I remember heated arguments with Arab men who would bleat about how 'their women' had more freedom than Pakistani women. In these instances, I would refuse to back down until the man in question had conceded that he knew nothing about either women or Pakistan. The other women at the table would watch silently or make feeble attempts to change the subject. Or, there were cab rides in which I lied to cab drivers about where I was from, because there had been too many instances of being held captive audience to a stranger's musings about how the place I called home needed to be bombed.

Many conversations about Pakistan would contain the expectation that perhaps I might have more to say on the failures of the country (these usually revolved around an excess of Islam and a general shortage of women's rights) by virtue of being from there. But this would be coupled with the assumption that I could not be entirely objective about Pakistan given that I was, after all, from there. Unless I nodded and agreed like a good native informant on the failed state that was Pakistan, I was either out of touch with reality, or sentimental about the place for unknown reasons. The word 'Pakistan' itself would summon up a cluster of images with fire in them – assassinations, suicide bombs, and car burnings, and always the bearded men. But my map of everyday violence in San Francisco was populated by several actors of whom none had beards and none believed themselves to be violent, but whose attacks invaded almost every space I occupied.

Two instances of kindness stand out because each happened when I was feeling more ragged than usual. In the first, a Palestinian shopkeeper offered me his condolences on the disintegration of my country. 'I'm so sorry at what you must be going through,' he said, 'being this far away from family, reading the news, and dealing with everyone's stupid questions.' I had responded by saying that things had to be bad if a Palestinian felt sorry for me. 'I had the same thought myself!' he had exclaimed, and we had both laughed uproariously. In the second, I had been at one of many gatherings in which Obama's victory was being celebrated. I had thought about drone attacks and the escalation of American invasions into Pakistan. But the suffering of a small, distant country seemed almost inappropriate to bring up in the midst of celebration about American's first black president. As I prepared to leave, an American colleague told me quietly that she was sorry that I had to keep hearing people celebrate. 'I know what this means for your home,' she said, and for the first time, I allowed myself to tell someone about the dread in my stomach and the difficulty I was having sleeping. I left before she could see my tears.

Of the first three years I taught in San Francisco, what I remember most is the thickening of my silence, and a stubborn, bordering on outright perverse desire not to share Pakistan with anyone, as though the act of sharing the country would dilute what made it mine. I had no words for the twisting feeling in the center of my chest for Pakistan, the knot of pain in my right shoulder, homesickness so intense that it had in fact become physical pain. The more Pakistan appeared in newspapers, the more difficult it became to explain the place. Even if I tried, I would be one voice against too many burning images. I began to pretend to be on the phone when taking cabs, I avoided colleagues interested in Pakistan, and I stopped going to Muslim social gatherings after realising that Pakistan-bashing would be a central theme in these. The sheer fatigue of deflecting questions left me with little room to know what it was I would say if allowed to speak on my own terms, or even what these terms would be. Most of the time, I maintained what looked like Pakistan-conversation to others, but involved defensive maneuvers that brought on the kind of exhaustion an athlete might feel at the end of a harrowing race she has lost despite her best efforts.

When I began to consider taking a fourth-year sabbatical to go to Pakistan, I was told, predictably, that this was a bad idea. The country was volatile and dangerous. No writing would get done and I desperately needed academic publications if I wanted tenure. I planned to teach while I was there—for both the fall semester of 2010 and the spring semester of 2011—and this would take even more time away from research and writing. Was I out of my mind to risk losing tenure at a private liberal arts college in San Francisco? But I suspected that something much larger was at stake if I didn't leave and go back home, to the place I had surrounded by a silence so thick that I was terrified that I had lost my capacity to put feeling into words, to write anything at all. I had always been certain of my ability to write, and the loss of language was paralyzing, as was the silence into which I had retreated.

Landing in Karachi is like running into the arms of a lover I've been forbidden to see for years. My sabbatical leave has been granted and I'm home. No one searches me in this country. Here is the place I finally feel safe. There's nothing menacing about the immigration officers. I laugh and joke with them, produce both my passports, the blue American one and the green Pakistani one, and eventually saunter off, grinning. I'm home. And I'm going to be home for a year, the longest time I've spent in Pakistan since I left for college thirteen years ago. When I was in college and the country hadn't yet come under siege, I took it for granted and didn't miss it much. But after I began graduate school in September 2001, it became increasingly difficult to leave and go back to the US after my visits home. I would dread the interrogations of Homeland Security, the cold, long winters in Ann Arbor, and the constant feeling of alienation that comes from being asked where you are from originally and then hearing people talk about where-you-are-from-originally as a dangerous place.

Even though I spent a great deal of time being homesick in graduate school, I wanted a PhD in history, so there wasn't a whole lot to do but get on planes and get on with the degree. I figured that I could go home when I was done. But in my last two years of graduate school, I was told that getting a PhD in history would be a waste if I picked up and left for the homeland. Instead I needed to Get a Job, Publish Things, and Be Successful. I didn't have a counter-argument, so I applied for jobs. On the job market, I told myself that I would go back to Pakistan unless I landed a tenure-track job at a small liberal arts college in New York, Boston, Chicago, or San Francisco. These parameters were impossible; I had only written two chapters of my dissertation and would be competing with people who had completed theirs for jobs in desirable locations. But after interviewing in San Francisco, I flew back to Ann Arbor thoroughly charmed and invested in the place. When I got a job offer, I cancelled my other interviews and accepted immediately. The academic job market crashed the next year.

The semester I began teaching in San Francisco, Pakistan had become the country around which I built walls to prevent it from being attacked in conversation. From the handyman who came to my apartment to fix a bookshelf and began ranting about terrorism when he found out where I was from, to the woman at my phone company who couldn't give me rates to Pakistan without commenting on the place, being Pakistani meant that like the country, nothing was off limits when it came to the kinds of attacks to which I was subjected. The sense of threat would begin after I would stumble out to the airport in San Francisco, bleary-eyed and homesick, and a stranger in a uniform would take me aside, search my bags, and leave my clothes in a heap somewhere. The questioning would begin, particular in its brutality. Why was I bringing back 'native costumes' to America? Why did my parents move back to a place like Pakistan when they could have lived here, in America, the country where I was born? And there would be the impossibility of saying 'because of you' to the man sifting through my things. At the end of the interrogation, an immigrations officer would finally stamp my American passport and say 'Welcome home.'

The threat would continue at work; a particularly vexing colleague who has now learned names like Salman Taseer and Benazir Bhutto would greet my return by drone-bombing me with his latest predictions about the steady demise of Pakistan and jokes about the duplicity of Pakistanis. Or, he would ask me about 'the current situation,' the amorphous phrase that has come to represent the entire country in the inquiries of the well-meaning. The last time I spoke to him, he said I must be happy to be back in America. I had thought of the airport in Karachi, and the road to my house. I had thought of my mother's garden at night, with flowers and pools of water, and of the peace that waits for me there. All this was safe somewhere in a place neither he nor a homeland security officer could ever reach. 'Oh, sure,' I had said lightly. 'I'm happy to be back.'

I'm home, I'm thinking, on the drive back from the airport in Karachi to house in which I grew up. There's no need for evasions here, no need for silence.

In the first class I teach in Lahore, the air seems to shimmer from the beginning. That September, something knotted suddenly unfurls. I'm in Pakistan. The line around it is no longer needed. My armor clanks to the floor. 'Let's talk about Pakistan,' I say to my students. And we do. There are no secrets to protect, no fear of being hurt from a stranger's inadvertent prodding of a private bruise. These are not strangers. I've never felt such complete trust while standing in front of a classroom, and it makes me remember my own years in college, and the openness with which I seemed to walk around, a product of being ten years younger, but also of being Pakistani before the country came under siege on so many fronts. My students draw out from me pain that I would not allow to see the light of day, and I trust them easily, and allow them to ask anything they like. This country belongs to all of us, and I'm not standing in front of a room alone, weighed down by belonging that no one else can understand.

'Look Taymiya, I know you love this place,' says Khadija, who I've known since I was thirteen. She's come to visit me in Lahore, and we are walking around on campus. 'But you don't know how hard it is to live here. Pakistan has a way of wringing us of the well-intentioned idealism we come back with. Trust me. It's not the country we grew up in.' I know what she means. There seems to be a collective trauma that has settled over Pakistan like a fog, and stories keep surfacing in everyday conversation—the house that washed away in the floods, the cousin blown up at a marketplace, the uncle who was shot, the father detained in prison in the US somewhere because he was at the wrong place at the wrong time. Another close friend tells me that her biggest heartbreak isn't a person, it's Pakistan. 'Be careful,' she says. 'You come back, this place welcomes you with open arms, and then it knifes you.'

There's a kind of lover you meet late at night even though your head is full of your friends' warnings and their concern. But then his car pulls up, silver and smooth and full of possibility, and you swear you've never felt more alive as you do in this instant. You join the world of other people in daylight, you pour tea and meet guests and go to your office, but there are hidden scratches on your arm, which you grazed when you ran out hurriedly to meet him, and you think of the open road and his sidelong glance and your heart speeds up. You forget about the warnings. Maybe he breaks everyone else's heart, but he won't break yours. And even if he does, you're not sure you care. I don't want to think about the damage Pakistan can cause me. I'm already damaged. And being here is the balm.

In late October, the moon hangs impossibly low. At night, the canal is gleaming moonlight and the reflections of trees. The air is beginning to cool down. It's soon going to be the season for steaming bowls of soup in cars, shawls and sweaters. Gas heaters will burn orange in darkened rooms. Later there's going to be the mist that envelops the city. Haniya, who I've known since college, is driving us to dinner at a restaurant she loves. But we have been stuck in a traffic jam for half an hour and I know she is annoyed. This kind of traffic jam is the bane of Pakistanis everywhere. A politician has blocked the road and no one can move. Haniya fiddles with the music. I peer out onto the road.

A woman is walking in our direction, obviously agitated, pounding on car windows. She comes to Haniya's window and raps on it. Haniya rolls her window down. The woman says her sister has been burned in an accident and she needs to get her to the hospital. Will we help her get the road open? I think of my sister Jawziya and how I would do the same for her. 'Yes,' we say. Car doors open, women and men rush out into the night. The woman argues with the police. The crowd backs her up. The policemen say they are doing their job. 'Is this politician's life worth more to you than my sister's?' she yells. They seem shamefaced. The crowd gathers momentum. A man says he is recording this because he is a journalist from GEO. The policemen open the road. This is the Pakistan I know and love, I'm thinking. These ordinary victories, nothing short of heroic. When the long-awaited winter fog descends on Lahore, I am convinced that the city is magic, and the magic is compounded because it will never make it to newspapers abroad. This magic is ours, you think, disappearing into the night with your secret lover, and no one needs to know.

Deeper into winter, Mav calls me early in the morning and says enough is enough, I am a Mughal historian and I need to go with her to the old city because what's the point of depriving her of my expertise? I crawl out of bed and go to her apartment. She drives us to Capri, where we order halwa puri, warm and sweet and delicious. We walk through the old city and I read her the inscriptions outside the Wazir Khan mosque, relieved that she doesn't know Farsi because I am out of practice. At night, she wants to buy flowers, and I soon learn that my new friend is the only person I know as obsessed with flowers as me. Many nights, we drive home with our arms full of heady, fragrant tuberoses, gladiolas in combinations of peach and pink, red and white, and always the motia and rose bracelets that smell like home. Mav likes mixing her colors. I like making entire combinations of one color. The man at what becomes our regular flower place loves both of us. The first time I went there, I refused to buy the waxy flowers from Dubai. My flower-patriotism had made him happy, and now he goes out of his way each time Mav and I show up.

News from the other country trickles its way to me all year. There's something about a mosque in New York that everyone is upset about. There's someone called Peter King and there are hearings of some sort. A cab driver gets stabbed for being Muslim. Mosques are being infiltrated with FBI agents and spray-painted with hate. Muslim activism is being arranged around the premise that Muslims are American too; the premise is banal and lacks dignity, but is necessary for these times. Later there's news of people holding a national celebration because Osama bin Laden got assassinated in a place called Pakistan. 'You're so lucky you are not here,' a friend from San Francisco says to me on the phone. 'It would make you sick—the jubilation, the crowds, and all the hatred for Muslims and Pakistanis.' I imagine my office in San Francisco, and the flurry of emails asking me if I want to give a guest lecture. I think of the questions in corridors and classrooms and the burden of having to respond to those. America seems the way Pakistan does from a distance, violent and dangerous. I hang up the phone. Khayyam and Aurangzeb want to meet for dinner, the night is starry, and someone is playing the guitar outside.

That winter, my apartment-mate Ned decides that I need to learn how to drive, even though I've been terrified of driving for as long as I can remember. With her, I take the car out to what seems like the edge of the city and drive by fields and trees, of which there's one that we both decide to climb. On another drive, we find the stream that feeds the fields and sit down to dip our feet in it. Or, we get lost, and feeling like Indiana Jones, I use the setting sun to navigate us back home. I thought I couldn't drive. I thought I had no sense of direction. This is not the case in the city where anything seems possible. When we return to campus, the car is covered with dust and the tank is nearly empty, and we stumble out of it brimming with triumph and elation. When it gets warmer, there's falsa juice at four in the morning with Haniya, who likes staying up late the way I do. We gulp down our falsa juice. 'This country,' Haniya declares, 'is like no place on earth'. I grin at her. 'Agreed,' I say, raising my glass. The falsa juice is cool and thick and there's nowhere else we want to be.

It's always so with a secret love, the one of whom all your friends disapprove. They tell you about his bad track record with women, her tendency to be fickle, things that are either common knowledge, or form rumors of uncommon proportion and against those you put moments in which you know your lover the best. His hair with the sun in it, her honey-gold voice, the thing in the air that burns between you, the smell of motia at night, a season with falsa juice and a moment which turns on the figure of a woman and the crowd behind her who is willing to stand up to policemen with guns. Against all that, you hold the worry of others and their warnings, and dismiss them the way poets dismiss the nasih for the mehbub. To some invisible holy force outside yourself you offer complete surrender. No one would fault you for not accepting the invitation to heartbreak. But you would be left with a day that is exactly like the one before it and the ones after.

It's a new semester and classes begin in late January. February ends with a hailstorm that coats the city in white, and after that, everyone feels the warmth in the air. The winter in Lahore is coming to an end. Ned and I have bought a takht for the balcony, perfect for chai in the evenings, and for breakfast in the mornings, which are still pleasant. There are few evenings left when sitting outside will be bearable, and we cherish each one. The sun is going to bear down on us, the electricity will go, petrol will run out, and everyone will want to emigrate. Days get warmer and warmer, but nights are still cool. The winter fog is the first to leave. I miss looking outside my window and watching couples walk through it, hand in hand early in the morning and late in the evening. I miss how it whittled down all the sharp edges of the sun and made mornings softer. After the fog leaves, the coolness of the air follows fast, and one morning, I wake up hot and uncomfortable. The heat makes the winter seem distant, as though it never happened.

Days in April begin too early, and their brightness is monotonous. Each day begins with the realisation that I can't hide from the things about being here that leave me troubled and edgy. Getting out of bed is an effort, the way it used to be in San Francisco, when each day felt like an assault from many sides. This semester, I realise I have lost some of the openness with which I began my first class. After Salman Taseer's death, we've been told to stay away from the topic of religion and blasphemy in the classroom and I am tense and anxious because there have been too many instances in which I have either been accused of attacking Islam or of defending Muslim fundamentalists.

At a conference, where I am presenting a paper on the pre-modern Muslim past, a young bearded student who has heckled every single female speaker begins to shout at me. He tells me I should be ashamed of myself for teaching students about the Mughals, who were bad Muslims. The stereotypes that both of us represent are staggering. I am an America-returned woman speaking in English about gender. He is a bearded Muslim male yelling at the woman for attacking Islam. What I feel, strangely enough, is betrayal. I'm on your side, I want to tell him. I've been threatened with violence, spat on, yelled at, and called names for being a Muslim. If anyone in my classrooms abroad says anything derogatory about angry, misogynistic Muslim men, I don't let them get away with it. My heart starts pounding and my hands and feet are cold. I respond by making fun of him, and I know that the sympathies of the room are with me. Now, I am angry at myself. He is a minority here by virtue of having a beard and he believes that something precious to him—Islam—is being attacked by me and he needs to defend it at all costs in a hostile environment. Don't I know that feeling? The reason I retreated into silence about Pakistan when it was being attacked was because I knew that if I started speaking, I would sound exactly like him.

I think of going to him and saying I'm sorry. But there's a chasm between us, and I'm not sure I can offer him anything for the kind of pain from which his anger springs. I express my discomfort to an old family friend who has been a professor for twenty-five years. He tells me that despite his silver hair, newly-bearded students feel quite comfortable coming up to him and asking him why he has not been seen at Friday prayers. In my time, he tells me, it would have been inconceivable for a student to question his elder like this. But, he says, mazhab now trumps adab even though for him and his teachers each was part of the other. 'It's what these kids see around them,' he tells me. 'We grew up in less turbulent times.' He says it helps to have one thing that stays still and unchanging within you when everything around you is on fire and you feel attacked from all sides. This, I understand. His eyes are sad. He has lived his life and doesn't regret spending it in Pakistan. But he worries about the country his generation has left behind.

That night, I'm at a dinner party and a feminist activist who has lived through the Zia years expresses interest in my work. I like her immediately, and we begin a long conversation about how literature has shaped our world views. The younger brother of a friend comes up to us and I introduce him to her. I tell him we were talking about poetry. He says that he would like to read more contemporary poetry from South Asia, and asks her for recommendations. Something freezes in the air. She stares at him coldly, and I see him through her eyes. He has a beard. He is wearing shalwar- kameez. Nothing else about him is relevant. 'Why do you want to read poetry?' she says. 'Isn't that against Islam? Just stick to the Quran.' He tries to engage her in conversation, and she turns away. She is also no longer interested in talking to me. 'I can't believe this!' I say to him later. He smiles. 'It happens all the time,' he says. 'Just chill. Or, if you really want to show me solidarity, start wearing the hijab. People who thought you were intelligent and cool won't want to be seen with you in public. I never thought I'd lose friends if I grew a beard but I did. Even if I shaved it off now, I don't know how I'd be friends with people whose loyalty to me was conditional in the first place.'

At another party, a woman becomes belligerent when I refuse a drink. She starts telling me about how 'the mullahs' are destroying Pakistan. She is proud, she says, of finding people who fast in Ramzan and eating in front of them. 'If I could have my way, I would shave every beard and rip off every hijab and drag the country into being secular and tolerant like myself.' I make a dig at her by saying something about secular fundamentalism. She dismisses me and says there is no such thing. She asks me why I don't drink. The skill with which I lied to cab drivers about where I was from comes back to me. 'I'm a recovering alcoholic,' I say. She doesn't believe me. I tell her I am sticking with my story because it's more acceptable to her than commitment to religion. This has an impact, and she doesn't ask me about drinking again.

The next time I meet her, she's talking about how the mullahs hate women. She's happy that Veena Malik told a mullah off on TV. I'm irritated and wonder if I can leave early. People like her are generic. They come to parties and you can't pass them a plate without them saying something or the other about the mullahs. I go out into the garden. It's nearing summer, the air is hot and still, and mosquitoes buzz around us. She follows me outside and lights a cigarette. 'Why do you hate mullahs?' I ask impulsively. She tells me she was married to one. She met her husband in college and they fell in love over the kinds of revolutionary plans students hatch late at night. But after they got married, her husband joined the Talbligh. 'It was worse than seeing him with another woman,' she says, lighting another. 'They took him away from me. Nothing I did was right. My hair was uncovered so I was shaming him in public, music was haram and I couldn't sing anymore even though he used to love my voice, and I was just an obstacle on his path to God. It was either me or God. Guess who won?' Again, I'm ashamed of myself. 'I'm sorry,' I fumble, 'I know you must have loved him and—.' She cuts me off. 'You can't love someone like that,' she says. She tells me she used to be religious too but bits of her faith kept disappearing until there was nothing left.

There's a god who lives here in Pakistan, who used to be khuda around the time I left for college, but who is now Allah. His name is etched onto the Mughal monuments of the city. Or it's written in the leaves of the tree outside my window, and in the patterns the stars make at night. When I pray to him, I ask for forgiveness. Sometimes it's because someone's pain has been thrown in my direction in the form of anger, and I've been unable to separate the two. Or I've been angry and trampled over another person's sacred values and then caused them pain. There are minefields in this place, and I respond by doing what I did in San Francisco. I draw a line around something I want to protect, and in Lahore, this is my classroom. In the class I am teaching now, I tell my students that we are living under siege, but this room is safe. We are going to have difficult conversations, and no one is allowed to disengage, not even me. This is the only way we can prepare for the country outside, and the attacks to which it subjects everyone who lives in it.

The trust that sustains the imaginary line around our classroom is difficult to build. Sometimes, we are angry with one another and confused about ourselves. The pain in the room is tangible when one person's sense of threat clashes with another's. I know there are times I've been irreverent towards things my students hold sacred, and I love them for the generosity with which they tolerate this. We talk about Pakistan, even when it gets difficult to reconcile one person's Pakistan with another's. And we talk about blasphemy, even when it means flooding the room with religious beliefs and their opposite and bracing ourselves for more hurt. We talk about how much we hate this place and we hurl our rage at each other and expect to be forgiven. Or, there are periods of calm in which we remember that we hate this place because we feel betrayed by it, and because somewhere underneath anger, there's love. I read them poetry from the Divan-i Shams-i-Tabrizi. The room is divided on the question of love and the price it extracts. On some days, there is laughter in the room, and complete understanding between us. Other days, in and out of the classroom, are exhausting, and I have to force myself to get through them.

I was naïve to think I would remain unaffected by the place I read about in newspapers. It has affected me. I am wracked with doubt, and often apprehensive and afraid. Did I come here like any other deluded expatriate, hoping to 'do something' for the country? What was I thinking? Your lover with the silver car is going to drive away and leave you devastated, and you won't be the first or the last. You may have defended him to your friends but he is in fact, exactly as they warned he would be—dangerous and unpredictable, entirely unconcerned about you—and your heart sinks when he drives away for the last time.

For the first time in years, I did not cry when I left Pakistan. I arrived in San Francisco on a characteristically cold day in June, and this time, when I was pulled aside and questioned by Homeland Security, I didn't feel angry or helpless. The questions seemed innocuous; they were just the questions of people who believed they were protecting their country, as though such a thing is even possible, as though a land enclosed by imaginary lines can ever belong to you or be yours to protect. My father jokes that wanting to emigrate is central to the experience of being Pakistani, and I understand this now. The indignity of being Muslim in America is still better, for many, than living in a country where either religion or its opposite is constantly being rammed down their throats. I understand the appeal of safe roads and electricity and running water, and of shiny, promising lives in peaceful cities abroad. I understand too many things I wish I didn't.

My parents come from Karachi to visit me in San Francisco the first winter I'm back — December 2011. Jawziya and I drive with our parents down Highway 1, from San Francisco to Santa Cruz, and the ocean gleams up at us, cold and blue. Driving in Pakistan did not scare me, but here I'm afraid of these long, isolated highways, and I'm afraid of accidents and insurance companies. I trust Jawziya at the wheel. We drive through vineyards and pumpkin fields. 'There's so much land here,' my mother says, with sadness in her voice. I know she's thinking of the refugee camps she visits outside Karachi, where people are piled on top of each other, and there isn't enough to eat. She's thinking of Pakistan. And I'm thinking of it too. News is never good. Pakistani soldiers are dead at American hands. There's Memogate and Husain Haqqani. There's Baluchistan. And there are the northern areas of the country, where we spent many family vacations, and which are no longer safe to visit. I wish I had saved more pictures; I thought we'd always be able to go up north, just as I thought I'd always be able to go back home. Pain the shape of Pakistan catches in my chest. It's only love, I tell myself. Nothing else can cut with such precision.

Either there is the news and my mother's sadness, or there are emails such as the one Khayyam sends me. Lahore is dreamy this time of year, he writes, and the winter of a year ago comes back, haunting and soft. I think of breakfast with Ned and Haniya on the balcony of what used to be my apartment and of buying flowers with Mav late at night. I think of the evening my students came over to say goodbye, and the signed picture frame with all of us together that I left in Karachi because I couldn't fit it into my suitcase. And I think of the old city waking up, and Badshahi mosque at night, moments in which I felt the kind of joy that borders on otherworldly. Outside my office, the San Francisco fog is cold and damp. I wish I could be back in Lahore and I envy Khayyam for being there. The city is a silver car speeding through the night with someone in it who isn't me. That the joy I felt in Lahore should necessarily have contained its opposite, from this distance, does not feel any more personal than the changing of a season.

There are loves about which people think the end was inevitable, and you were a fool, like all the others, for thinking you could change him. Finally, they think, you've come to your senses, and bitterness sets in when you agree with their judgment. But if you don't, you know you didn't choose him despite the certainty that he would break your heart; you chose him because of it. You had built a wall around your heart to protect yourself, but then you found yourself trapped behind it, afraid of suffocating, and your wall put you in greater danger than you were in the first place. So you chose him. He smashed the wall and broke your heart open, as you knew he would. He was being himself. You were the one who needed to change.

Questions about Pakistan are now a fact of living here, no different from damp weather or calls from salespeople. Some I deflect, and others I frame around my own terms. It always helps to ask people who know names like Salman Taseer if they can name Pakistan's four provinces or its major political parties. Pakistan makes its way into my classrooms, and I assign Sara Suleri for a course on autobiography. And when a student wants to interview me about my sabbatical year in Pakistan, I don't refuse, even though I talk only about teaching history in the city that I came to love, and not about the country that appears in newspapers. And at a gathering of the same Muslims I had begun to hide from because of their Pakistan-bashing, I am asked what it was like being in Lahore. The disparaging nature of the curiosity is obvious. 'It was glorious,' I reply. 'Weren't you afraid of dying in a suicide bomb?' someone says, and others laugh and agree. Snide comments about terrorism follow. 'Not at all,' I say. Then I ask him, 'Aren't you afraid of dying slowly, a little bit at a time? That's a lot worse.' He laughs nervously and changes the subject.

I can see Pakistan from his eyes, and I know the newspaper images that fuel Pakistan-bashing. I know the minefields of personal sorrow and betrayal that don't make it to newspapers. I also know a Pakistan beneath these images that is rich with extraordinary possibilities, in which I made friends from whom I could ask more after a month of knowing them than I could ask of people I've known here for years. That place is unlike anywhere else on earth. I walk back to my apartment and realise that for the first time, words that would once have bruised are easy to dust off and walk away from. It's as though Pakistan has sent me back with something that remains, like the place, difficult to translate but that acts slowly on my silence, thinning it when necessary, and giving me words when needed. It's only love. Nothing else can mend with such precision.

ART AND LETTERS

PRINCESS MAHRUKH AND THE MAGIC HORSE

A R Khatoon

Once upon a time there was a king who had only one daughter. She was beautiful and accomplished in every way and famous for her horse riding skills. The king and the princess were keen on acquiring horses. Whenever any merchant presented a pedigreed horse the king would buy it for the asking price.

One day, a merchant brought a white horse to the king who was stunned at his beauty. He had seen thousands of horses but none as appealing as this one. He said to the merchant, 'We will pay whatever you ask for this horse!'

The merchant folded his hands respectfully, 'Sire, you are the lord and master. I will accept whatever sum you are gracious enough to give me, but this is a wondrous horse. He does not consume oats or grass like other horses, nor does he drink water. That is why no one wants to buy him. Since I knew that Your Majesty is keen on horses I brought him here!'

The king and his ministers looked astonished and asked, 'What does he eat?'

The merchant replied, 'Sire, instead of oats he has almonds, pistachios, walnuts and raisins! Instead of grass he eats saffron and drinks only milk!'

The king smiled. 'That is all right! We will feed him the same things!'

The merchant submitted. 'Sire, I do not want to deceive you. He does have a fault as well!'

The king asked, 'Very well, what is it?'

The merchant said, 'Sire, he does not let anyone ride him. That is why no one has made a bid for such a beautiful animal!'

The king declared. 'It does not matter. We have plenty of other horses to ride!'

The king then ordered his vizier, 'Tell the treasurer to pay this merchant a hundred thousand rupees, and have the masons build a spacious and clean stable near the palace by the evening. Also have some gold and silver buckets made for him!'

No sooner had the order been given when tons of dried fruit and fragrant saffron was stocked for the horse. Milkmen were asked to provide gallons of fresh milk morning and evening. Two smart young grooms in expensive smart uniforms were appointed to care for the horse. In the evening the king himself tied the horse with a silk cord that was loosely looped around a gold hook. He patted the horse affectionately and returned to the palace.

The next day the city was buzzing with the news of the remarkable horse the king had acquired that grazed on saffron instead of grass and nibbled on dried fruit instead of oats! People flocked to the palace grounds to see the horse and there were scores of people around the stable. No one was allowed in the stable and the horse could only be viewed from outside. This went on for many days and the news also reached the palace. Princess Mahrukh was already very keen on horses and was eager to see this one.

She said to the king, 'Sire, I have heard that you have bought a unique horse that eats dried fruit and drinks milk. Do I have your permission to see this animal?'

The king said graciously, 'My daughter, I wanted to show you this horse myself but our people were anxious to see it as well and I thought you could see it at your leisure. I will arrange that you visit the stable on your own. However, do not try and ride it! He is a spirited animal and will not let anyone come close to him!'

Thus, the next day kanaat screens were placed from the palace to the stable. Mahrukh came to see the horse along with her friends and handmaidens and found the horse quite beautiful. She approached the horse to stroke his back and fed him dried fruit from her own hands. She was tempted to ride such a beautiful animal and thought, 'He seems quite good-natured. I should try to ride him. At the most he will throw me off!'

She warned her handmaidens, 'Do not let this get to my noble father – I would like to ride this horse!'

Her companions tried to dissuade her but she jumped on his bare back without a saddle. The horse remained quite still. The princess smiled at her friends, 'You were making a fuss about nothing. Look, he is quiet!'

She jumped off and stroked the horse while warning her handmaidens not to mention this to her mother either. After a while, the princess returned to the palace.

That evening the horse did not touch his meal of dried fruit. When the pail of milk was placed before him he turned his face away and ignored the saffron offered to him. The grooms thought that perhaps he was full as the princess had fed him during her visit but even the next morning the horse did not touch his food or milk and stood with his head bowed down. The grooms reported his behaviour to the keeper of the stables who was worried and went to the stable. He stroked the horse lovingly before trying to feed him with his hands but the horse did not touch anything.

The keeper was now alarmed as this valuable animal was the king's favourite. He went and reported to the vizier who sent for an animal healer to examine the horse. He declared that the animal was perfectly healthy and suggested purgatives in case there was a problem with the digestion. However, the horse resisted all attempts to medicate him.

Eventually, the vizier went and related the whole story to the king who came to the stable and tried to feed the horse his diet of dried fruit and milk but to no avail. The king sent for the royal grooms who appeared with their palms folded. He questioned each of them and declared that if someone had mistreated the animal he would be beheaded. They all submitted humbly, 'Sire, we treat him with love and affection. We keep his food pails spotless and clean out the stable several times a day.'

One old groom moved forward, 'Sire, if you spare my life, may I say something?'

The king declared, 'Your life is spared! What do you have to say?'

The old groom said, 'Sire, I would like to say it privately to you!'

The king ordered everyone to leave the stable. The old man whispered, 'Sire, this is the third day since the noble princess came to see the horse. I was leaving a sack of dried fruit when the screens were drawn and I hastily hid behind the sack. The princess was delighted to see the horse and fed him with her own hands. She kept stroking the horse for a long time and the horse was perfectly content. She told her companions that he seemed mild natured and she would like to ride him. They tried to stop her but the princess climbed on his bare back. He remained quite still. The princess was happy with him and then left after patting him on the back. Sire, since then he has been very quiet. He has stopped eating and his eyes are watering. It seems as if he is weeping.'

The king was silent for a while and then said, 'Very well, you can leave now but I am warning you not to say a word of this to anyone or your family will be thrown in the oil presser!' The old groom fell at the king's feet and promised not to breathe a word.

The king returned to the palace to send for the princess and said, 'My daughter, our favourite horse has been unwell for three days. He is not eating or drinking but stands with his head down.'

The princess looked sad, 'Sire that is terrible! He should be treated at once. He is a rare animal.'

The king said, 'Yes daughter, I am worried as well. But how can we treat him? He kicks anyone who comes close to him!'

The princess said, 'Father, with your permission, may I have a look at him? I really liked that horse!'

The king also wanted her to visit the horse to see whether the groom was right. He arranged for the kanaat screens to be put up at once and escorted the princess to the stable. As soon as the princess arrived the horse looked up. She stroked his back lovingly and took a handful of dried fruit to feed him. He nibbled at it eagerly and lapped up the pail of milk the princess held up for him. She then offered him the saffron which he also munched happily. The king was watching all this silently and thought that the groom had been proved right.

The princess exclaimed, 'Father, he seems to be fine. You were worried for nothing!'

The king replied, 'Yes daughter, the grooms may have been careless with him!' After some time, the king took the princess back to the palace. The next day the grooms reported that the horse was not eating or drinking again. The king then sent for the old vizier and after confiding in him, asked, 'Now what do you suggest we do?'

The vizier said, 'Sire, the princess cannot visit the horse daily to feed him with her own hands!'

The king said thoughtfully, 'And yet, I would not like such a rare and beautiful animal to die of starvation!'

The vizier suggested, 'Sire, there is a simple solution. When you convene your durbar tomorrow, announce that since the princess really liked the horse you have decided to gift it to her. Then order me to have a stable built in her palace and the horse will be moved there. Instead of the grooms, the princess's slave girls will look after him!'

The king was pleased with this idea. The next day a stable was constructed in the courtyard of the princess's palace and the horse was taken there. The princess was overjoyed with her father's generosity. She would make it a point to be in attendance on the horse at meal times and feed him with her own hands. A young slave girl was appointed to clean the stable. The princess had some chairs moved to the stable and would often sit there to play chess with her friends.

Several months passed by in this manner. During that time several princes proposed to her but the princess refused each one. She would think, 'If I get married, who will look after the horse? He only feeds and drinks from my hands. No one I marry will tolerate this and once I leave him the horse will starve himself to death!' She would often joke with her friends, 'It seems that I am married to this horse!'

One night Mahrukh woke up with a start. She tossed restlessly in her bed and then came out for a stroll. She went as far as the stable and saw the strangest sight. Her slave girl Champa who cleaned the stable was sitting with her long lustrous hair open and a handsome young man was sitting next to her. The princess could not believe her eyes. She stood silently watching this scene and noticed that the horse was missing from the stable. The princess was mystified but being an intelligent and wise girl she returned to her bed in silence. She could not sleep that night for sheer anger.

Mahrukh was unusually quiet the next day but did not confide in anyone and pretended to have a headache. She did not visit the horse that day and in the evening she sent for Champa to confront her with what she had seen last night.

Champa was terrified and confessed immediately, 'Mistress, since you have seen for yourself, that horse is actually a prince. He has taken a liking to my hair. At midnight he transforms into a man and makes me open my hair to see it, and then he becomes a horse again!'

The princess controlled her anger and said, 'If from today you open your hair in front of him I will chop it all off! Moreover, I will inform the king and you will be shot to death with arrows!'

The princess locked Champa in a hut and went to bed. The next morning, she was informed by another slave girl that the horse was missing. The princess immediately asked the girl to bring Champa from the hut. A little later she was told, 'Mistress, Champa is not in the hut!'

The princess went to the stable and saw a piece of paper. She picked it up and it read:

'Who will come to Kanggan *desh*? Who will cut off Champa's *kesh*?

I am a prince from the kingdom of Kangan. I know an incantation that enables me to change my form. I had come to your kingdom in the guise of a horse when I was caught by a horse trader who sold me to your father. You came to see me and I fell in love with you at first glance. You kept me with great love and comfort but I really liked your slave girl Champa's hair. I used to make her open her hair for me but you saw us yesterday and threatened to cut off her hair! I was really saddened by that. Therefore, I am taking her away, just to be able to see her hair! I will not forget you for the rest of my life, nor will I marry anyone else!'

The princess was absolutely furious upon reading this letter but controlled herself in front of her servants. She went back to the palace but did not have any breakfast or change her night robes. With the paper clutched in her hand she went straight to her mother who was startled to see her that early in the morning and asked, 'My daughter, is all well with you? You look upset!'

The princess fell in her arms and wept without restraint. Her mother embraced her and asked, 'Tell me daughter, if anyone has offended you I will have her blinded! If anyone has raised a finger at you I will have it cut off! My darling, why are you weeping?'

The princess sobbed helplessly, 'Mother…the…horse…has…vanished!'

The queen caressed her hair and said, 'Let him vanish! It is just as well! I always suspected that the horse was from fairyland!'

The princess wiped her tears and said, 'Mother, it would not have mattered if he had vanished on his own but he has taken the slave girl Champa with him!'

The princess related what had happened the previous day and gave her the letter. The queen abused Champa roundly and said, 'Daughter, do not grieve about this. Your father has gone on a mission. When he returns, we will have that wretched Champa arrested and brought back!'

The princess declared, 'I have sworn not to rest until I cut off Champa's hair! I have come to have your permission to leave for the kingdom of Kanggan!'

The queen looked alarmed, 'My child, where will you go? I have never even heard of this kingdom before!'

The princess said, 'If you do not give your permission I swear I will consume poison this very day! I cannot bear to be insulted in this manner!'

The queen tried to reason with her daughter and wept as she tried to convince her not to go but the princess was quite determined and she gave in at last.

The next day, the princess had four pairs of men's garments stitched to her size. She took a small quantity of precious gems and gold coins, some dried fruit and selected a swift-footed horse to leave the city disguised as a man. She promised her distraught mother that she would return within three months.

After leaving the borders of her kingdom she travelled without any idea of which direction she should choose. She travelled through forests and plains and would only stop at night under the shelter of some tree to rest her horse. Her anger made her fearless. At every settlement or village she would ask about the kingdom of Kanggan but no one had heard of this name. A month passed by but the princess had not lost hope and knew that she would succeed in her quest one day.

One morning she woke up to see that she was close to a thick forest that seemed to have a wall of trees blocking her way. She was distressed at this new obstacle and thought, 'What will happen now? Will I have to turn back? I will never do that! I will cut off Champa's hair or be eaten by wild beats in this jungle!'

She stood up with a fresh resolve and used her dagger to start cutting the branches of the trees in front of her. After an hour of hard work she could see a faint light and finally made a way through a small opening. She lay down to rest a while and left her horse to enter the forest. To her surprise, the trees gave way to a large clearing with a hut visible at the far end. She peered inside to see an ancient sage sitting on a deerskin. His eyelashes were down to his naval and his beard flowed down to the ground. He sat with his eyes closed with a rosary of a thousand beads in his hand.

The princess was terrified at the sight of him and trembled so violently that the dagger slipped out of her hand. The old sage swept up his eyelashes with both hands to looked at the princess, then looked down at the dagger and asked, 'My daughter, have you come to kill me?'

The princess fell at his feet in fear and said, 'Baba, how can I dare to do that? I am but a needy girl and have left my house for a reason!'

Baba patted her head and asked, 'My daughter, tell me what troubles you.'

The princess related her story. Baba smiled and said, 'That boy is a rogue! I was the one who taught him the incantation to assume any disguise. He will forget the incantation now that he has deceived you!'

The princess folded her palms and said, 'Baba, just give me the directions to Kanggan land! I want to avenge my insult!'

'Daughter, you must promise not to kill anyone!' Baba said.

The princess declared, 'No Baba, I will just cut off my slave girl's hair and return to my land!'

Baba said, 'Beyond this jungle is the land of Kanggan. If you cross the forest you will enter the city of Kanggan before sunset!'

The princess said. 'Baba, how will my horse enter the forest? It was difficult enough for me to enter!'

Baba declared, 'Take the name of God and lead him in!'

The princess returned to the small opening she had hacked through the trees. When she led her horse by his reins she found the entrance had widened. She said farewell to Baba and went on through the forest easily. After some time she could see the walls of a city at a distance and joyfully rode faster as her quest seemed to be over. Before sunset she entered the city.

Her horse trotted slowly through the city that seemed hostile and alien to her and she wondered where she could spend the night. People looked with wonder at the young handsome boy and several of them offered a place to stay. She thanked them politely and at her request someone eventually directed her to a *sarai*. The landlady welcomed her and opened a small room which was simply furnished but very clean. The princess sent a silent prayer of gratitude. She stabled her horse and washed her face and hands before settling down on the bed.

The landlady came in with a tray of food with a piece of meat and a small potato in bowl of thin gravy, a watered down lentil curry and two thick pieces of unleavened bread. When would the princess have had a meal like this one? But she was so hungry that it seemed like a blessing from heaven to her. She ate heartily before stretching out on the bed and falling into a deep sleep.

The next morning the landlady woke her up and said, 'Traveller, did you swear not to wake up today? Your breakfast is cold!'

Mahrukh got up abruptly and asked, 'Could you feed my horse?'

The landlady laughed, 'Young man, my life has been spent in this work. I look after the guests and my husband tends to their horses and mules!' She left smiling archly at her guest and returned with a glass of watered-down milk. Mahrukh praised the quality of the milk and asked, 'I am in this city for the first time. Who is king here and how does he treat his people? Which buildings are worth seeing here?'

The landlady said, 'Young man, you are fortunate to have come now to the city. A month earlier this city was in mourning and plunged in darkness every night. Our king has only one son, who was missing for several months. The king had stopped convening his durbar and both he and his wife wept day and night for their son. With God's Grace he returned a month ago but instead of being overjoyed the noble king and queen are very sad!'

Mahrukh asked, 'And why are they sad?'

The landlady said, 'Young sir, all parents dream of marrying their children in an exalted family. We have heard that the prince has returned with a hideous young girl and has kept her in his palace. People tell us that she looks as if she is a slave girl! No one is allowed into the prince's palace. The king does not allow her to come to his own palace!'

The princess smiled, 'Well, everyone has different likes and dislikes!'

She felt a little better after hearing this story from the landlady and was quite delighted that no one had any respect for Champa!

The landlady picked up the tray and said, 'Young sir, you can have a bath and get ready, then go and see the city. People come from everywhere to see the royal gardens!'

Mahrukh looked uneasy, 'Landlady, I am not used to bathing at the well. Take me to a more private bath!'

The landlady chuckled knowingly, 'Young sir, you are as bashful as a young girl! Very well, you can bathe where I bathe!'

Mahrukh had a bath and changed her clothes. As she went to the stables, the landlady said, 'There is no need to ride to the royal gardens. It is close to this place and someone will direct you there!'

Accordingly, Mahrukh walked to the royal gardens. She noticed an old woman picking flowers on one side and approached her to remark, 'Respected one, you are bent from the waist and must be tired of picking flowers!'

The old woman looked up to see a handsome young boy and asked curiously, 'My son, where have you come from? Whose son are you?'

Mahrukh said, 'Mother, I am a traveller. I had heard good things about your city and have come to see it!'

The old lady asked again, 'Son, where are you staying?'

Mahrukh was now helping out the old woman by picking flowers and said, 'I am staying at the sarai and thought I should see the gardens!'

The old woman said, 'My son, my heart is gladdened at the sight of you! I live alone. Do not stay in the sarai but move to my house. These wretched landladies swindle young men like you!'

The princess said, 'Very well mother, I will move to your house. But tell me, why do you labour so much? Let me escort you back to your house.'

The old woman looked gratefully at him and said, 'My son, how can I eat without working? I will go home now and cook. After that I will make some flower jewellery. I will take it to the palace of the prince tonight for his wife. No one is allowed to step in there except me!'

The princess guessed that the flower jewellery was made for Champa and felt a hot wave of anger. She thought that moving to the old woman would be a good opportunity for her. She carried the basket of flowers to the old woman's house and said, 'Mother, I also have my horse with me.'

The woman said, 'Son, I have a large courtyard and you can keep the horse under the neem tree.'

The princess returned to the sarai for lunch and then informed the landlady, 'I had come in search of my aunt and found her. Now I am moving to her house.'

The landlady was delighted with the two coins of gold the princess handed over to her. The princess then promptly rode to the old woman's house. For several days she observed what the woman did and then helped her by stringing the flowers into garlands. The old woman protested, 'Son, you are a boy and should not do this work!'

The princess replied, 'Mother, you cannot see too well. Just watch, within a few days I will be able to string the garlands into jewellery!'

Gradually, the princess grew quite proficient at this work and one day she made some very beautiful jewellery out of the flowers.

The old woman exclaimed, 'My son, this jewellery is so good that the prince's wife is bound to ask me who has made it! How will I answer her?'

The princess said, 'Mother, just tell her that your niece has come to visit you and made the jewellery today!'

The old woman was satisfied. At eight that night she went as usual to the palace and opened her basket to bring out the flower jewellery. The prince's wife exclaimed, 'These are beautiful! It does not seem as if you have made them! Tell me truthfully, whose handiwork is this?'

The old woman repeated the princess's words, 'Mistress, my niece is visiting me and she made them today!'

The prince's wife said, 'Bring your niece with you tomorrow. We will have her braid our hair and dress them with flowers and reward her!'

The old lady looked frightened and said, 'Mistress, her husband is with her and he is a very strict. I will try to bring her but cannot promise anything. God knows whether he will let her come!'

The prince's wife frowned, 'You know that no one is allowed to come here. The prince comes late at night. If you do not bring your niece I will punish you!'

The old woman folded her palms, 'Mistress, I will try my best!'

The old woman stumbled out with her basket. As soon as she returned to her home she told the princess, 'My son, you have caused my living death! The prince's wife has sent for you!'

The princess laughed, 'Mother, why are you worried? I will disguise myself as a girl so that no one will suspect anything. Just go to bed!'

The old woman thought to herself, 'Well, he is young enough to pass off as a girl at night!'

The next day the princess went to the bazaar and had a skirt stitched to her size. The matching chemise and veil were heavily worked with shiny gold braids. She also bought a pair of sharp scissors. She returned home with these items and then attended to the flower ornaments. This time she made them particularly appealing with silver tinsel threaded through the flowers. A braid of flowers to adorn Champa's hair was made every day. The princess made an elaborate braid with several strings of flowers and arranged them artfully in the green and red wicker basket that she covered with a red cloth.

After finishing this work she mixed dark colouring in some oil and applied it to her face and hands and feet and then painted the soles of her feet with a red dye. She had bought some silver jewellery for herself as well. When she emerged from her room in her new clothes and silver jewellery the old woman stared at her amazed at the transformation. She asked, 'My son, why did you make yourself so dark?'

The princess replied, 'Mother, she might wonder why the niece is so fair when the aunt is dark! It's better to be disguised properly!'

The old woman happily escorted her to the prince's palace. The princess saw that Champa was reclining in all splendour on a jewel-inlaid bed. She was furious and wanted to use her dagger on Champa right then but controlled herself. The old woman bowed low to greet Champa and the princess had to bow as well.

Champa said, 'Your niece is splendidly dressed but why is she hiding her face under a veil?'

The old woman opened the wicker basket and said, 'Mistress she is shy of you!'

Champa was delighted to see the flowers and said, 'Today, your niece will braid our hair!'

The princess got her dearest wish at that time. As Champa opened her hair she set to work by cleverly cutting off Champa's hair and arranging the flower braids instead. After she had finished she told the old woman, 'Aunt, we should leave. You know he has only allowed me to be here for a short while!'

Champa gave her a good sum of money and said, 'As long as you are here you must come every day!'

Both women greeted her respectfully and returned home. The princess changed her clothes quickly and washed the colour off her face and limbs. She said to the old woman, 'Mother, my head aches after wearing that veil! I want some fresh air!'

She left with her bag and rode out of the city swiftly. Within two hours she had gone a long distance. The horse had also been idling for several days and galloped at the speed of wind.

That night the prince came into Champa's room at his usual time and said abruptly, 'Champa, open your hair!'

Champa first unpinned the flower braids and wanted to open her hair only to discover it was missing. She looked ashen at the prince. He said, 'Why do you use these flower braids? I do not like all these pretensions! I just want to see your hair. You know well that I brought you here because the princess threatened to cut off your hair. She looked after me so tenderly and I loved her as well but your hair made me forget my loyalty to her!'

Champa sat on the bed frozen with despair. The prince asked harshly, 'What is the matter with you today? Why are you not obeying me?'

Champa folded her palms to say, 'Sire, I am not disobeying you! I seem to have lost my hair!'

The prince stood up in alarm. He went over to see for himself and saw that Champa's hair had been chopped off quite ruthlessly. He shook her hard and shouted, 'You are of no use to me now! I just liked your hair! Tell me truthfully, who came here today!'

Champa gasped in fear, 'Sire, no one came here except the old woman and her niece who dressed my hair today!'

The prince barked angrily, 'Why did she come without our permission? I had only allowed the old woman to come here!'

The prince paced up and down the room in rage and kept repeating the words, 'Who came to Kanggan desh? Who cut off Champa's kesh?'

Suddenly his eyes fell on the doorway through which the old woman came to the room. On it was written in a large script,

'We came to Kanggan desh! We cut off Champa's kesh! Princess Mahrukh.'

The prince stood there looking at this completely stunned. He turned to Champa and said. 'Princess Mahrukh cut off your hair and you were not even aware of it, you stupid girl!'

Champa looked astonished, 'But sire the princess is so fair! That girl was dark!'

The prince snapped, 'In truth, an ignorant person cannot reason. Look, she has written on that doorway!'

The prince stormed out of the room and summoned his soldiers, 'Go now to arrest that old gardener woman and whoever is in her house!'

The soldiers marched briskly to the old woman's house. It was midnight and the old woman was waiting for her guest to return. The soldiers broke into the house and tied her arms. She began shouting, 'Help! Help! There are robbers in my house!'

The soldiers were angry with her, 'We are not robbers! We are the prince's soldiers and he has ordered us to arrest you! Who else is in the house with you?'

The old woman thought that the prince's wife must have discovered the identity of the boy and trembled with fear. She gasped out, 'There is no one in my house. My nephew was visiting me. He went out at eight and has not returned yet. I was waiting up for him!'

The soldiers said, 'Well, then you come with us! The prince has summoned you!'

Two soldiers took her to the palace while the others waited at the house for her nephew. The prince brought the old woman to his room and picked up his whip, 'Tell me whom you brought to the palace this evening or I will whip your hide off!'

The old woman folded her palms, 'Sire, I did not want to bring him here but the mistress insisted that I must bring the maker of the jewellery. He is a young boy and disguised himself in women's clothes to come here. I was with him all the time!'

The prince said sternly, 'Why are you lying? That was a girl, not a boy!'

The old woman related the story of how she met the boy and said, 'Sire, I live on my own. I thought he was a traveller and offered him shelter!'

The prince declared, 'Tomorrow morning you will be hanged!' The soldiers took the old woman to the prison.

The prince remained awake the whole night. He was sorry that Champa had lost her hair but even more amazed at the princess's daring and bravery in crossing the dangerous forest to reach Kanggan land. He was chastising himself for having chosen the low-born, silly Champa over the beautiful princess and realised that this was a huge insult to the princess and thought, 'Her father had spent so much money on me. The princess would feed me from her own hands and would sit for hours with me in the stable. She had refused the proposals of so many princes because of me. I remember her telling her friends that she was married to a horse! I went after an illusion. After her locks were shorn off, Champa had no appeal for me. I hate the very sight of her!'

Meanwhile, the prince's soldiers had reported to the city magistrate that the prince had given orders for the old woman to be hanged in the morning. The magistrate went to the vizier with this tale. The vizier declared, 'Without the king's permission no one can be sent to the gallows! Besides this, the old woman took the boy there because the prince's wife insisted on it. She is also to blame. I will report this to the king and we will act according to his orders.'

The vizier requested a private audience with the king and was summoned at once. He related whatever the magistrate had reported to him. The king looked thoughtful and said, 'You can leave. We will speak to the prince!'

The vizier withdrew respectfully and the king ordered his special attendant to summon the prince. The prince arrived forthwith but looked obviously disturbed. The king looked closely at him and asked, 'We have heard that you have given orders for the old gardener woman to be hanged. My son, this punishment is meant for those who commit a grave crime. If the woman has taken someone's life then she deserves to hang. What is her crime?'

The prince said in a low voice, 'Father, she brought a boy disguised as a girl into my palace. I was so furious at this that I gave the orders to hang her!'

The king said, 'My son, if we start hanging people for such minor transgressions they will turn rebellious and we will have trouble!'

The prince remained silent. The king ordered his attendant to present the old woman. Shortly, the old woman was brought forth, tied up in ropes. The king dismissed everyone except the prince and the old woman. The king asked her, 'Who was the boy you had slipped into the palace disguised as a girl?'

The old woman replied, 'O Protector of the Poor! One day, I was picking flowers in the royal gardens when a boy came and stood near me. He was quite young – perhaps thirteen or fourteen years old...he had not sprouted hair on his upper lip yet! I have not seen a more beautiful boy in my life and I really liked him. He told me that he was a traveller and staying at a sarai. I invited him to stay with me and he came with his horse and his luggage. I make flower jewellery for the prince's wife. He used to help me and within days he learnt to make it better than I ever did! One day I brought the jewellery he had made for the mistress who really liked it. When she asked me who had made it I told her that my niece had made it as that is what the boy had suggested I do. The mistress ordered me to bring my niece the next day. I was terrified and made all kinds of excuses but she threatened to punish me if I did not bring her. When I told the boy this he told me not to worry and said he would disguise himself as a girl for a little while and no one would know. To my misfortune, I was convinced by him and brought him to the palace. But

Sire, I was watching him all the time. He did not even talk to the mistress. He just arranged the flowers in her hair with the veil drawn low over his face!'

The prince interjected angrily, 'Arranged her hair..?'

The old woman said, 'Yes Sire! After that I left with him. He changed from women's clothes into his own and then went out for some air. I was waiting up for him when the soldiers arrested me! Sire, you can punish me as you will!'

The prince asked, 'Did he ride out on his horse!'

The woman replied, 'I was in my room. I cannot tell you how he went. But when the soldiers arrested me at that time his horse was not there.'

The prince got up and untied the old woman, 'Go, you are pardoned. Now do not appear before me again!'

The old woman called blessings on him and stumbled out of the room. The king looked at his son and said, 'You had condemned her to be hanged and now you have pardoned her completely! She did take a man into the ladies palace and that was a crime!'

The prince looked sheepish and said, 'Father, it was not a boy but a girl!'

The king looked surprised and asked, 'How do you know that?'

The prince replied, 'Father, it was Princess Mahrukh and she had come to wreak revenge on me. I had run away with her slave girl Champa as I really liked her hair. The princess came and cut off Champa's braid!'

The king looked amused and said. 'She must be a brave girl! I admire her tenacity and daring but you have still not disclosed to me why you were missing for six months and where you were!'

The prince then related the whole story to his father; how he had met a sage in the forest who had given him the incantation to change his form and how he had transformed into a horse.

The king reflected silently on the prince's story and then said, 'It would embarrass me now to send your proposal for Princess Mahrukh! You should return to them and beg forgiveness of the princess and her father. After that we can formally propose for you. It is a great pity that you showed preference for a slave girl over a princess!'

The prince looked down, 'Father, I am ashamed of my behaviour. I tried to read the incantation again but cannot seem to remember it!'

The king said, 'If you really like the princess then write to her father, other-wise, we can arrange another marriage for you but you will have to get rid of

Champa! We have been shamed before everyone because of her. Your mother has been very depressed on your account!'

The prince said, 'I turned Champa out last night. I just liked her because of her hair!'

Now hear about the princess. She crossed the forest that night and saw a faint light in Baba's hut but the door was closed. She thought that if she stopped here the prince's soldiers might find her and so she left quietly holding her horse's reins. She rested a while in the morning and let her horse graze in a meadow before pressing on. Thus, travelling swiftly, she reached her kingdom within fifteen days.

The king and queen had given up on their daughter and there was a funereal atmosphere in the palace. When Mahrukh suddenly appeared the slave girls and handmaidens ran happily to inform the queen. Mahrukh marched straight to her mother's room and threw Champa's long braid at her feet. 'Mother, I have succeeded in my mission!'

Her mother embraced her with joy. The king also rushed in to meet her and said, 'You should have waited for us to return! We would have taken an army and attacked his kingdom!'

The princess explained, 'Father, no one can go there!' Then she related her adventures to her parents. That night the city was illuminated and the poor and needy were fed. The princess rested for a week after her gruelling journey but she looked quiet and sad. She was no longer interested in riding or entertainment but would keep to her room laid up listlessly on her bed.

One day her mother sent for her and said, 'Daughter, it is my wish and your father's that you should get married now!'

Mahrukh replied, 'Mother, as long as the prince remained in the form of an animal he loved me. You know that he would only eat from my hand. I also loved him very much but he deceived me when he transformed into a man. Perhaps that is a human trait. Now I am determined not to marry. Men have a strange disposition. Even if you marry me off to another prince, he might like another slave girl! Many of my handmaidens are beautiful but he liked Champa who was the ugliest of the slave girls! Now I do not trust anyone. I am happy as I am and I would like to spend my life in the service of God. I am building a sarai for travellers. A poor and needy person who enters our city will have room and board in it for three days!'

The queen mother was silent and thought that Mahrukh was heartbroken now but would recover in time.

Thus the princess's sarai was built. She would distribute the food herself to needy travellers. One day the keeper of the rest house informed her, 'Mistress, a beggar woman has come and the rest of the travellers shun her. No one eats with her. Her clothes are torn and her feet are blistered. She has no hair and does not talk to anyone; she just keeps weeping all the time!'

The princess told the keeper to bring the woman to her. When she was taken to the princess she fell at her feet and cried, 'Mistress, I am your slave girl Champa!'

The princess stepped back instinctively and turned her face away but then felt pity for her and asked softly, 'How did you leave your bejewelled bed and sumptuous clothes to end up here?'

Champa wept as she said, 'Mistress, the prince only liked my hair. When you chopped it off he kicked me out of his palace! I wandered in forests and plains until I came across an elderly man. He stroked my head and told me the way here. When I left that forest the remaining hair on my head turned wiry and frizzed up!'

The princess's handmaidens murmured, 'Serve you right! This was your punishment for disloyalty to your mistress!'

The princess sent Champa to the queen with the message, 'I have forgiven her. She has been punished enough. You should forgive her as well!' Thus Champa was reassigned to the princess once again.

The princess was still not satisfied and still dreamed of humiliating the horse prince. One day, an ambassador from the kingdom of Kanggan arrived in her father's durbar with many costly gifts and a letter from the prince. He had begged the king's pardon and asked for Princess Mahrukh's hand in marriage. The king had the ambassador stay in the royal guest house and consulted with his vizier.

The vizier advised, 'Sire, Princess Mahrukh will have to be consulted before composing a response to this proposal. You had gifted that horse to her and he betrayed her. Now we should do as she says!'

The king came into the ladies palace and showed the letter to his wife, 'Show this letter to Mahrukh and let us know what she says.'

The queen summoned Mahrukh and showed her the letter before saying, 'The king would like to know your opinion on this matter.'

Mahrukh was quiet for a while and then said, 'Mother, give me a day to think this over.'

That night the princess stayed up late reflecting on this new development. She thought of the trials and difficulties she had undergone after the horse prince has left and how she had refused all proposals of marriage because of him. Now the prince was contrite and wanted to marry her. It was not right to refuse him but she should make him suffer a little. She thought of a plan and then went off to sleep. The next day she conveyed a message through a companion to her mother: 'The king should be informed that if the prince was true in his resolve to marry her then he should come and speak to Mahrukh himself. She will decide whom she marries!'

The king sent the ambassador with gifts from his land and this message. The prince was quite ready to fulfil this condition and travelled with his companions and advisors to the princess's land. When he entered the city the king sent his vizier to welcome him and he was lodged in a splendid palace.

The next morning Mahrukh arranged to meet him on a plain which she used for riding. She wore her richest robes and set off with her companions and handmaidens. Champa was also part of this group dressed as a prince with a shining crown and a fine horse.

When the prince was led to the garden he saw the princess riding with a young slave boy. He trembled with fury at the sight and drew his dagger from the waist. Mahrukh saw him and came forward to meet him. 'I thank you for coming here!'

The prince made no reply and just handled the dagger but was so overawed at the sight of the beautiful princess that he could not raise it to attack her. He asked abruptly, 'Who were you riding with?'

Mahrukh smiled, 'With your slave boy of course!'

The prince asked, 'How did my slave boy come here?'

Mahrukh replied, 'In the same manner that my slave girl went to Kanggan land!'

The prince lifted his dagger in a red rage, 'Did you bring him with you!'

Mahrukh retorted, 'You liked my slave girl and I liked your slave boy!'

The prince looked baffled. 'Did you call me here to humiliate me? I will first cut off this lowly slave's head and then kill you! I did not realise you would fall so low!'

Mahrukh smiled, 'Prince, why are you in such a rage? Women cannot fall so low! They only love once. I had loved a horse and he deceived me by running off with my slave girl leaving me a challenge, "Who will come to Kanggan desh? Who will cut off Champa's kesh?" I could not bear this insult and if you had not challenged me I would never have gone to Kanggan land! You know that my parents brought me up in all comfort but I combed the deserts for months! While you were indulging yourself with Champa I was trying to save myself from wolves and lions! Even then you thought that I was a weak girl and even now you want to use force on me. Kindly sheath your dagger and try and recognise this slave boy'

She signalled to Champa to come closer and threw the crown off her head, 'This is your chosen one Champa! If you still want to take her you are welcome to do so! I will have no objection!'

The prince looked down and said, 'I am very ashamed for having wronged you. You have avenged yourself on me. I was so furious when I saw you with that slave boy!'

The princess smiled, 'And when I learnt that the horse that I doted on and fed with my own hands had fled with Champa, how do you think I felt then?'

The prince looked rueful, 'Do not remind me of this wretched incident. I apologise for my behaviour!'

The princess ordered her companions, 'Bring a chair for the prince. He has been here for some time!'

The prince smiled, 'I want to see my stable!'

The princess said, 'The stable was useless without a horse so I converted it into a rest house for needy travellers. One day when Champa arrived there in rags she informed me that you had kicked her out when she lost her hair. That was not a good thing to do. It means that when a man tires of a woman he mistreats her!'

The prince looked embarrassed and said, 'Leave that for the moment. Tell me whether I can gain what I have come for?'

The princess was quiet for a few moments and then said, 'You can speak to my father. I cannot refuse him!'

After some time the prince went to the king and proposed formally for Mahrukh. The king said, 'My son, I am happy to meet you but this proposal should have been conveyed by your father. If I accept this match he may not approve!'

The prince looked down and said, 'I have come with his approval but he is embarrassed to face you because of me. I have hurt you and the princess with my behaviour. He was the one who urged me to beg your forgiveness!'

The king embraced him warmly and said, 'Son, I forgive you. Convey our greetings to your father and tell him that we have only this one daughter. If he accompanies you we are ready to accept this match!'

Accordingly, the prince left the same day. The two kings arranged the wedding date by corresponding with each other and the wedding was solemnised with great pomp and splendour, and now this story has also come to a happy end!

(translated by Shahnaz Aijazuddin from Kahaniyan by A R Khatoon)

Glossary

Kannat – cloth screens

Desh – land, country

Kesh – hair

Baba – respectful way of addressing an old man or father

Sarai – inn or hostelry for travellers

Neem – azadirachta indica – a tree in the mahogany family native to the subcontinent

KIRATPUR

Yasir Shah

Kiratpur: a city hundreds, hundreds and hundreds of miles away from Islamabad. A small, modest city – from what I hear – in the Bijnur district of UP, India, where people gladly drink goat's milk and eat only *khaalis ghee* and *paneer*. Also a city that, every afternoon, my grandfather would visit for one whole hour, sometimes even an hour and a half, before returning to our home in Islamabad to curve his lips into the sweetest smile. The kind you only saw on those who dreamt of yesterdays.

But I, back then, dreamt only of tomorrows. Never knew what Kiratpur was, oblivious to its existence as a word let alone as an actual city. Yet my earliest childhood memories are of afternoons when my grandfather – whom we lovingly referred to as Dada jee – would roll over on his side of the bed and announce '*Ab may Kiratpur jaa raha hun.*' (I'm off to Kiratpur now).

As far as I can remember, I never asked him what Kiratpur was. Later, when I was told by my father that it was a city far, far away where Dada jee grew up, I never got around to asking Dada jee how a trip to Kiratpur every afternoon was even possible. Now I know. Not just the what and the how but also - and especially – the why.

Because today all I have are memories! Of spending my summer afternoons besides Dada jee on the bed reading children's books in large-print. Afternoons, while I devoured Enid Blyton, Roald Dahl, Encyclopedia Brown and Apple Paperbacks, he went through stacks and piles of all the digests he'd brought with him from Lahore in an old, leather suitcase. That old leather which also contained his thick black reading glasses (the kind that made you dizzy if you tried them on), several cotton *kurtas* (all white,

all stitched the same) and medicines (lots and lots of medicine). Lazy afternoons, when I chewed my nails and read about talking rabbits, British
boarding schools, giant peaches, big friendly giants and American high
schools, Dada jee would gurgle his hookah with one hand and turn the
pages of his Urdu digests with the other. Then, with the last *grr grr grr* of his
hookah, he would place his reading glasses back on top of his digest, his
digest beside his pillow, roll over and announce …

'I'm off to Kiratpur now.'

'Why do you sleep so much Dada jee?'

'Because I get to go visit Kiratpur…' Always his reply, always with a
smile.

And when three pm would turn into four, the sky's scorch would eventually bestow a breeze of misery to those who napped without roofs. Dada jee
would also wake up next to me… stretch… smile.

'So how was it? Kiratpur?' I would ask, only slightly interested.

'Still as beautiful as ever.' Always his reply. The *grr grr grr* of his hookah
punctuating each syllable.

'Did you drink goat milk like Gandhi?' I asked, my eyes only following
the large words in my book.

'Yes…' The rest of what he would say, I honestly can't recall. All I
remember is that I would be too engrossed in my own world….of talking
rabbits, giant peaches, British boarding schools and American high
schools.

I would spend my summer with him in Lahore. Boring afternoons when
I got tired of playing with my aunt's pets and after the kids from the servant
quarters informed me that 'Ma says we shouldn't play with rich boys
because rich boys get hurt more easily and they cry when they get hurt and
we get blamed…' That was when I would return to the bed besides my
Dada jee to pacify my boredom with books. When I would finish all the
books I had brought from Islamabad, I would pick up my *Phuppo's* Sydney
Sheldons and Danielle Steeles. I even read the flimsy, ten-page Urdu books
we could buy for a rupee with silly stories of *Umer-oo-Ayar* and *Tarzan*. All
the cousins my age were in Model Town at my Nani's enjoying their afternoons with relay-races, *pithoo garam* and *Tilo Express*. However, my siblings
and I were told we had to spend some of our days at my uncle's house in
Mayo Gardens – a pristine house with manicured lawns and a back yard full

of pigeons and peacocks, parrots and hens, even a German Shepherd. So, with no one to play Tilo Express with, I resorted to spending my afternoons on the bed besides my Dada jee, reading whatever I could lay my hands on, from Enid Blyton to Sheldon to eventually Dada jee's Urdu digests. At first I waited till he went to Kiratpur in his sleep. Then I would sneak a digest over to my side of the bed and begin reading. Urdu, I soon realised, was more beautiful as well as more expressive. It also contained a different world of fiction from what I was accustomed to; here short stories were called afsanas, and protagonists from modest Pakistani households could narrate a real eye opener of a tale. So I read, and I read more. Every afternoon that I spent with Dada jee napping beside me, I secretly read his digests and smoked his hookah. Once, when he woke up from his nap, he looked up and said:

'Yasir *beta* you're too young to read those digests...'

'But if I can understand the words and what they say doesn't that mean that I'm old enough to read them?'

His response was only a smile, maybe a chuckle along with it. But from that day on, he never stopped me from reading his digests.

In fact, later we began to discuss some of the *afsanas* too. He would recommend a story to me, and when he took off for Kiratpur, I would read it with the usual furtive puffs of his hookah. Then – at those brief moments, when afternoons were almost over and evenings had not quite begun – we would discuss the characters and the plots.

My father appreciated the afternoons I spent with Dada jee. He wanted to do the same but was always very busy with his work. There was no doubt that Abu had a very stressful job back then. It required lots of travel and he was hardly ever home before seven, but the sight of him walking through the door with a briefcase full of important files made Dada jee proud.

My greetings for my father only began with 'Abu, did you remember to....?'

Dada jee, on the other hand always greeted him with 'You must be tired...?'

'But he naps a lot in the afternoons' I once told Abu. I never mentioned reading his digests or smoking his hookah. 'He calls it going to Kiratpur.'

That was when Abu told me what Kiratpur was: 'Dada jee's childhood home, like Sialkot is mine...' Abu also added '...where the happiest moments of our lives were spent.'

It was probably true. Because each time Dada jee spoke of Kiratpur he had that distinct smile. The one which stretched across his face and lit up his eyes. The only thing that made me smile was when I imagined my future, the life I had yet to live, the one I couldn't wait to. Sometimes I wished I could fast-forward ahead to the good parts; cars instead of bicycles, dorm rooms instead of classrooms, driver's licenses not backseats, height and muscle instead of skin and bones, and a salary instead of pocket money. To me, those things were far more exciting than the past. But Dada jee always smiled – that distinct smile – when he reminisced of days when he struggled financially just to put himself through school, and how he paid rent by tutoring neighborhood kids. Now I know why. It was a time when his whole life lay before him. A future of endless possibilities to look forward to.

But back then, I did not know that. So, when he slept and dreamt of moments already lived, I continued to dream of promises my future had made me: high school parties, a car, my own place, cigarettes, college and fancy jobs. As for my past, I really did not remember much of it but bits and pieces of me crawling around. My present? Well it was just that, a time that couldn't pass quickly enough to give way to the exciting times that lay ahead.

By the time I started my O-levels, boredom could no longer be pacified with stories of giant peaches or by the *afsanas* found in Dada jee's digests. I quickly replaced the space underneath my pillow with Bronte, Desai, Manto, even Ismat. I also spent most of my afternoons talking on the phone because now I had lots of friends – friends with crushes, friends with gossip. So afternoons became those anticipated moments when we could secretly talk on the phone with the opposite sex while mothers, fathers and grandparents napped.

Even then, the only reading next to Dada jee's pillow remained his Urdu digests.

'Dude, who's that in the background?' my friends would ask if they heard him coughing.

'Oh that's my Dada jee. He just returned from Kiratpur...'

'Oh, okay…'

Along with a heavier book-bag and ink-pens, O-levels also introduced us to dance parties, begged permissions to go to birthday dinners and Muddys Café – the only discotheque we had ever seen. Friends back then also carried around their parents' diplomat passes to these couples-only events, and I was lucky enough to always be invited as the plus one. I was also completely aware that since permissions to even a lunch with friends had to be begged and bargained for with parents, there was no way I would be allowed out all night. So friends, neighbours and sometimes even strangers carefully racked their brains to plan ways to sneak out at nights to go dancing. When we finally did, we spent merely an hour in those living rooms turned into dance floors – carpets rolled up, furniture removed – before we would sneak back into our beds. The more I risked getting caught, the more it excited me and the less I could wait to grow up and attend grown-up parties where no one worried about words like permission and curfew. When I would be able to stay out all night and not have to sneak in and out of bathroom windows, climbing up and down pipes.

And although I smiled at being one of the only ninth graders at Muddys Café or parties where they played bubblegum beats like Mr Vain and Saturday Night, I knew my Dada jee was also smiling, fast asleep…visiting Kiratpur.

By my A-levels we had moved to Karachi and it felt like moving from a suburb to an actual city. I was now also at that stage in my life when I just wasn't supposed to care. I wore only black and replaced my Ace of Base cassette tapes with CDs of Garbage, Prodigy and angry female rockers. This time, when it was suggested that I was going to have to share my room with Dada jee, I expressed dismay instead of the usual excitement. In my eyes, I was no longer a kid who thought it was cool to smoke a hookah and read Urdu digests. I was now a rebel who wanted to change the world by playing loud music and chatting with friends all afternoon on the latest craze – the internet.

TQ17: Sup! I'm so bored this afternoon? LOL
Getlost: Yeah! My Dada is sleeping in the same room as me!
TQ17: LOL…you loser jk
Getlost: hahahah =P

TQ17: Have you heard back from any colleges yet? I only got an acceptance from Mt Holyoke!

Getlost: Nope. Just a pile of rejection letters. Man I can't wait to leave for college. Life will be so much fun!

Even in my rebellious days, I knew it was time to log off when Dada jee pulled himself off his bed with a grunt and shot me that distinct glare before stomping off to the bathroom. I also knew that he was trying really hard to go to Kiratpur but I kept waking him up with the tapping of my keyboard. I did want to apologise. Maybe even ask him what he missed so much about Kiratpur, and whether he had written a new poem. But I didn't. On those afternoons when I found an excuse to go out with my friends, he probably cherished the peace and quiet of not having to listen to angry lyrics and dark beats. An afternoon when he could go to Kiratpur in peace.

In the fall of 1999 I left for college. Although I was sad to bid my friends farewell, I was told by everyone that these next four years were going to be the best years of my life. So I waited anxiously to begin these next four years. I had deliberately chosen a small liberal arts college in Pennsylvania where I would not know a soul. A place full of strangers waiting to become friends, where parties didn't need permissions and internet access didn't have to be purchased in the form of hours from an office in Boat Basin. I hoped to attend a Garbage concert once I got there and maybe even go dancing at a goth club! When it was time to say goodbye to my Dada jee, I repeated his words back to him verbatim – 'Heath and Time', 'Respect your own person, others are bound to respect you', 'Don't let your parents down.' Words of advice I had heard him utter countless times before, yet words I rarely ever paid attention to.

Once in college, afternoons didn't exist. Neither did nights, nor mornings. Hours were never enough, so we prayed for insomnia and studied wherever we found a place to sit with a staple diet of ramen noodles and pop tarts. As far as reading was concerned, I only got time to highlight mundane passages in textbooks. Yet every now and then I would soak myself in the newly discovered prose of Toni Morrison and Jack Kerouac or in the poetry of Nikki Giovanni and Sonia Sanchez. Strangers also quickly became friends. Nights we spent awake in computer labs and dance clubs. Days we spent taking several naps on different couches and bean bags on each other's floors. There were 8am classes, just like there were 3pm association meetings. Of course, there were also those Wednesday night rituals of dancing at Otters, nickel and dime wings at Chippers and pickled eggs with hot sauce before last call at the Penny Bar. If I ever stopped to think about Dada jee during those times, I could only picture afternoons. Him lying on the bed in my room: the *grr grr grr* of his hookah, those thick black reading glasses on top of Urdu digests. Him rolling over and falling asleep, hoping to relive his Kiratpur childhood for one whole hour. Sometimes... even an hour and a half.

Dada jee passed away during my junior year of college. I was told a couple of weeks after it had happened. Once the news hit me, I did not know what to do or how to feel. The only realisation that hit me was that I would no longer be able to see him again. There were no more chances left for me to tell him that I loved him. Neither could I go back in time to ask about Kiratpur, to read a poem he had written or even to share my own writing and ask him if he understood. No longer would I ever be able to spend an afternoon on a bed beside him reading his Urdu digests.

No longer hear the word Kiratpur replace the word nap.

And I didn't.

Today, I watch my father when he naps in the afternoons, a man who has achieved everything he ever aspired to in his career. His children now grown up, out of the house, settled, married, working. A grandchild of his own that he tries to cuddle up with in the afternoons. I then wonder what he dreams of during those afternoons. I also wonder if he will ever tell my niece that he goes to Sialkot when he naps. I wonder if she will ever ask my sister what Sialkot is. I wonder if my sister will ever tell her that 'Sialkot is your Nana's childhood home....a city far, far away from Washington DC.'

Then I wonder about myself. Of a time when I too would stop dreaming about the future and dream of a life already lived – even if for an hour or an hour and a half.

And then I wonder what those dreams would be like? Would I dream of crazy nights that turned into mornings, starting off in massive clubs in DC and New York and then giggles with friends in 24/7 diners? Would I dream of college life with friends pulling all-nighters together to finish papers with 4am caffeine breaks at gas stations and Wal-Mart? Would I dream of high school dance parties and how happiness meant spending every minute with friends out of the house whether at yearbook meetings, community service trips, school-play rehearsals or lunches at Copper Kettle? Would I dream of sneaking out of bathroom windows and climbing down pipes to meet my friends on the weekends? Maybe I would dream of scorching summer afternoons in Lahore and Islamabad reading Enid Blyton and Urdu digests next to my Dada jee and secretly smoking his hookah.

I honestly don't know.

Because today I'm still too busy planning for the future.

But tomorrow...

maybe...

I may find myself in bed...

... hoping to dream of today. Just this very day.

INTIMATIONS OF GHALIB

Like all poets of the ghazal, Mirza Asadullah Khan (1797-1869) is best known by his *takhallus*, Ghalib, the pen-name with which he signed his ghazals. He was born in Agra, moved to Delhi at an early age, and but for an absence of three years during which he visited Calcutta, he never left Delhi again, not even during the great rebellion of 1857.

Although the British became sovereigns of much of India by 1803, they found it useful to maintain a titular Mughal emperor in Delhi where he kept court, with some of its former trappings but powerless outside the walls of the city. The reign of the last of these Mughal emperors, Bahadur Shah Zafar, produced a final but brilliant flowering of Urdu culture in India. Ghalib was the leading light of this Delhi florescence and in 1854 he became *ustad* or poet-mentor to the Mughal emperor who was an accomplished poet in his own right.

Ghalib is commonly regarded as the greatest of Urdu poets. He wrote much of his poetry in Farsi and believed this was superior to his work in Urdu. Nevertheless, although his Urdu ghazals were written mostly in his early years, many before he was twenty, his claim to fame rests primarily on his slim Urdu divan and secondarily on his Urdu letters. In a society that was outwardly ruled by the shariah, poets used the ghazal to celebrate love and longing, and, under the cover of symbols and metaphors, questioned, criticized, and even made light of the religious and social conventions of society. Ghalib covers these subjects in the most exquisite manner, bringing a new and sharper irreverence to his dissent, but nearly always his barbs are softened by his inimitable wit and humour.

Ghalib offers observations on life that anticipate the doubt, skepticism and angst that have come to define the modern age. For all these qualities, his ability to memorialise the varied moods of a lover, the breadth of his vision, his deep humanity, the unforgettable music of his lines, his use of new imagery and new uses of old imagery, all the nuances of meaning captured in his dictions, his wit and playfulness, and the multiple layers of meaning in his ghazals – and notwithstanding the difficulty of his diction and syntax – Ghalib remains the poet of poets as well as the common man. He is quoted by politicians and housewives, and his ghazals have been set to music by the best singers and music composers of the last few generations.

1.

عشرت قطره ہے دریا میں فنا ہو جانا
درد کا حد سے گزرنا ہے دو ہو جانا

A drop becomes bliss when it enters the sea.
In a night of excess pain rises to remedy.

After years I could play the right notes.
On our first tryst, fate changed the melody.

No one masters his soul without this.
Not love, only her sword will set us free.

So weary, my tears turn to sighs. I like
This crossing over from liquid to levity.

How shall I cleave flesh from my bone?
I am your touch: you dream inside me.

A lover sheds tears, clouds disperse in rain –
Till sorrows part, setting his spirit free.

Ghalib, dew-laden roses take us to discovery.
In every light discover – your eye in beauty.

2.

ذکر اس پریوش کا اور پھر بیاں اپنا
بن گیا رقیب آخر تھا جو رازداں اپنا

She has such beauty: and I had a way with words.
So I lost a confidant and he is courting her.

Give me a lofty perch clear beyond the sky:
And I will sketch a vista that soars still higher.

Be done writing your lovesick letters: go show her
Your bloodied pen and blistered fingers.

My rivals now will never squeal on me.
I got them to sign my screeds against her.

I had no lock on wit nor danced with charisma.
Ghalib, How did I offend the higher powers?

3.

دل مرا سوزِ نہاں سے بے محابا جل گیا
آتشِ خاموش کے مانند گویا جل گیا

It was a fire unlike any I have seen. It went
To work inwardly, the heat was extreme.

There was nothing I could save, a memory,
A face. I lost a whole life without any trace.

Every wound, every scar was a radiant star.
This festival of lights was lost in a blaze.
Ghalib, I seek solace in ruins and ashes.
Get me away from these false painted faces.

(introduced and translated by M Shahid Alam)

Sohni Mahiwal by John Siddique

Part I - Izzat Baig (Mahiwal)

I
Each moment is the first moment.

II
I have seen this day many times before.
At night the moon's face on my face.

III
Made smooth by the hands of day,
a cheap vase for tourists to buy.
What have I made with my hands?

IV
It was day. It was night.
I thought that the passage of time
was what life was about.
The moment before I met you.

V
It was day. It was night.
The face of the moon in a black blue sky.
Some things would catch my eyes.
Though I was mostly counting time.
The moment before I met you.

VI
Coiled clay – the rope of the heart.
Every moment is the first moment,
this is the secret of the cup we share.

We are made in fire; we are the hand
and the turning of the wheel.
It is day, and then it is night.

VII

The rules which we try to make against the river
of the heart. Rules and castes. Notions of
respectability, unlived lives.

Shame on their faces for the things
They would love to make with their own hands.
They take you from me, but the clay has been fired.
There is no legislation against the river of the heart.

VIII

It is nothing to choose what others see
as poverty to be near you.

I let go of the old life.
There is no poverty except
for selling the heart cheaply
for trinkets, money, caste and respectability.

I will wait in moonlight on the far side of the river.
I will pray in moonlight as she guides your crossing.

IX

Eat my flesh – I am all for you; blood for blood.
Turn the world with your fingers my love.
The space inside is only ever filled by love.
Life moves the river.

We sleep side by side.
My fingers move over the line
of your arm, caress your waist.
I watch your face as you sleep
in moonlight. Coiled rope, clay heart;
painted with the only colours we have.

X
The world hates lovers. It fears beauty.

It cuts its own face to prove its point.

Ingests poison and then waits for us to die.

It places a porous jug in your hands
so that the river may pull you down.

It tries all of its tricks
to unname, to unmake us.

There is no one richer than we are.
We have painted our love brushstroke
by brushstroke on the clay of our flesh.

Part II – Sohni

I
The space inside is only ever filled by love.

II
The inside is unspoken
– outside we paint our lives in colour.

III
There is a river flowing between us.
Between sleep and wakefulness.
Between one meeting with love and the next.

IV
The hands of day turn each moment over,
poetry speaking through touch.

Moments painted brushstroke by brushstroke
with the only colours we have.

V

The potter throws the clay to the wheel
– a moment, a movement. The whole of
the artist's being defined in a single action.

Each moment is the first moment.
There is only trust and touch to go by.

VI

It is not art that makes art.
In is not the desire to write
which puts ink on paper.
It is not the value of an antique vase
which gives it value.
It is life moving the river.

VII

At night we meet despite
what has been chosen for us by others.

At night we make the dreams
of the day into reality with our bodies.

Painting our love brushstroke
by brushstroke on the clay of our flesh.

There is no one richer than we are.

VIII

The vase is filled, kept buoyant, by love,
its inner space allowing the body to exist.

Fingers and hands shape the outside.

Giving our lives in this instant to throw this pot.

Bigger on the inside: cups of love,

a vase of dreams, containers of oil and wine,
a bowl of salt - cupped hands of treasure.

IX
You feed me with fish caught from the river.
Every moment apart is a river between us.

On the nights when we are poor,
you feed me with the flesh of yourself.

Your bandage makes me cry. Never cut
the meat of yourself for love.
I want you whole.

Painting our story on this vase,
its being, its beauty, its form is our flesh.

X
The clay turning on the wheel, placed
in fire and in time. Fingers having learned
to shape the life moving through us.
The inside of the vessel is alive
with the shadow of our souls.

Others make bread, build houses, hammer in nails,
fix car engines, write poetry and hold babies.
Some lie with the words in their mouths and faces,
their hands always give them away. Love and poetry
course through our fingers making shapes of our clay.

Zehra has not written much for many days by Zehra Nigah

Zehra has not written much for many days
Although during those days she has seen everything
But if she writes, what should she write? And if she thinks, what should she think?
Thought has dimmed a little, her hand trembles a little
Zehra has not written much for many days

She is not so naive as to say anything that comes to her mind
Her lips are not sealed without reason
Nor is she that old to tire easily
She has deliberately decided to be like this
She has kept everything in a suitcase of memories
It is the only way of living at ease
Zehra has not written much for many days

She thought the house and its effects were a fortress of protection
She learnt that the housekeeper is like a plaything made of clay
Be it clay or stone, diamond or pearl
Authority over the house belongs to the householder
What to say of helplessness when being governed
That stone in your hand is a prize for being a believer
Zehra has not written much for many days

The mandate of friendship which she hung on a wall
Has the tide of time destroyed that wall?
The sanctity of love's mandate is just this
A quivering of the lips, a tie which is present from the beginning
Zehra has not written much for many days

Having raised two sons this naïve woman thought
She alone owned the wealth of this world
But time has revealed a mirror in which
A perspective of the picture has only now become clear
The world is an oyster for growing children
As it opens, each chapter is a spectacle

Parents are like an overly familiar map
Upon which all the colours are faded
Zehra has not written much for many days

She had thought that brothers and sisters are rivers of love
She saw that sometimes the river changes its course too
Brothers too are trapped as obligatory carers
Sisters too undergo that which fate decrees
There is a mother who talks to the trees
There are ten children to think of, but still she is lonely
Zehra has not written much for many days

(translated by Amina Yaqin)

ATIA JILANI: WRITING THE QUR'AN

Syed Haroon ur Rasheed Ahmed

Atia Jilani is a self-taught calligrapher, a painter and a writer living in the village of Mohammad Abad. She is the first Asian woman to inscribe the entire Qur'an in the elegant calligraphic style of Naskh, despite never attending an art school. She inscribed the verses of holy text on cardboard paper with the help of two handmade calligraphic pens. The entire project took seven years to complete. Her calligraphic Qur'an has been compiled in six volumes, each containing five Qur'anic sections (*paras*). Her exceptional talent has been widely recognised, and her Qur'anic art has been exhibited twice by the Al Hamra Art Council.

Jilani belongs to a family that is deeply connected with art in its various forms. Her great grandfather, Syed Bilal Shah Jilani, grandfather, Syed Mubarak Shah Jilani, and uncle, Syed Anees Shah Jilani were prominent writers. But her major inspiration comes from her mother Syeda Ameer-un-Nisa Jilani, who not only recognised Atia's artistic talents but also encouraged the artist within her. Ameer-un-Nisa was a thoughtful observer, a realistic poet and a fluent narrator of feelings and thoughts, and Atia has discreetly adopted her nature and qualities.

During her childhood, Atia fell deeply in love with words, their shapes and the feelings that are associated with their appearance. She spent her childhood drawing alphabets in the air and on the surface of waters, adoring the vivid movements of her hands when they drew words instead of just writing them. These alphabets drawn on water in water tubs gradually transformed into words and then sentences; the artist inside her grew stronger with the passage of time. Later, she practised different approaches for drawing words with simple pens on pieces of paper, on water with handmade waves, and by melting candles on cloths. To satisfy her passion, she also worked on her handwriting skills, to make sure that the words she wrote were drawn beautifully on the paper.

Later, she started inscribing Qur'anic verses for her grandmother, who gave them to anyone who wanted them. Arabic words and letters have their own unique composition, which openly exhibits artistic style. And it is the splendid architecture of Arabic letters that inspired Atia to pay more attention to Arabic calligraphy.

Once she decided to inscribe the entire Qur'an, says Atia, she found herself thinking about the purpose of her project. 'Why am I doing this?' She did not know. Was it for fame? To stand out as an individual? Her questions brought vague and obscure answers. In the end, she says, she realised that the purpose lay somewhere in her love for God. She thought only of God, and never thought of reasons and purposes again. Calligraphy became a consistent element of her daily routine; she finds it impossible to separate it from her own self.

She lived in the countryside with no access to art supplies or painting accessories. So she made her own pens. In her entire project, she used only two pens, which she dipped in and wrote with regular ink. She drew on ordinary paperboards, which are rough and rigid, bought from the local market. At the beginning of her project, Atia found it quite hard to arrange the chapters of Holy Qur'an as they are arranged in conventionally published copies. She wanted an arrangement which left no empty space on the page, a task that turned out to be exceptionally hard. She kept changing the font size and rearranging the order but to no avail. Finally, she decided on a sequence of two-page spreads. It worked.

Atia wrote every day after breakfast. She had to be extra conscious of her work: a careless mistake would mean disrupting God's message. As she inscribed holy words, she says, her shoulders grew heavier, as if they were carrying the weight of God's message. She found herself engraving these feelings in the form of words. Some invisible force empowered her and the appetite for perfection kept growing. She used a Qalmi Qur'an from Mubarak Urdu Library and a copy of the Qur'an published by Taj Company for help, as they had been certified and checked already for any kind of printing mistakes.

She started her project in 1985 and completed in in 1991. When she finished writing the final chapter of the Qur'an, she called everyone in her family and showed them her achievement. Her mother cried, her brother cried, and along with them, she cried. 'It was the most blessed day of my life', she says. She still remembers her mother saying, 'When I realise that you have inscribed the entire Qur'an, I'm enthralled.' But Pakistan itself did not recognise her achievement till 2006, when Atia's family moved to the city of Lahore and her work became widely known.

Atia is now working on a new project, calligraphing the Qur'an in bigger font thus making it easier to read for people with eyesight problems. But this project is an even bigger challenge. Inscribing Qur'an in life-sized letters requires more skills and perfection and she did not consider herself qualified enough to give a professional touch to this project. It was time to learn from a master calligrapher. She has successfully completed the first five parts of the Holy Qur'an, in two of which she was helped by her elder brother, Syed Ahmed Shah Jilani.

Atia Jilani says her work would have been recognised much earlier if she had lived in a city. But then in a city, with all its distractions, she might not have succeeded in keeping her promises even to herself. Country life is like the air; and its peace, like water. Because it helps you breathe, and satisfies your thirst. She believes that.

ET CETERA

THE CATALYST FOR KNOWLEDGEABLE GENERATION

SELANGOR FOUNDATION

For further details, kindly contact us at :

Corporate Affairs Unit
Menara Yayasan Selangor, No 18A, Jalan Persiaran Barat
46000 Petaling Jaya,
Selangor Darul Ehsan,
Malaysia.
Tel : +603 - 7955 1212
Fax : +603 - 7954 1790
Email : Info@yayasanselangor.org.my
www.yayasanselangor.org.my

IMRAN KHAN

Ali Miraj

On a visit to Karachi in 2011, I witnessed a surprising spectacle. Imran Khan, Pakistan's legendry cricketer, was in town. His Pakistan Tehreek-e-Insaf (PTI) party was holding a rally in the shadow of Quaid-e-Azam Mazar, the mausoleum that houses the tomb of Mohammad Ali Jinnah, the founder of the nation. Jinnah, a Lincoln's Inn-educated barrister with a penchant for suits tailored in Saville Row, died barely a year following the creation of the state, providing insufficient time for democracy to take root. The country has suffered much since then. Now, sixty-five years later, the former playboy who is seldom seen these days out of shalwar kameez, the national dress of the country, was offering the nation a new hope.

The 'Imran' bandwagon rolled into town on 25 December. By all accounts there were over a hundred thousand people there. Leading industrialists with little interest in politics, feudal landlords and urban middle class 'aunties' joined rickshaw drivers and mobile phone sellers to attend the rally. A surprising number of my own relatives and friends were also there. The atmosphere was electric. There was a sense that history was being made. A desire to say 'I was there' when the 'tsunami', as Imran Khan himself refers to it, began.

Where has this tsunami come from? Khan established PTI in 1996. For years his party was considered to be a one-man band. It won no seats in the 1997 general election. It won only one seat in the next 2002 elections: Imran's own. Yet here he was striding into town in a cavalcade that a US president would be proud of, addressing a crowd that global pop stars cannot generate. In all my frequent trips to Pakistan over the last thirty-seven years, I had never witnessed anything like this. He had stardust; but there was also something more.

Khan has captured the zeitgeist. He speaks the language of the vast majority of Pakistanis, particularly the young, who feel desperate. It is more than just being fed up with President Asif Zardari, the narcissist widower of Benazir Bhutto, branded 'Mr 10 per cent', who many regard as a national embarrassment. They are tired of the dynastic merry-go-round of the Bhuttos on the one hand and the Sharif brothers, the leaders of the Pakistani Muslim League (N), on the other, with smatterings of military rule in-between. All of them have shown themselves to be rapacious, kleptomaniacs who see power as a vehicle to amass personal fortunes. Imran Khan offers a real alternative. If many are not yet prepared to give him their full support, they are at least willing to give him a fair hearing.

So how did a dashing cricketing hero come to carry the hopes of a great number of his countrymen on his shoulders and what chance does he have of fulfilling them?

Imran Khan Niazi was born in 1952 and brought up in the pleasant surroundings of Zamman Park in Lahore. A Pashtun by origin, his father came from Khyber Pakhtunkhwa (formerly known as North-Western Frontier Province), associated with providing a safe haven to elements of the Pakistani Taliban. His mother was from the Burki Pashtun tribe in South Waziristan in Pakistan's notorious Federally Administered Tribal Areas (FATA). He had an idyllic childhood in a close-knit family where his mother played a pivotal role in his life. When he was not being doted over by his four sisters, he was playing cricket with his cousins, shooting partridge, or trekking in the Karakoram Mountains. The Pashtun traditions of loyalty, honour, and hospitality were drilled into him from an early age. He attended the prestigious Aitchison College, the Eton of Pakistan. Established in 1886 in the tradition of British public schools, Aitchison, with its prefects, head boys, team captains, military service and its focus on sports and teamwork, ingrained leadership qualities in Khan.

But Khan's initial interest was not in political leadership but cricket. He wished to follow on the footsteps of his uncle, the formidable batsman, Majid Khan. He completed his education at the Royal Grammar School Worcester and then went straight to Oxford University. He was obsessed with cricket and spent most his time playing, showing no inclination towards the political path he would later pursue. This was in stark contrast to his contemporary, Benazir Bhutto, the former Prime Minister, and leader of the Pakistan's Peoples Party (PPP). She lobbied hard to secure the Presidency of the Oxford Union, and then followed her father into politics. Her son, Bilawal, became the Chairman of PPP while still at Oxford, aged just nineteen, after her own death in December 2007. Politics is a family business in Pakistan. Lineage trumps ability, experience and merit.

Khan began his cricket career against England in 1971 aged just eighteen. He would go on to become one of the most prodigious all-rounders in history, amassing 362 wickets and 3,807 runs in the test arena. But it was not an easy ride. His test debut was a disaster. He was taken aside after the match by the senior players and told that he would be better off focusing on being a batsman. His coach concluded that he had neither the physique nor the action to be a fast bowler. But Khan did not give up. He changed his action and practised relentlessly. His next appearance in a test match in 1974 was successful. The rest is history. He became one of only eight players in the world to achieve the 'All-rounder's triple', scoring over 3,000 runs and taking over 300 wickets in test matches. In a global culture which is increasingly driven by a desire to achieve instant fame, Khan is an exemplar of what hard work, focus and determination and indomitable self-belief can achieve.

Some leaders are born great, as the saying goes, but Khan had greatness thrust upon him. A naturally shy individual, when he was given the captaincy in 1982 at the age of thirty, he felt uncomfortable speaking to the players directly and requested the manager to mediate. But his leadership abilities were so established that following his decision to retire from international cricket in 1987, he was persuaded by the then President, General Zia-ul-Haq, to resume the captaincy for the good of the nation. He would later go on to reach the high point of his career, leading Pakistan to victory in the 1992 world cup, the only time Pakistan has won the competition.

Following his retirement from international cricket, Khan could have taken the easy path and pontificated on matches from the comfort of a television studio or coached the national team. But he eschewed this for pursuit of his charitable work. He worked tirelessly to establish a cancer hospital and research institution in memory of his mother, Shaukat Khanum, who died of cancer in 1984. He ploughed a considerable amount of his own personal wealth into the project and flew all around the world raising funds, auctioning all his cricket trophies in the process, while refusing to compromise on his aim of treating 75 per cent of patients for free (currently 65 per cent receive free treatment with a further 10 per cent paying just a fraction of the costs). The process of raising funds brought him into contact with ordinary Pakistanis who displayed their extraordinary generosity by donating whatever they could. A key method he employed was to get children enthusiastic about the project by visiting schools. He called them 'Imran's Tigers'; and they proved instrumental in championing his cause with their parents and relatives. Incidentally, while he got no support either from Benazir or her husband for the hospital, they wanted to attend the opening ceremony and cut the ribbon to bolster their fledgling popularity. Khan refused, requesting a ten-year-old cancer patient to do the honours instead. That made him a political enemy of the couple. Shortly after announcing his intention to form a political movement, the hospital was bombed in 1996, killing seven people; the finger can be pointed at any one of his myriad of enemies. He has expanded his philanthropic pursuits to education by establishing a technical college in the Mianwali District, his father's home town. Namal College was opened in 2008; and made an associate college of the University of Bradford of which he is Chancellor. When the floods in Pakistan took hold in August 2010, he immediately launched an emergency fund-raising appeal while President Zardari visited his chateau in France.

So Imran Khan, the cricketer and philanthropist, is a tried and tested entity. But what about Imran Khan the politician? And what drove him to enter the political fray in a country where the pursuit of power is a blood-sport?

His answer is simple: 'to end corruption'. The principal rationale for individuals to enter politics, Khan has explained, is to 'plunder the country'. In an interview with the former cricket player turned sports pundit, Jonathan Agnew, he explains that to refrain from politics is to condemn Pakistan to be run by criminals. Corruption destroys governance and meritocracy. The country's potential goes 'down the drain'. He has a point. If elected, he plans to establish a National Accountability Bureau and to strengthen the judiciary so that it can hold politicians to account and is not just a de facto extension of the executive. His second priority is to tackle tax evasion. In a country of 180 million people, only 2 per cent pay income tax.

There are three things that can be highlighted in his favour. First, Khan is without doubt the cleanest politician in Pakistan. He has even opened his personal accounts to public scrutiny. His probity is unquestioned. He refused offers to join the governments of General Zia-ul-Haq, Moeen Qureshi and General Musharraf, on principle. For fifteen years since the launch of his party, he has been an outsider. Second, he has tenacity by the truck-load. His cricketing career provides ample proof. Politics is an inherently dirty business the world over, but in Pakistan, intrigue, conspiracy and murder go with the territory. It is dominated by a troika of vested interests: the feudal aristocracy, the upper echelons of the civil service and the all-powerful army. He will be up against seasoned campaigners who would not hesitate to use dirty tactics against him, and will thus need all the perseverance and resolve he acquired on the cricket pitch. Third, Khan understands the youth of Pakistan. His 'tigers' are now young voters. In a country where more than 60 per cent of the population is under the age of twenty-five, this ability to connect with the young is invaluable. One reason why his *jalsas* are more like concerts than political rallies.

But there is another side. His views on religion are rather simplistic; and he has been closely associated with and supportive of the right-wing Jamaat-e-Islami, that sees Islam as an unbending, monolithic and authoritarian ideology. In his autobiography, *Pakistan: A Personal History,* Khan says that a simple man called Mian Bashir, who he met in 1988, is 'the single most powerful spiritual influence' on him. He encouraged Khan to focus on compassion and humanity, not on the rituals that the mullahs he had encountered were obsessed with. That may well be the case but Pakistan is full of 'simple' religious soothsayers who have led millions up the garden path. It is good to see that as an international celebrity who is often asked questions about his faith, he is forced to read. But he ought to read more than just the works of converts and the *taqwa* (God consciousness) brigade. A familiarity with the intellectual tradition of Islam, and the literature of reform, would be helpful. The only real thinker he appears to focus on is Muhammad Iqbal, the poet-philosopher and spiritual founder of Pakistan, who was deeply concerned with issues of freedom and social justice. However, he needs to go beyond Iqbal and discover the true complexity and interdependence of the contemporary world.

Then there is the naked nationalism. Khan's rhetoric is often couched in conformist ideology, jingoism and anti-Other (India or America) phobias. He wants the Kashmir issue to be resolved before agreeing to increase trade with India, currently a paltry US$3 billion a year compared to India-China trade flows of US$75 million a year. Resolving the thorny issue of Kashmir, which has been a festering sore and a cause of a number of conflicts between the two neighbours, before increasing commercial ties may play well with the nationalist gallery at home but it is exceptionally short-sighted.

Khan's anti-American pronouncements verge on hysteria. Of course, there is a great deal to be angry about. He has rightly suggested that Pakistan should be a friend to America but not a 'hired gun'. He has also rightly called for the immediate withdrawal of US troops from Afghanistan and an end to drone attacks which have served as a recruiting sergeant for the Taliban. He wants Pakistan to be economically self-sufficient, not a hostage to perpetual hand-outs from the US government. He feels that Pakistan's leaders have taken US money in return for bombing their own people. He points to Raymond Davis, a CIA operative, who shot dead two people in Lahore, supposedly in self-defence, in January 2011, as evidence of the government allowing foreign intelligence agents to operate unimpeded throughout the country. He also highlights that the twenty-five million Pashtuns living in Pakistan do not recognise the Durand line – the border between Afghanistan and Pakistan – and feel a natural loyalty to their fifteen million brethren living on the other side. All this is right and proper. But unbridled hatred of the US is something quite different. This venom has affected the Pakistani psyche to such an extent that many Pakistanis start to foam at the mouth at the very mention of America. Such hatred, which Khan inflames at every opportunity, would have little effect on American foreign policy but would consume Pakistanis themselves.

Then there are his vaunted claims. He will end corruption, he says, in ninety days; with the aid of computers if necessary! He will also reduce government expenditure, solve the energy crisis which is seeing power outages for up to eighteen hours a day, and improve the woefully inadequate education system, introducing a common curriculum in all schools and ending the elitism of English-medium schools – all in a matter of months.

It is difficult to say whether this is simply electioneering or genuine naivety. He often cites Mahathir Mohamad, the former Prime Minister of Malaysia, as a great example to follow. However, there are numerous allegations of corruption against Mahathir who is regarded by some as one of the most authoritarian leaders in the history of Southeast Asia. And a country ruled by a single alliance dominated by a single party for over six decades is hardly a thriving democracy whose example should be followed.

It is evident that whilst Imran Khan has articulated an attractive vision of a country based on meritocracy rather than nepotism, where the rich pay their fair share and wealth is shared more equitably, he is short on detailed policy. His views on the Pakistani Taliban verge on dangerous simplicity. He refuses to talk about home-grown terrorism and its daily toll of death and destruction of innocent citizens. He wants a ceasefire with the Taliban and sees problems in the Federally Administered Tribal Areas (FATA) on Pakistan's western flank as a 'fight for Pashtun solidarity against a foreign invader'. He sees no threat to Pakistan from the Taliban's ideology and claims that 90 per cent are simply resisting occupation with 10 per cent actually posing a threat which can be eliminated in ninety days. And he has no suggestions for how the simmering insurgency in Balochistan, Pakistan's largest province by land-mass and rich in natural resources, should be handled.

There are also worrying trends in his own party. Politicians of questionable reputation have jumped ship to join the PTI. Party stalwarts have been side-lined to accommodate the new luminaries who have been given positions of authority and influence. And a cult of personality has emerged around Khan. His supporters seem incapable of tolerating any criticism of the great man.

However, these shortcomings may not matter. Khan is riding a wave of dissatisfaction. With a growing number of Pakistanis yearning for change, Khan offers promise of change and hope where there is no hope. In a You-Gov poll in April 2011, Imran Khan was favoured by 61 per cent as first choice to lead the country. The second most popular candidate, former President, General Pervez Musharraf, received 12 per cent of first preference votes. The current President, Asif Ali Zardari, received a dire 2 per cent. The survey was clearly angled towards urban rather than rural Pakistanis but it highlights Khan's increasing popularity.

So can he still succeed? It is an open question. In a country where political parties are treated as family heirlooms and seats in the National Assembly are won by entrenched operators through a combination of kinship and patronage via local henchmen on the ground, Khan faces an uphill battle. Attracting thousands of adoring supporters to rallies is one thing. Turning that into hard votes is much more challenging.

There are two key risks that Khan needs to be mindful of. First, what we might call the 'Obama syndrome' – the risk of promising too much and delivering little. His party's website states that it will secure a 50 per cent increase in per capita income and achieve full literacy in five years. Drive and ambition are admirable qualities, but reality is also a vital ingredient of statecraft. Second, whilst he is considered a 'clean' politician, untainted by largesse, his brand is in serious danger of being tarnished by his fellow travellers. If his loyal supporters feel that they don't matter and can be passed over in favour of serial defectors from other parties, their resentment will grow.

That said, I get the impression that Khan is at peace with himself, and has found a mission and purpose in life. He is a man of faith who feels a responsibility towards the society he lives in. Principled, courageous and patriotic: he is a man of conviction. Pakistan would be lucky to have him as a prime minister. But I think the odds are stacked against him.

TEN THINGS WE LOVE ABOUT PAKISTAN

A country allegedly and perpetually on the edge of chaos. A nation shrouded in darkness, thanks largely to power cuts, toxic religion, feudal politics, a corporate military and the ever present threat of violence. A state teetering on economic collapse, political fragmentation and imminent breakdown. Is there anything to love about Pakistan? We think there is.

1. The People
They have endured everything. From Biblical floods and massive earthquakes, military dictators and kleptomaniacs; mad Mullahs, terrorism, drone attacks and suicide bombers; ethnic feuds, gang violence and target killings; stagflation, austerity and food riots; to the humiliation of being described as a 'failed state' and being both 'loved' and bullied by the US, often simultaneously. And yet their resolve remains undiminished, their hospitality unparalleled, and their determination to overcome bedlam and turmoil unwavering. It's time we recognised the courage and indefatigable passion of Pakistan's people.

2. Poetry
There isn't much that can send a heart racing more than a few choice verses of the best Urdu poetry. At around 66 per cent, illiteracy rates in Pakistan may be among the highest in the world, but tap a peasant-farmer on the shoulder and ask him about his favourite poet and you'll be lucky to escape before having heard an entire *divan*, or a collection from one of the Urdu canons of Mirza Ghalib, Mir Taqi Mir, Khwaja Mir Dard and more. We love Urdu poetry: all the way from the first Urdu poet, Amir Khusro, to countless grandmasters down the ages, right up to Iqbal and Faiz Ahmad Faiz. However, we must also admit that our knees get a bit wobbly when we hear Bullah Shah, and other Sufi poets, in Punjabi. But you don't have to take our word for it; or feel sorry for yourself if you are not an Urdu speaker. Listen to ghazal and qawwali singers, artists who popularise and keep the tradition

alive, such as Noorjehan, Mehdi Hassan, Farida Khanum, the Sabri Brothers and Nusrat Fateh Ali Khan, and discover the magical beauty of Urdu and Panjabi poetry yourself.

3. Classical novels

When the iPhone runs out of juice or when iTunes freezes, we turn to novels from Urdu's classical age. From the accounts of Delhi gripped by a plague in Deputy Nazir Ahmed's Toba *tun nasuh* to the adventures of a speck of dust by Abdul Halim Sharar, the beauty of Urdu prose surely cannot be matched. We particularly love the novels of Deputy Nazir Ahmed, Maulana Rashid-ul-Khairi, Mirza Hadi Ruswa, Qazi Abdul Gaffar, Aziz Ahmad, Abdul Halim Sharar; and the exponents of Urdu literature claimed by people on the other side of border: Premchand, Krishan Chander and Ismat Chughtai.

4. Ingenuity

The ingenuity and 'can-do' attitude of Pakistan's people is a marvel to behold. Pakistanis can design and build anything. Whether you want a nuclear device or a non-stick frying pan, there will always be a road-side or pavement workshop ready to deliver your order. It will all happen while-u-wait, by a technician who won't have had more than a few years of primary schooling, and all for one-tenth of its 'normal' price. As far as Pakistan's concerned, Dr Who's Tardis is not a work of fiction. The nation's transport planners know exactly how to shoehorn impossible numbers of people into the tiniest spaces. A humble scooter can be turned into a transport system for the extended family; a rickshaw for two can easily squeeze a dozen passengers — sitting atop handle bars, on the driver's lap, or dangling from the vehicle's sides. Sadly the ingenuity trait also seems to be shared by Pakistan's criminal underworld, and by its political classes who continue to break records for diversity in fraudulent methods. Pakistan frequently finds itself in top-ten lists for political corruption. Pakistanis like to joke that the only reason their country isn't right there at the top is probably because its politicians managed to bribe the eventual 'winner'.

5.*Young talent*

We celebrate the amazing young men and women who've transformed —
and are transforming — Pakistan's cultural landscape, and in particular the
country's phenomenal movie scene. Inspirational film directors include the
Oscar-winning Sharmeen Obaid-Chinoy, honoured for her 2012 documentary film *Saving Face* about the lives and hopes of women who suffer acid
attacks. Then there's Shoaib Mansoor, director of the hard-hitting *Bol*
(Speak) from 2011 in which a young woman on death row narrates her
tragic life story before she goes to the gallows; and who also directed *Khuda
Kay Liya* in 2007 (For God's Sake), which explores the phenomenon of
Islamist activism among the country's secular elite. No list would be complete without a mention for Hasan Zaidi, founder of the Karachi International Film Festival who directed *Raat Chali Hai Jhoom Ke* (The Long Night)
in 2000, which has one of the most delicious femmes fatales you have ever
seen. We also applaud the nation's fashion designers; the producers, writers,
and actors in comedies and TV plays; a legion of younger musicians and
singers; and not forgetting the thousands of young journalists and bloggers
who put their lives on the line to expose corruption.

6. *Paklish*

'We find there is a very great desire among Pakistani people to become
acquainted with the peculiarities of the English language and they have great
curiosity regarding it.' 'Be therefore as it may therefore be' many Pakistanis
speak English. We 'have, indeed, occasion to express our sincere and heart-
felt gratitude' for preserving 'the same' in fossilised late Victorian idiom.
Public transport is 'conveyance', career is 'carrier', a bathroom is 'latrine',
a lounge is a 'drawing room', and a range of other examples 'can be had'
from local newspapers and books. Even internationally published authors
slip into Paklish. We plead guilty too as an odd 'nefarious plot' or a 'Kara-
chite' may have inadvertently crept into this issue of *Critical Muslim*. As 'your
obedient servants' we seek your forgiveness. 'Thank you, please'.

7. *Sweets*

It's official: Pakistan is the world capital for people with a sweet tooth.
Travelling in a nation of hospitality-conscious sweet-lovers means it is near-
impossible to go anywhere in Pakistan without being greeted with a glass of

a red-coloured sugary drink called 'Rooh Afza', served on a tray next to a plate of some choice *mithai*, or 'sweetmeats' in Paklish. The sticky and intensely sugary *barfis* and *cham-chams* once exclusive to Lahore or Multan are now of course a global phenomenon, but in our humble opinion nothing beats the taste of a crisp *jalebi* made fresh in front of your eyes. Indeed, nothing beats *mithai* unless you happen to have a health condition in which sugar could be fatal. Sadly, that includes most of Pakistan where diabetes is virtually a national emergency. We fear that this may put the sweet-meat vendors out of business, unless they embrace 'modernity' and start using artificial sweeteners.

8. Mountains and Mangoes

Switzerland has the Alps; Peru is blessed with the Andes, but Pakistan, yes Pakistan, scorns these bumps from a great height, for three of the world's highest ranges meet in its territory — the Himalayas, the Karakorams, and the Hindu Kush. When it comes to mountains, Pakistan looks down its nose at the rest of the world, and its nose is as high as K2. Pakistani mangoes, 'the king of fruit', are just as colossal in taste and juiciness.

9. Missiles

Defence is the one sector of Pakistan's economy that forever seems to boom, boom, boom. No matter which government of whichever party is in power; no matter if the president is a general, or an elected politician, he will have no problem sucking funds out of health and education and firing it in the direction of the bomb-making Pakistan Ordnance Factory. Pakistan, it seems, has a missile for every day of the year. Many are appropriately named after Islam's warrior heroes, the Ghauri, Shaheen, the Ghaznavi. They are also public property, standing phallic and shining at the centres of roundabouts, squares, and even, sadly, universities. Now all the nation needs is to find someone they can be thrown at.

10. 'Load-shedding'

The Paklish for power cuts is an apt metaphor for the efficient corruption of politicians and energy providers as they fill their pockets and secure their families' right to rule. What a great display of familial provision as the rest of the country sweats in the dark, patients die in hospitals, the factories come to a grinding halt, and productivity takes a nose dive. We love to get those candles out and wave our fans frantically in the 40-degree heat. Load-shedding is also preparing Pakistan for the future — when the oil runs out and lights throughout the planet go off, Pakistan will be way ahead and well prepared to cope.

CITATIONS

Introduction: That Question Mark by Ziauddin Sardar

The annual ranking of failed states index is prepared by the Washington-based Fund for Peace: http://www.fundforpeace.org/global/?q=fsi. In 2011, it ranked Pakistan thirteen, below Yemen, Iran and Central African Republic. Robert Browning quotation is from *Ring and the Book* (1 :410); it is available at: http://ebooks.adelaide.edu.au/b/browning/robert/ring/book1.html

Robert Kaplan's article, 'What's wrong with Pakistan', published in *Foreign Policy* (July–August 2012) can be accessed from: http://www.foreign-policy.com/articles/2012/06/18/whats_wrong_with_pakistan
Ralph Peter's testimony to the Congress can be found at: http://foreignaf-fairs.house.gov/112/HHRG-112-FA-WState-RPeters-20120208.pdf; and Michael Hughes article on why Pakistan should be balkanised is available at: http://www.huffingtonpost.com/michael-hughes/balkanizing-paki-stan-a-co_b_635950.html

U. Rahman's article on Karachi's three cultures was published in *Dawn*: http://dawn.com/2011/09/15/karachis-three-cultures/
See also, Ayesha Siddiqa's *Military Inc.: Inside Pakistan's Military Economy* (London: Pluto, 2007); and the American trilogy by Ziauddin Sardar and Merryl Wyn Davies: *Why Do People Hate America? American Dreams — Global Nightmare,* and *Will America Change?* (London: Icon Books; 2002, 2004, 2008, respectively)

Breaking News by Ehsan Masood

Maya Khan's exploits can be watched on You Tube. A summary of the Shamsul Anwar hoax is here: http://www.thenews.com.pk/TodaysPrint-Detail.aspx?ID=86770&Cat=6
And 'I told Shamsul Anwar's story', an article from Sehrish Wasif, the journalist who first broke the story, is here: http://blogs.tribune.com.pk/story/9886/i-told-shamsul-anwars-story/

Ibn-e-Safi, BA by Ziauddin Sardar

A number of Ibn-e-Safi novels have been translated into English; most recently *The House of Fear*, translated by Bilal Tanweer and *The Dangerous Man*, translated by Taimoor Shahid (both Random House, India, 2009 and 2011). But no translation can do just to ibn-e-Safi's playful language, full of innuendos and puns. He is best read in original Urdu; and a number of his novels are available for free as downloads from a host of sites, such as http://imranseries.urdunovels.org/category/imran-series-by-ibne-safi/ and http://freeurdubooks4u.blogspot.co.uk/2011/03/ibn-safi-jasoosi-dunya-novels-complete.html
The ibn-e-Safi website (http://www.ibnesafi.info/), clearly a labour of love, contains all one needs to know about Ibn-e-Safi. For more on the adventures of Hakim Sahib, see Ziauddin Sardar, *Balti Britain* (Granta, 2008).

Paperback Writers by Bina Shah

Some of the recent novels mentioned in the essay include Mohsin Hamid, *The Reluctant Fundamentalist* (Penguin, 2008); Muhammed Hanif, *A Case of Exploding Mangoes* (Vintage, 2009) and *Our Lady of Alice Bhatti* (Jonathan Cape, 2011); Daniyal Mueenuddin, *In Other Rooms, Other Wonders* (Blooms-bury, 2010); Aamer Hussein, *Another Gulmohar Tree* and *The Cloud Messenger* (both Telegram, 2009 and 2011, respectively); Kamila Shamsie, *Burnt Shadows* (Bloomsbury, 2009); H.M Naqvi, *Home Boy* (Penguin, 2011); Uzma Aslam Khan, *The Story of Noble Rot* (Rupa, 2009) and *Trespassing* (Harper

Perennial, 2010); Sehba Sarwar, *Black Wings* (Alhamra, 2004); Maniza Naqvi, *On Air* (OUP, Pakistan, 2000) and *Stay with Me* (Sama, 2009); Feryal Ali Gauhar, *No Space for Further Burials* (Akashic Books, 2010). Muneeza Shamsie's anthology, *A Dragonfly in the Sun: An Anthology of Pakistani Writing in English* was published by OUP Pakistan (1998).

More recent editions of Manto include Chughtai, *Saadat Hasan Manto, Selected Stories* (Modern Penguin Classics, 2010); *Bitter Fruit: The Very Best of Saadat Hasan Manto* translated by Khalid Hasan (Penguin, 2009); *The Crooked Line* (Kali for Women, 1995) and *Lifting the Veil* (Penguin, 2003).
Granta 112, devoted to 'Pakistan' and edited by John Freeman, came out in 2010. Issue 1 and 2 of *Alhamra Literary Review* were published by Alhamra in 2005 and 2007. Faiza S. Khan and Aysha Raja's *Life's Too Short Literary Review 01* is published in India by Hachette (2011); and the 'Life's Too Short' blog can be accessed at: http://lifestooshortreview.wordpress.com/

Coke Studio by Bilal Tanweer

Coke Studio Seasons are available on YouTube: http://www.youtube.com/user/cokestudio
Some of the songs popular during the MCC days can be heard at: http://www.defence.pk/forums/general-images-multimedia/84235-music-channel-charts-mcc-pakistan.html
Ahmer Naqvi's *Dawn* interview with Rohail Hyatt is available at: http://dawn.com/2011/08/07/the-artist-must-shine/
and to read Safieh Shah's *The Friday Times* reviews of Season 4 begin here: http://www.thefridaytimes.com/beta/tft/articlephp?issue=20110617&page=24
The Fasi Zaka and Friends Show on the Pakistan's Radio One FM 91 is widely available on YouTube.

Discovering the Matrix by Muneeza Shamsie

The women of Muneeza Shamsie's family mentioned in the essay include Begum Habibullah, (Inam Fatima), *Tasirat-e-Safar Europei* and *Nazar-e-Aqeedat* (both Lucknow: 1924 and 1955); Jahanara Habibullah, *Remembrance of Days Past: Glimpses of a Princely State During the Raj* translated from the Urdu by Tahira Naqvi (Karachi: Oxford University Press, 2001); Attia Hosain, *Phoenix Fled* and *Sunlight on a Broken Column* (both London: Chatto and Windus, 1953 and 1961); Rashid Jahan, *Wo: aur Dusray Afsaney Dramey* (New Delhi: Rashid Jahan Yadgar Committee, n.d.); Rashid Jahan, Mahmuzaffar Khan, Sajjad Zaheer, Ahmed Ali, *Angarey* (Lucknow: Sajjad Zaheer, 1932); Hamida Saiduzzafar, *Autobiography: Hamida Saiduzaffar 1921-28* edited by Lola Chatterji (New Delhi: Trianka, 1996); Zohra Segal and Joan L. Erdman, *Stages: The Art and Adventures of Zohra Segal* (New Delhi: Kali, 1997); Kamila Shamsie, *In the City by the Sea* (London: Granta, 1998) and *Salt and Saffron* (London: Bloomsbury, 2001); and Hamida Sultan, *Rang Mahal* (Delhi: Zafar Adib, 1960).

See also Muneeza Shamsie '"Imperial Shadows" A Tale of Two Childhoods: Colonial and Postcolonial in *Journal of Commonwealth and Postcolonial Studies* 16 [1], 2009; and Kamila Shamsie, 'Literary Line' *Guardian,* 2 May 2009, p16–17.

Imran Khan by Ali Miraj

Imran Khan's Pakistan: A Personal Journey is published by Bantam Press (New York, 2011). The report on 25 December 2011 rally in Karachi can be found at: http://www.guardian.co.uk/world/2011/dec/25/imran-khan-rally-karachi; the Jonathan Agnew interview can be seen on YouTube: http://www.youtube.com/watch?v=ElaGlvtnudQ

ON VISITING PAKISTAN

Shazia Mirza

When I was a child, I was really naughty. I used to steal, fight, and tell lots of lies. I was a disruption in the classroom. The only thing that ever scared me was when my mum shouted, 'If you don't stop this bad behaviour, I'm going to send you to Pakistan.' Pakistan must be worse than Coventry, I thought.

At school one of my friends told me that when she left school she might have to get married to her cousin 'back home in Pakistan'. The word 'back' always seemed to be followed by the word 'Pakistan'. To me it was a backward place, full of backward people, where all the failed despots from Birmingham ended up. I also wondered why people were always being sent to Pakistan 'to get married'. It sounded like some Guantanamo Bay for naughty girls under eighteen.

My parents did not portray Pakistan in a good way. They had good reasons. My mum was born in India in 1944. At Partition in 1947, her mother and father were killed by the Indians. She was three and her sister six; they were now orphans. They were adopted by a Pakistani Colonel driving his truck through the town picking up small children left by themselves. He adopted them both, took them to Lahore and brought them up as his own children along with the family he already had. My mum had bad memories of Pakistan. Once she married my father and left the country in 1970, she never returned. My father had better memories, but once he moved to

England he preferred Birmingham to Pakistan. In the 1970s when I was growing up he would say, 'Birmingham is an upmarket version of Pakistan. Its got the same people, the same conversation, just better toilets.'

My dad would go back to Pakistan to visit family that he still had there, but he always went by himself, and never took my mum, or me and my brothers and sister. This was because my mum never wanted to go and neither did we. I always wanted to go to Spain or France because I wanted to be like my friends. I thought I was white and was ashamed of being Asian. It wasn't cool to be Asian then like it is now. So I wasn't bothered that I hadn't visited the country.

My dad used to bring back presents from Pakistan. Like wooden jewellery boxes with gold patterns that smelt of a market. At the time I just wanted a Ra Ra skirt and ballerina jewellery box — that's what all my friends had. My dislike of Pakistan continued until I was nineteen. I had Pakistani friends at university who seemed surprised that I had never been to Pakistan. They told me they had been many times and how much fun they had. I was surprised; it wasn't a place I had thought of as 'fun'.

Then one day I asked my father to take me. He was shocked and then turned the tables on me: 'Why do you want to go to Pakistan?'

I said, 'Don't you want me to go?'

He said, 'I have been trying to drag you there for years and now at nineteen you want to go?'

My mum still didn't want to go. Too many bad memories, she said. But my dad said, 'Ok I'll take you. I can visit my family and I'll take you to Chucklala Rawalpindi where I grew up.'

So I went with my dad to Pakistan for the first time. We went to Karachi, Lahore, Rawalpindi and Islamabad. This trip was really about family, visiting all these fat aunties I'd seen in pictures who were much fatter in real life. These aunties and uncles would grope my face and smother me with saliva, then start whaling and crying about why they have never met me and how beautiful I am and how there is a nice man who lives just round the corner who happens to be single and would be just right for me.

I experienced a small bit of Pakistan this time round. It was to do with the people. The warmth and generosity of people in Pakistan. I had never been so well looked after by people I didn't know. They would cook for me, care for me, talk to me, be interested in my life and would be incredibly pleasant and kind. In all the houses I visited there was no shouting or fighting or war of any kind. It was peaceful and fun. There was a lot of sitting around philosophising. Most conversations ended with 'what will be will be, that's life, Insha'Allah.'

A few years later I went back again with my dad. My mum still had no interest in going. But there is only so much fun you can have with your dad. I wanted to go out and explore the nightlife and meet people. Men and women seemed to socialise just like they did in England. But I couldn't do that with my dad in the next room. I had experienced a slice of Pakistan and I thought well that's it, if I never go again at least I've been.

Then in October 2008 I received an email from my manager. Usually she would say 'this would be good to do', or 'you should definitely consider this'. Basically wherever there is money she is more than encouraging. She's not Pakistani but Scottish. On this occasion she sent me this guarded email: 'Do you want to perform here? It's an English Medium Festival. 500–700 capacity indoor venue at Lahore's Alhamra Complex. They had an Irish Comedian last year who went down well. They say do your normal set, as they have no restrictions. There is good security at the venue. They are providing a fee, flights, accommodation, food, ground transfers, etc. You'd have to do three shows — an hour each night. What do you think?'

The first thing I thought was what on earth was an Irish comedian doing in Pakistan? And what do you mean: 'they have no restrictions but there is good security at the venue.' What were they trying to say? Do what you like but you might get killed? But I wanted to do it straight away. I had done shows in India, so why not my parents' country? I flew to Lahore for eight days. I didn't know what material to do, who the audience would be, or what it would be like. But for some reason I didn't expect much. Pakistan may be famous for Imran Khan and terrorism, but not comedy.

I arrived at the Alhamra stadium to discover the most well-organised, elaborately decorated, professionally laid out display of performance tents I had ever seen. It was like a cultural village with giant-sized puppets walking around, arms stretched to greet the visitors. There were drivers to drive us from our hotel to the venue, a hospitality tent for performers with the best food I had ever tasted. Performers — musicians, actors, dancers, puppeteers, and comedians — had been flown in from all over the world, from France and Spain to Ireland and America. I have performed at many festivals all over the world but this was not only the most well-organised but also the most diverse, most colourful, and most spectacular.

The World Performing Arts Festival in Lahore has been running since 1992. It is organised by a team of four brothers from the Peerzada family, which is known for its artistic prowess. It is, as I later discovered, one of the largest festivals of its kind in South Asia. The Peerzada brothers, led by Faizaan, are credited with rescuing a dying art: the traditional puppetry of Punjab. In 1974, they set up Rafi Peer Theatre Workshop (RPTW), a non-governmental, non-profit organisation that promotes arts and culture in Pakistan. RPTW has grown in the past three decades to include not only theatre and puppetry, but a host of other art forms in its repertoire. It is now Pakistan's largest arts organisation, promoting education through the arts and committed to building collaborative links through cultural forums. RPWT has also created the country's first ever Museum of Puppetry, a cultural complex, and a national theatre company called Nautanki, which tours Pakistan, taking theatre-on-wheels to the masses. If that's not enough, it is building an Art Village, where indigenous arts and crafts will be show-cased, contributing to Pakistan's 'creative economy'. All of this and in Paki-stan! I didn't know any of this, and neither did any of the performers who I was working with. Pakistan was turning out to be a normal, civilised, crea-tive, and dynamic place just as vibrant as London, Paris and New York — but without the glamorous reputation and good-looking men.

RPTW hosts four major festivals in Pakistan: the World Performing Arts Festival; the International Youth Performing Arts Festival, which encourages and displays the talent of the global youth; the National Folk Puppet Festi-val, which celebrates and revives the art of folk puppetry; and the Interna-tional Mystic Music Sufi Festival which has been held in Lahore and Karachi, and is touring the world, spreading the message of peace espoused by Sufi mystics who have rendered some of the most beautiful poetry and music known to mankind.

When I decided to accept the invitation to perform in Lahore all I heard from other comedians and my non-Pakistani friends was: 'are you sure you want to go? It's a bit dangerous. They might not get comedy. They might be easily offended. You might not come back alive.' I thought of all these things too. But when I actually got to Pakistan it was another story. The audiences all spoke or at least understood English, they wanted to laugh and enjoy themselves, men and women sat outside the venue, smoking cigarettes, laughing, joking, music playing in the background. There were old Aunty Ji's with their sons and daughters, there were young people, teenagers, students — everyone. It was like being at Glastonbury or Notting Hill Carnival but much better.

I played it safe during the first two shows. I did my safest jokes talking about my parents, Pakistan International Airline, hairy women, arranged marriage and trying to get into America. People were laughing and the shows were going ok. I was relieved no one had sworn at me, complained about me, or tried to kill me. On my last show I felt so relaxed with such a great audience that I decided to use more risqué material. The jokes I do everywhere else in the world. I did a rude joke. I said that I had never drunk alcohol in my life because it was against my religion but I had anal sex a couple of times. Sometimes, you have to shock an audience to bring them together. And no one likes coarse sexual commentary from an unassuming woman with a British accent more than the Pakistanis. The room erupted. The older audience members, the aunties and uncles, laughed the most. One woman was laughing so much her *dupatta* fell off and her husband fell on top of her. It was a scene from Benny Hill and the atmosphere was euphoric.

As the laughter went to a new level, I thought: why didn't I do this before? I carried on and said, 'In America they have the American dream. Well in Pakistan they have the Pakistani dream, which is if you murder your wife you become president.' It was like a firework had gone off. There was stamping, cheering, whistling, screaming and clapping. And the woman with the fallen *dupatta* had her face in the ground gasping for oxygen. I had joked about the things that mattered to these people; this is what they wanted to hear. They wanted to laugh at all the things they cannot openly laugh at in their newspapers, magazines, TVs and theatres.

I should never have listened to people who kept telling me, 'don't tell jokes about sex, politics, religion, terrorism, or news. People would just get offended.' But these were exactly the topics that people wanted to hear. I was so scared to offend that I forgot that almost anything can offend and that it is my job to offend! Performing my last show felt like I was not in Pakistan at all. It was like doing a show in Birmingham on a Friday night. The audience was fantastic, and the show was so much fun. The Pakistanis were not the backward, narrow-minded, humourless terrorists that other people had portrayed them to be. The last show was such a success that the festival added two more dates and both were sold out. I ended up doing five shows to 4,000 people. I had expected to be deported after two.

I went back to Pakistan again in 2010 to perform at Lahore University of Management Science, and T2F, a performance space in Karachi. This time my mother came with me, visiting Pakistan for the first time in forty years. She loved it. The shows were a hit and we had a great time visiting Anar Kalli, the famous bazaar in Old Lahore, staying on our aunt's farm in Sargodha, and meeting the real people of Pakistan. They are intelligent, fun-loving, care about their country and are very politically aware. They are also the best audiences I have ever played to, dying to laugh at the unlaughable.

I love Pakistan. I am so pleased that my fondness for the country is something I have discovered for myself.

CONTRIBUTORS

Mahvish Ahmad is a freelance journalist and a lecturer in Political Science at Quaid-e-Azam University, Islamabad ● **Muhammad Idrees Ahmad** is Senior Lecturer in Journalism, De Montfort University, Leicester ● **Syed Haroon ur Rasheed Ahmed**, who describes himself as 'a struggling writer of 25', is currently looking after his agricultural farms in Mohammadabad, Pakistan ● **Shahnaz Aijazuddin** is a translator and writer; her translation of the Urdu classic *Dastan Tilism-e-Hoshruba* was published by Penguin under the title *Tilism-e-Hoshruba: The Enchantment of the Senses* (2009) ● **M Shahid Alam** Professor of Economics at Northeastern University, Boston, has published his poetry in *Prairie Schooner, Chicago Review* and *Beloit Poetry Journal* ● **Merryl Wyn Davies** is the Director of the Muslim Institute ● **Mirza Ghalib** (1797–1869) is/was a legendry Urdu poet ● **Aamer Hussein** is the author of five collections of short stories, including *Mirror to the Sun* (1993), a novella *Another Gulmohar Tree* (2009), and a novel, *The Cloud Messenger* (2011) ● **Robin Yassin-Kassab,** author of *The Road From Damascus*, is working on his second novel ● **Taimur Khan** is a freelance journalist based in New York ● **A R Khatoon** (1900–65) whose real name was Amtur Rahman, was an Urdu writer whose romantic novels have been in print ever since her first iconic book *Shama* was published in 1941; her other novels include *Tasweer, Afshan, Fakiha, Chashma, Hala* and *Romana* ● **Ayesha Malik**, a photographer, is currently pursuing graduate studies ● **Ehsan Masood**, a science journalist, is Editor of *Research Fortnight* ● **Ali Miraj** was a member of the Conservative Party Commission on International and National Security 2005–07 ● **Shazia Mirza** is an award-winning stand-up comedian and writer; you can follow her adventures on twitter:@shaziamirza1 ● **Zehra Nigah** is one of the most prominent and respected female Urdu poets of Pakistan ● **Bina Shah** is a writer and journalist living in Karachi; her novels include *Where They Dream in Blue* (2001), *The 786 Cybercafé* (2004), *A Season For Martyrs* (2010) and *Slum Child* (2010) ● **Yasir Shah**, who works in Public Health and lives in Washington DC, was twenty-one when his first novel *Shrine* (2008) was published in Pakistan; it was later adapted as a television film ● **Ziauddin Sardar** is Chair of the Muslim Institute Trust ● **Muneeza Shamsie** is the editor of *And The World Changed: Contemporary Stories by Pakistani Women* (2008) ● **John Siddique** is the author of six books of poetry, the most recent of which is *Full Blood* ● **Bilal Tanweer** is writing his first novel ● **Taymiya R Zaman** is Assistant Professor in the Department of History, University of San Francisco.